Ethics in the Alcohol Industry

Ethics in the Alcohol Industry

Simon J. Robinson
and
Alexandra J. Kenyon

First published 2009
PALGRAVE MACMILLAN

Palgrave Macmillan in the UK is an imprint of Macmillan Publishers Limited, registered in England, company number 785998, of Houndmills, Basingstoke, Hampshire RG21 6XS.

Palgrave Macmillan in the US is a division of St Martin's Press LLC, 175 Fifth Avenue, New York, NY 10010.

Palgrave Macmillan is the global academic imprint of the above companies and has companies and representatives throughout the world.

Palgrave® and Macmillan® are registered trademarks in the United States, the United Kingdom, Europe and other countries.

ISBN 978–0230–21988–5

This book is printed on paper suitable for recycling and made from fully managed and sustained forest sources. Logging, pulping and manufacturing processes are expected to conform to the environmental regulations of the country of origin.

A catalogue record for this book is available from the British Library.

Library of Congress Cataloging-in-Publication Data
Robinson, Simon, 1951–
    Ethics in the alcohol industry / Simon J. Robinson and Alexandra J. Kenyon.
        p. cm.
    Includes bibliographical references and index.
    ISBN 978–0–230–21988–5 (alk. paper)
    1. Alcoholic beverage industry—Moral and ethical aspects.   2. Drinking of alcoholic beverages—Social aspects.   3. Social responsibility of business.   I. Kenyon, Alexandra J., 1966–   II. Title
    HD9350.5.R63 2009
    174'.96631—dc22   2009013634

10   9   8   7   6   5   4   3   2   1
18   17   16   15   14   13   12   11   10   09

Printed and bound in Great Britain by
CPI Antony Rowe, Chippenham and Eastbourne

Contents

♪

List of Tables, Figures and Boxes

Tables

Figures

Boxes

Preface

I was brought up in a Yorkshire village in the 1950s. Church, chapel, primary school and cricket club kept the village alive and gave the villagers shared meaning, and alcohol did not play a huge part. There was the occasional excess, but a village of less than 2,000 people meant complete transparency, and anything out of the ordinary was soon spotted. On the whole, people preferred not to be spotted. Alcohol was not frowned upon. It simply did not figure that much in a place where you had to be careful with your money and did not have time to get drunk. In my first profession – psychiatric social work – alcohol was at the centre of life. We sat in groups twice a day, each session lasting one-and-a-half hours, each reflecting on the effect of alcohol in the lives of patients, and what they would replace the empty bottle with. Alcohol here was a matter of life and death, and I remember to this day an animated conversation with a very articulate man, who had become a friend, about the effect of alcohol on his liver. The next week he was dead.

In this book, we hope that the reflections on alcohol, and the ethical issues that surround it, will be more than merely an academic conversation. The aim is to focus on the meaning that alcohol makes for individuals and communities and, beneath that, on ethical identity and the importance of responsibility for all concerned with alcohol. The first man to help me see something about responsibility and community lived close to me in that first Yorkshire village – my grandfather, Hardy Rhodes. Joiner, undertaker, builder, choirmaster, organist and maths lecturer, he has influenced many of my attempts to develop responsibility even to this day. It is to his memory that I dedicate this book.

Advent 2008   Simon Robinson

I have lived in, worked for and researched the licensed retail and alcohol industry for many years. My first job was as a waitress in a gastro pub and I enjoyed the convivial atmosphere, the banter and the camaraderie – so much so that I kept returning to it, working in local boozers and pre-club bars. When I changed careers and moved to a new town, I needed to establish a social network with fun loving people: what better place to do that than in a pub, after work on a Friday night. Pubs have a long history of being happy, welcoming spaces where communities are brought together, friendships are formed, loved ones are found and lost ones mourned. When the values of community spirit, friendship and warmth are at the forefront, and alcohol secondary, a wonderful evening can be shared. I dedicate this book to my husband Steve (who I met in a pub), and Kelly, Lynn and Kevin, with whom I have shared many memorable times.

Advent 2008   ALEXANDRA J. KENYON

Acknowledgements

We thank the following for advice and for permission to reproduce material:

The Advertising Standards Authority
The British Beer & Pub Association
Professor Cary L. Cooper, CBE Pro-Vice-Chancellor (External Relations), Distinguished Professor of Organizational Psychology and Health, Lancaster University
Eurobarometer
The Cabinet Office: Reduction Strategy for England
The European Advertising Standards Alliance Brussels
The International Center for Alcohol Policies
The Stationery Office (TSO)
The World Health Organization

For his support and advice, we would like to extend our thanks to Professor Cary L. Cooper, CBE, Pro-Vice-Chancellor (External Relations), Distinguished Professor of Organizational Psychology and Health, Lancaster University. Our thanks also go to the Cabinet Office for permission to present Figure 2.5, and the European Advertising Standards Alliance, Brussels, for Tables 2.2 and 3.1. The Cabinet Office, the European Advertising Standards Alliance, Brussels, and the International Center for Alcohol Policies have also been the sources for general information referred to in the text.

For the design and artwork of the front cover to this volume, we gratefully acknowledge Toby Montague BA (Hons), Graphic Arts and Design Student at Leeds Metropolitan University, with the support of the Facilitator of Design Ian Truelove, Principal Lecturer, Leeds School of Contemporary Art and Graphic Design, Leeds Metropolitan University.

List of Abbreviations

AA	Alcoholics Anonymous
ABV	alcohol by volume
ADS	all-day session
AHRSE	Alcohol Harm Reduction Strategy for England
ASA	Advertising Standards Authority
BAC	blood alcohol concentration
BACC	broadcaster compliance team
BACP	Committee of Advertising Practice (broadcast)
CAP	Committee of Advertising Practice (non-broadcast)
CR	corporate responsibility
CSR	corporate social responsibility
DALY	disability adjusted life
DHSS	Department of Health and Social Security
DISCUS	Distilled Spirits Council for the United States
DSM	Diagnostic and Statistical Manual
EESC	European Economic and Social Committee
EFRD	European Forum for Responsible Drinking
EGTA	European Group on Television Advertising
IAS	Institute of Alcohol Studies
IBLF	International Business Leaders Forum
ICAP	International Center for Alcohol Policies
ICD	International Classification of Diseases
NGO	non-governmental organization
NHS	National Health Service
Ofcom	Office of Communications
PHSE	personal, health and social education
PND	penalty notice for disorder
SHT	stakeholder theory
YFJ	European Youth Forum
YLD	number of years a person has physical or mental disability, or poor health (known as 'years lost')
YLL	potential life-span of a person that has prematurely been cut short

Introduction

In a book about ethics and the alcohol industry, it would seem right to begin with ethics. The conventional way of doing that would be, first, to set out what is meant by ethics. The problem is that we can hardly expect everyone to understand the term 'ethics' in the same way. Postmodernism suggests that any convincing overview of ethics has gone. The effort of sustaining some overarching prescriptive framework of deciding what is right and wrong is now too great (Connor 1989). In any case, so the argument goes, we all have very different, personal or local views about this. Moreover, it is argued, we have every right to follow what we feel is morally acceptable, unless it is harming another. Whatever view is taken regarding theories about postmodernity, it is clear that in many areas of life there is no shared moral discourse. Moreover, regardless of views about content, perceptions of the nature of ethics differ according to experience. If, for instance, an individual has been brought up dominated by prescriptive and legalistic ethical practice, he or she might well be inclined to be suspicious even of the term 'ethics'.

The study of ethics has traditionally been the concern of philosophy, theology or religion. However, with the rise of applied ethics it is becoming less clear that any of these disciplines or traditions can 'own' ethics in its entirety. Disciplines such as psychology and sociology increasingly have insights about the nature of ethics (Williams 2004), and the many professions seek to locate a particular perspective of applied ethics in their area. Nonetheless, the traditional ethics disciplines have a key part to play in clarifying ethical concepts, developing and critically assessing ethical theory and underlying views of the world that inform value, and reflecting on how these theories and values are embodied in practice.

Traditionally, philosophy and theology tended to focus initially on two views of ethical theory: the *deontological* and the *utilitarian*. The first

1

of these argues that ethical meaning is found in principles, such as the Ten Commandments, applicable to all situations. The second argues that moral meaning is discovered in calculating how any action might maximize the good. Both offer perspectives that are necessary, but not sufficient, for understanding ethics in practice. Principles are an important summary of accumulated wisdom, but all have exceptions. Hence, they cannot be applied uncritically. Equally, whilst it is important to assess the effects of any ethical decision, this does not itself tell us what we mean by, or for that matter justify, the good that we want to maximize.

At least five other different approaches have emerged since 1900, each trying to develop a view of ethics that is richer, more complex, and focused in practical reflection:

- Virtue ethics
- Feminist ethics
- Post-holocaust ethics
- Discourse ethics
- Global ethics.

Virtue ethics

Building on the ethics of Aristotle, this argues that ethics is not so much about determining what is right or wrong but, rather, about building a good character. The character is informed and sustained by the stories of the community, which embody the virtues. The virtues are learned through practice in community (Macintyre 1981), and good character will lead to good ethical practice.

Feminist ethics

Feminist writers contrast justice with care (Koehn 1998). Justice, they argue, is solution driven and based upon power. This approach to ethics has dominated Western history. In contrast, 'care' as the foundation of ethics is concerned not simply with solving ethical dilemmas but, rather, with understanding the nature of any dilemma and including all those involved in working it through. This is an ethics that looks to develop trust, and is dependent upon key attributes such as empathy.

Post-holocaust ethics

Writers such as Bauman (1993) reflect on the experience of the Holocaust. The Holocaust happened because of the way in which certain groups of people were excluded from humanity. Responsibility for the other was, in these cases, denied. This denial was exacerbated by management techniques such as the division of labour, which further distanced any sense of responsibility. The basis of this ethics is inclusive awareness and appreciation of the other. Hence, ethics begins with taking responsibility for the other, and the rest is how that responsibility is worked out, with others.

Discourse ethics

Habermas (1992) suggests that ethical meaning emerges from discourse, enabling reflection on values and the discovery of shared norms. Getting the process right for such discourse is, thus, of the highest importance, and Habermas suggests basic conditions for this. Benhabib (1992) goes further, noting that whilst the discourse might reveal shared moral meaning, the conditions of discourse themselves already embody moral meaning – not least, respect. This, in turn, requires attributes such as empathy (Benhabib 1992: 52).

Global ethics

Building on the sense of connectedness stressed by the feminist ethics, global ethics stresses our responsibility for the environment and humankind globally. In one sense, this is also a natural progression from post-holocaust ethics, stressing responsibility for all on a global scale, and a concern for structural global response to issues that dwarf the all too often individualistic focus of ethics (Kung 1991).

These approaches overlap. All have some reference to:

- character, involving virtues or qualities
- awareness of, and openness to, the other
- process focused on reflectivity and dialogue that embodies core values
- a starting point of taking responsibility for the other.

Ethics, then, is a not a simple application of predetermined theory. It is always twin track: working through from many different theoretical perspectives to how we judge something to be right or wrong, and working out the particular issues of any situation. And no situation stays still for long. Situations comprise real people, with different needs and concerns.

There are few more complex situations than alcohol and the alcohol industry. Alcohol is a unique product that relates closely to personal and social identity, leading to good and bad consequences. It involves elements of corporate, political and personal ethics. Hence, this book will begin by looking at alcohol in society over time. In Chapter 1, we will outline the origins of alcohol; discuss major events in social history where governments, social activists and the licensed retail industry challenged consumption patterns due to changes in moral attitude; fashions within alcoholic drinks; and distributors and manufacturers through to the present day.

Chapter 2 will focus on the social responsibilities at international, national and local levels, including those of the alcohol and licensed retail industry. Each area has its own set of rules or codes attempting to embody social and ethical considerations. This begins with the World Health Organization's recommendations, which emerge from a global understanding of the health, economic and social issues surrounding alcohol. It then moves down to the social responsibilities of governments around the world, local authorities, suppliers of alcohol and the licensed house manager. The chapter will consider the legal aspects and self-regulatory codes to which organizations have to adhere.

Chapter 3 centres on the world of advertising and marketing of alcohol. It will consider three areas. The first is self-regulatory voluntary codes of practice for the advertising of alcohol, worldwide and nationally. Regulations change and evolve rapidly, and we will discuss the changes and how they have affected the advertising industry. The second area will review the extensive scholarly activity with regard to rhetoric, lifestyle and humour in alcohol advertisements, and their reflection of society. The chapter will close with an examination of today's major sponsors, and the brewers and manufacturers of alcoholic drinks. Changes in regulations to abide by social, ethical and moral codes have affected sponsorship in many ways, and these are also considered in light of legislation and self-regulatory codes. This chapter will argue that the situation with regard to advertising and sponsorship is complex, and requires more careful strategy than simply a blanket ban.

Chapter 4 revisits issues about corporate and related responsibility through the perspective of the Nuffield Centre for Bioethics Report on public health policy. It notes some core ethical approaches, focused in different perspectives on freedom and best interest. The Report argues for a developed liberal position summed up in the concept of stewardship. This argues for coercive responses to the issues of alcohol that give appropriate attention to individual freedom.

We argue that the Report does not make enough of the concept of responsibility that lies at the heart of any view of stewardship. Analyzing responsibility in terms of imputability, accountability and moral liability, we seek to apply this to corporations and the alcohol industry, as well as to wider stakeholders. Noting the case of Brown-Forman, we argue for a sense of shared responsibility that requires dialogue around the negotiation of that responsibility. This, in turn, requires a clearer sense of the identity and responsibility of the alcohol industry as a whole, encouraging dialogue and regulation that focuses on this and on good practice, rather than simply the unthinking adherence to ethical codes. We argue that this demands that the ethical agenda is moved away from polarizing dynamics, with the alcohol industry seen as inherently self-interested, to a view of ethics based around committed and critical dialogue, enabling creative response that engages the responsibility of all groups involved.

Chapter 5 will be divided into two sections. The first section will consider concerns that the European Commission and the nation have about the role of alcohol in young people's lives. Reports suggest that young people feel they are pressured to drink alcohol in order to be involved in the alcocentric (a state of mind that centres on alcohol) environment. There are numerous education driven strategies aimed at young people, to help them understand the dangers that extreme drinking can bring to their health and psychological well-being. Public service announcements have used television, radio, outside media (billboards) and 'in-pub' media ('Don't drink and drive' beer mats and posters) to provide young people with information about the social and health risks of extreme drinking. The initiatives outlined in the Alcohol Harm Reduction Strategy of England will be discussed, together with approaches to education in schools on the nature of alcohol, alcohol risks and the consequences of extreme drinking.

The second section will discuss how alcohol is part of a young person's social scene, his or her 'right of passage' into adulthood, recreational drinking and therapeutic drinking. This section will also discuss 'binge drinking' and 'extreme drinking' as two scenarios that are on the increase. This will guide the reader through the economic factors, changes in lifestyle and social freedoms that might have contributed to the increase in alcohol consumption. The chapter concludes that the most effective educational strategies need to focus on the development of moral responsibility, not simply information about alcohol.

Chapter 6 looks at the role of alcohol in religion and at the attitude of religions to alcohol. It will focus on the Judeo-Christian and Islamic religions. In the Judeo-Christian, alcohol is not only accepted as central to community identity, it is also used in positive ways to describe key doctrines such as that about the end of time, using pictures such as the

Messianic Feast. This also ties the faith history of this tradition into core rituals, such as Passover and the Eucharist. Any negative reference to alcohol is confined to drunkenness. A plurality of Christian views will be examined through a reflection on Augustine, Aquinas and Luther. Despite similar roots, Islam reaches opposite conclusions. Nonetheless, there remains plurality of interpretation and of practice in global Islam. All the religious views examined focus on the importance of community, and of the individual taking personal responsibility for his or her relationship with alcohol.

The chapter suggests that it is important to take into account religious perspectives, and that intra- and inter-faith dialogue should be encouraged, as well as the dialogue between religion and civic responsibility.

Chapter 7 focuses on addiction. Alcohol's addictive nature will inevitably mean that those with 'addictive personalities' will be drawn towards misuse. The understanding of the nature of 'addiction', both psychological and physical, has moved away from the moralistic and judgemental view of drunkenness, focusing on pastoral care and medical models. This, however, runs the danger of medicalizing the problem, taking away responsibility from both the individual and the industry, and placing it with medicine and government. This raises the issue of responsibility and therapy, and how far the ethical agenda should be addressed as part of therapy. We deepen the complex definition of responsibility noted in Chapter 4, and argue that therapy has to engage this in a challenging but non-judgemental way.

We examine the psychological and spiritual dynamics of alcohol addiction and therapy. The core ambiguity of addiction as an illness against the view of therapy as personal growth will be worked through. The spiritual and moral dynamics of alcoholic counselling and Alcoholics Anonymous will be analyzed, noting the importance of developing key virtues in the patient as part of the therapy, including integrity, empathy, commitment, care and the capacity to reflect on purpose in practice (practical wisdom).

Key insights from an ethical reflection on the dynamics of therapy are that personal responsibility is central, and that the development of personal responsibility is intimately connected to an empowering and responsible community. This, we argue, applies beyond the therapeutic arena.

The final chapter begins by placing the discussions on ethics and responsibility into the wider sphere of corporate responsibility. It will then review the earlier arguments, showing how the ethical focus has moved from traditional ethical theories to a focus on shared responsibility, involving shared data collection and the engagement of moral imagination, value analysis, negotiation of responsibility, and shared creative response. This moves the debate away from the polarized views about the different interests to practice centred dialogue that is more about the building of relationships around community, and enabling shared response that embodies and mutually supports personal, professional, community, industry and government responsibility.

1
History of Alcohol, Values and Legislation

Introduction

Alcohol contains ethanol (pure alcohol: C_2H_6O). The strength of the spirit, wine or beer depends upon the amount of ethanol in the drink. And it is often thought that if alcohol were invented today, it would be classed as illegal, due to its properties to change behaviour, the damage it does to a person's health and the social risks that it can cause. However, through nine millennia it has helped societies form communities; pay for crusades; helped us celebrate weddings, births, and graduations; and it is involved in virtually all forms of society, in one way or another. This chapter will explore how governments, lobbyists, activists, religion and celebrities have contributed to the role alcohol plays in our day-to-day lives. It begins with the age old question: 'Which came first beer or bread?', and discusses when alcohol became a 'problem' and how legislation has developed. The chapter sets the scene for the remainder of the book, which explores government intervention, alcohol problems in society, alcoholism as a disease, the social responsibilities of the alcohol industry, religious perspectives, and the part that the many stakeholders play in trying to control alcohol consumption and enable a positive community context for it.

The beginnings – did beer bring about social cohesion?

Scholars have long debated the view that beer changed man's nomadic lifestyle to one that was more sedentary (Braidwood 1953, Joffe 1998, and Katz and Voigt 1986). Man's nomadic lifestyle of following the herd or seasonal foodstuffs declined as people began cultivating and consistently producing items with which to brew beer, mead or wine. Ancient artefacts found in archaeological digs give pictorial and iconographic evidence that the production and consumption of alcohol, beers and wines were at the heart of social cohesion and Man's development.

Archaeological and scientific evidence from writings, agricultural sites and carbon dating suggest that beer drinking began in earnest in Mesopotamia by the Sumerians in around 7000 BC (Dornbusch 2006) and in Egypt during the Pre-Dynastic era, 5500–3100 (Hornsey 2003). One of the most recent 'finds' adding to the alcohol consumption debate came from Michel *et al.* (1992). A chemical test on residue from an ancient jug confirmed the jug was used as a vessel for storing alcohol. The vessel, housed at the Royal Ontario Museum, had been discovered in Godin Tepe, a prehistoric settlement in Western Iran, and had been carbon dated at 3500 BC. Where the 'first' alcoholic drink was drunk it is impossible to say, but beer might have been a major factor in bringing people together, advancing social hierarchies and developing political powers. This view stems from the evidence of organized agricultural sites in the Jarmo region of the Taurus Mountains of Mesopotamia (now Iraq). The oldest cultivated plants found were barley, which is used to brew beer, and emmer (a low-yielding wheat), used to brew beer or make bread. The Jarmo region would have had little rainfall, and so Sumerians joined together, formed villages and began to develop and irrigate the plains, using the water from the rivers Tigris and Euphrates. The mind-changing properties associated with beer drinking might have encouraged the Sumerians to work as a collective. It is interesting to note the ability to brew beer, therefore, happened in parallel to the 'civilization' of man (Alexander 2001). The question remains as to whether beer provided the stimulus for Man to become civilized and work together for the greater good. Of course, there is no conclusive evidence, but what is certain is that, in order to organize a large labour force in the Mesopotamian or Egyptian regions, social hierarchies had to develop (Hornsey 2003). There is evidence that the labour force was given sufficient quantities of alcohol to remain within the newly formed communities. Not only were they provided with alcohol as an appreciation of their labours, but also alcohol and intoxicated states became part of rituals and religious celebrations.

The British were not as cultured as their Mediterranean or near-Eastern counterparts. This was partly to do with Britain coming out of the Ice Age and with being populated far later than countries in sunnier climes. Neolithic brewing has been discussed at length by Dineley and Dineley (2000), who point to evidence that ale production took place from brewing matter found at Skara Brae (Scotland), an excellent example of a pre-historic village. Barley, the primary ingredient for beer and bread was found in Britain; brought from the near East before the fourth millennium BC. This is noted, in the main, from artefacts and plant matter. A European culture then began to develop that was male-dominated, and brought about feasts and ceremonies focusing on warrior kinship and the recruitment and mobilization of troops (Sherratt, cited in Hornsey 2003). One of the earliest written accounts of beer being drunk in the UK was from Julius Caesar, in 55 BC. When Caesar landed in Britain, he witnessed sophisticated mechanisms for beer production. He referred to the beer as a 'high and mighty liquor' (Butcher 1989). Caesar seemed bemused that the English often used vines as decorative plants for the garden rather than for making wine, but affluent families in the Iron Age did drink wine. Recently, evidence has shown that extensive vineyards were in mass operation during Roman Britain (Brown 2002). Despite that, beer was the main drink consumed during the first century AD. Archaeological finds have revealed that beer drinking, socialization and feasting events occurred in Britain during the Roman period (Pitt 2005). Beer remained the primary drink until the latter half of the twentieth century, when lager (known as 'beer' in all other European countries) and wine became more popular.

In Anglo-Saxon Britain (fifth to eleventh century AD), it was hardly surprising that beer was so popular. According to Bede (1990 edition), the highly salted meats that were then the norm (the salt being used to preserve the meat through the long winters) necessitated additional drinking to quench the salt induced thirst. During the Anglo-Saxon period, advances in technology included ox-drawn ploughs, better agricultural equipment, pots, drinking vessels and beer-tubs, all of which contributed to the mass production of beer. The increase in production was such that landowners and the monasteries began to employ increasing numbers of people, much to their financial advantage. This also saw an increased level of intoxication in Anglo-Saxon Britain, as production and availability increased. Monks and other clergy were included in this, and were not excused for drunken behaviour, suffering penance if caught vomiting in the streets! Students were also given a wide birth as they walked down the streets singing and shouting. These tales resonate with contemporary headlines.

From the Norman Conquest to the early 1700s

William I brought many changes to the nation. He developed the Old English lifestyle into the Middle English, redistributed the land and set up the first British 'breweries'. The Doomsday Book, completed in 1086, shows that half the land was 'owned by spiritual persons', and William I considered monks and nuns would be excellent facilitators for equipping their local community with education, medicine and beer. Previously, beer tended to be brewed in the family home rather than in 'purpose built' entities, with weekly allowances of 30 gallons (Maitland 1897 cited in Hornsey 2003). Historical scripts of this period recognize drinking and drunken behaviour, which was often punished. Punishments tended to be time in the stocks as a form of humiliation and, possibly, self-reflection. The Normans exported the first beer from England to France. Henry II wished for peace and an alliance with King Louis VII of France. One of the elements of the alliance was a marriage between the son of William II and the daughter of King Louis. William II felt a gift might ease the negotiations and sent William fitzStephen, Thomas Becket's clerk, to France laden with beer. The gift arrived with an entourage of fabulous horses, chariots and iron-bound casks of beer. The shelf life of beer was only a matter of days, as there were no appropriate preservatives in those days. It is assumed that the beer was very alcoholic in order to remain fresh throughout its long journey to France. And it was reported by fitzStephen that the French enjoyed the beer and thought it to be an excellent invention!

The Normans also used beer to finance wars, and the first national taxes were levied on the brewing industries. Following the attack on Jerusalem by Saladin in 1187, the Pope requested help, and Richard the Lionheart, son of Henry II, took up arms. Therefore, taxes from beer, as money or stock, had been collected in some form or other since the twelfth century. It was clear that the taxes from the 'Saladin Tithe' would be used for war. Today, taxes from the entire supply chain of the alcohol industry are distributed to many causes including prevention of crime, alcohol education, health, support groups, addiction centres and so on. Up until this point in history, there seems to have been little concern for the health and welfare of the nation. However, health and safety regulations were put in place for the buildings that brewed beer. Breweries therefore became licensed and had to have fire-precaution measures in place if they were built of wood or other highly flammable materials. Crusades and another war with France lay a heavy burden on the finances of England, requiring more money from the breweries. Naturally, the breweries were not happy, and their persistent demands, in addition to those of other notable businessmen and elders, brought forth the Magna Carta. Among the great book's many sections, Clause 35 set out information about standard weights and measures. From that day, throughout the land beer, wine and spirits would be served in standard measures.

As time moved on, kings of England introduced business ethics into the brewing industry. Ale-conners, also known as ale-tasters outside London, were noted in the London Letter Book D for 1309–14, but are considered to have been around since the eleventh century (Unger 2004). Germany had similar 'craftsmen' known as *Bier Kiessers*. The ale-conner fulfilled the equivalent role taken by modern-day legislation for weights and measures and trades description. The ale-conner was employed to ensure that the beer sold was acceptable and 'fit for purpose'. He had two main tasks: the first was to taste the beer, and the second was to sit in it. Ale-conners wore leather britches and sat in the pool of beer they poured onto a wooden bench. The ale-conner would sit for at least 30 minutes. If, after the allotted time, the ale-conner could rise from his seat without impediment the beer was passed and proclaimed satisfactory for sale. If, however, the ale-conner could not rise, because his britches were 'glued' to the seat, the beer was declared to be unsatisfactory and unfit to sell. The logic of the process is based in the fermentation process – specifically, the sugars turning into alcohol. If the fermentation process were not fully complete, sugar would remain suspended in the beer, thus becoming sticky and adhering to the leather britches. Hence, 'wearing trousers with a leather seat, he sat in the pool of beer. By trying to get up he was supposed to be able to decide on the strength of the beer by its pull or tenacity' (Grindal 1979: 129). Not only was it the responsibility of the ale-taster to check for the wholesomeness of the beer, he also had the authority to alter the price of the beer being sold. Price was relative to strength; inferior quality ale had to be sold more cheaply than bright, wholesome beers. Legislative bodies – kings, during this Tudor period – gave the ale-tasters powers, status and a code of ethics to abide by through an oath named *Liber Albus*. The oath not only declares the powers of the ale-conner, but also categorically states that bribery is unacceptable:

> You shall swear, that you shall know of no brewer or brewster, cook or pie-baker in your Ward who sells the gallon of best ale for more than one penny halfpenny, or the gallon of second ale for more than one penny, or otherwise than by measure sealed in full of clear ale; or who brews less than he used to before this cry, by reason hereof, or withdraws himself from following his trade, the rather by reason of this cry; or if any persons shall do contrary to any one of these points, you shall certify the Alderman of your Ward thereof and of their names. And that you, so soon as you shall be required to taste any ale of a brewer or brewster, shall be ready to do so the same; and in case that it be less good than it used to before this cry; you, by assent of your

Alderman, shall set a reasonable price thereon, according to your discretion; and if anyone shall afterwards sell the same above the said
price, unto your said Alderman ye shall certify the same. And that for
gift, promise, knowledge, hate or other cause whatsoever, no brewer,
brewster, hukster [sic: huckster – a woman who retailed ale she had
purchased from a brewer], cook or pie-baker, who acts against any one
of the points aforesaid, you shall conceal, spare or tortiously aggrieve;
nor when you are required to taste ale, shall absent yourself without
reasonable cause and true; but all things which unto your office per-
tain to do, you shall well and lawfully do. So God you help, and the
Saints. (Riley 1861, citing from *The White Book of the City of London*,
1419)

Tudor times also provided a logo to invite ale-conners. Brewers put a
stake with a branch or a bush attached to it – it became known as the
ale-stake. As competition grew in the larger cities, brewers made bigger,
wider and taller ale-stakes to attract the attention of the ale-conner. Similarly, brewers began to create their own logos to identify themselves from
one another. And gradually pub signs began to develop. Ale-Conners are
still honoured today with a beer named *Leatherbritches*, brewed by the
Falstaff Brewery. William Shakespeare's father was a man of note who
became an ale-conner in the fifteenth century. The post of ale-taster
lasted until 1878, when Spindle Dick (Richard Taylor) from Rossendale
in the North of England retired from the post. It seems Spindle Dick had
a sense of humour. When he was brought before the magistrate's bench
for being caught 'drunk and incapable', he protested and felt it a slight
to his long and respected career, claiming he was only carrying out his
duties.

The gin epidemic – the realization of addiction

All historical accounts, plotting changes in alcohol consumption
throughout the world, include the 'gin epidemic' that occurred in
England between the 1720s and 1750s. As noted above, from the Middle
Ages distillers were common throughout Europe, but less common in
Britain. Alcohol manufacturers provided an array of beers, ales and
stouts. However, following Parliamentary Council adjudication, imports
of French wine and spirits were virtually banned in 1689. This occurred
because William of Orange (1689–1706) wished to cut down the flow of
British sterling to France. By placing heavy tariffs on French wine and
brandy, sterling all but ceased flowing from England to France, and, in

turn, French wine and brandy ceased to be imported to England. At the same time, there was a surplus of corn that needed to be used up to raise money for a war against France (Greenaway 2003). Therefore, there was a gap in the market, in terms of drinks choice being restricted, and corn available to aid production of a new spirit. Entrepreneurs who could distil spirits and retail them seized on this gap in the market, and so the taste for gin was born. Business people who could afford a licence to distil gin set up entire supply chains of distilling, bottling and selling. At the same time, there was a glut of corn that outstripped demand within the existing food supply chain; therefore, a cheap and potent alcoholic drink grew out of economic conditions. Over the years, as more sellers came to market, the price of gin fell below the price of beer. As prices fell, gin consumption increased from one to two pints per person per year in 1700, to eight to nine pints per person per year by 1751 (Mitchell and Deane 1962). Consumption of beer remained constant during this period at three million gallons per year across the nation. However, it was the nature of the drink itself that caused consternation, leading Josiah Tucker, an eminent economist at the time, to say that gin brought on 'a kind of instantaneous Drunkenness, where Man hath no time to recollect or think whether he has had enough or no' (Tucker 1751 p. 21, cited in Nicholls, 2003). The strength of the drink (40 per cent proof) and the fact that gin is given in shot measures, unlike beer which was measured in pints, added to the intoxication over a short period of time. Due to the fact that there were many suppliers, competition became fierce and price promotions around that time included: 'Drunk for a penny; dead drunk for twopence; Free straw to sleep it off.'

Excessive gin drinking did not just occur in London; it also occurred counties such as Derbyshire, where new industries were introduced, creating wealth for the genteel classes. They were reported to enjoy their prosperity with merry-making, drinking and feasting. Villages and domestic staff replicated the upper classes and chose to drink gin, as it was new, cheap and plentiful (Hopkins 2008).

Therefore, drunkenness was not merely associated with the 'inferior classes', as middle and upper classes reflected upon alcohol excesses as just an amusing activity. Social commentators of the time, however, felt 'something must be done' to reduce the amount of alcohol drunk by the working classes, thus excluding themselves – and the upper class, as a whole – from the problem. Commentators and activists urged Parliament to take responsibility for the behaviour of the working classes. Whilst it seems that concern and responsibility for the welfare of the working classes was the main motivation in all this, having a reliable workforce to ensure economic growth might also have been on the agenda. Drunken workers would lead to premature deaths, affecting the workforce and possibly leading to calls for higher wages (Holden 1736).

The artist and social critic William Hogarth commented upon the drunken behaviour of the middle and lower classes. His engraving 'Midnight Modern Conversation' shows 'topers at play' enjoying a drink together in a happy social gathering, suggesting even through the title that they can enjoy the excesses of drink. Interestingly, the context is of a coffee house frequented by the gentry and assumed to be a place where sobriety over a cup of hot beverage took place. Another scene shows two engravings combined, each a caricature of working class life. One, 'Beer Street', shows a convivial atmosphere of bonhomie, with tradesmen working together and a healthy environment. Even the pub is called *The Sun*. The pawnbroker's signage in 'Beer Street' depicts a man who has fallen on hard times. In contrast, the pawnbroker in 'Gin Lane' has a queue at his door and a sign that intrudes into the sky. Was Hogarth suggesting that drinking gin was unpatriotic, as it was a brew that originated from overseas? There is no doubt that 'Beer Lane' depicts a happy community drinking 'good' English beer. Or did he support Tucker's suggestion that gin brought forth a new kind of drunkenness? The scene of 'Gin Lane' was of moral turpitude, laziness and carelessness. The woman at the font of this scene even lets her baby fall to its death, echoing the story of Judith Dufour, who strangled her baby to raise money for gin by selling its clothes. Gin has often been called 'Mother's Ruin'; could Hogarth's engraving have helped to formulate this phrase?

T.S. (1736, an anonymous writer), however, claimed that gin was being singled out as the drink that made consumers disturb the peace, whereas beer and wine drinking, afforded mainly by the upper classes, also disturbed the peace in equal measure.

Hogarth, Daniel Defoe and Henry Fielding, amongst other social commentators at that time, saw that gin drinking was giving rise to different fears, not least that it was the cause of the ever-increasing crime rates and general lawlessness. Thefts and social unrest at the time, however, had many other causes. Families were starving – due, in part, to poor harvests of barley, which drove up food prices for essential foodstuffs such as bread. Therefore, desperate people stole to make ends meet (Malcolmson 1981). Indeed, following the 'gin epidemic', crime rates increased.

Despite these arguments, and concern for the decreasing price of gin, the government felt responsible and intervened with the Tipping Act of 1751. The Tipping Act prohibited distillers selling gin to the consumer at retail prices, as it encouraged 'drunkenness'. Two things came out of the gin epidemic. First, there was an increased national awareness that intoxication, with its rippling effects through the social and economic environment, is a political problem. Second, alcohol was confirmed as an addictive substance, the consumption of which had to be controlled.

The Beer Act 1830 and the growth of the Temperance Movement

Moving to the beginning of the nineteenth century, which still had a 'gin haze', drinking was still considered to be both the scourge of the working classes and a social problem. When there were problems, especially with the 'masses', the educated and the activists often protested or demanded that Parliament add to existing laws, bring in new legislation and encourage the police force to use their powers to halt or change the problematic behaviour. London's police force was privately owned, paid for with taxpayers' money, but not the national police force known today. Political leaders and commentators at the time stated that the poor were drinking excessively, which, by definition, created an ugly social problem. The 'Drink Question' was discussed by activists and policy-makers, such as Samuel Pope, who wished to bring about prohibition. Government figures such as Lord Stanley, Lord Salisbury and Lord Chancellor Goulburn offered a more liberal view. They argued that prohibition and legislation was a top-down coercive approach, and 'No person ought to be punished simply for being drunk' (Mill(1946 [1859]): 73). It was suggested that discussion and persuasion would enable consumers of alcohol to form their own opinion and choose to drink or not, thus leaving the responsibility with the person rather than the law.

One of the reasons for the drinking excesses of the nineteenth century seems to be the massive population movement of that time. Thousands of families left the countryside to seek employment, exacerbating the overcrowding in major towns and cities. The Industrial Revolution 'offered' untold opportunities and riches in trade and commerce from Glasgow to Leeds through West Bromwich to London. The opportunity for financial advancement was achieved by only a few, and the majority of working-class people became desperately poor. Working-class citizens were poor both in pocket and in spirit, as families were housed in hastily built accommodation that often had no running water or bathroom facilities. Population movement also broke down the familiar caring family and community networks. The working classes, therefore, sought solace in alcohol. Pubs in towns and cities had bright lights, companionship, warmth and a jovial atmosphere, which seemed far better to many than the foul homes they occupied or their wretched working conditions.

It should be noted, once more, there was little or no debate regarding the excesses of middle-class ladies and gentlemen (and their children), who also drank throughout the day, on a daily basis (O'Daniel 1859).

Naturally, breweries and licensed traders, just as they are today, were worried about their businesses being heavily regulated or shut down, or taxes rising to such an extent that consumers could not afford to socialize in pubs. The breweries and traders wished for greater freedoms to expand their business and sell alcohol in more and more premises to meet demand. Potential for growth, however, was severely restricted due to the licensing powers being in the hands of the licensing justices. Therefore, alcohol brewers and suppliers called upon government to change legislation and take away the powers of the licensing justices. The licensing justices at the time were gentleman magistrates who decided who could sell alcohol and who could not. This led to a high incidence of corruption, some taking financial bribes, whilst others had cellars bursting with alcohol provided by the breweries. Additionally, the licensing justices were inconsistent in their decisions, favouring applications for licensed premises by people who supported the same political party or turning down applications from socially unacceptable people.

The government of the day were under pressure from several groups, including their own backbenchers, calling for a solution to the 'Drink Problem', and from businesses that wished for greater freedom to acquire licenses and sell their wares. Running parallel to these debates was another pressure group, a growing social movement that sought complete abstinence from alcohol. The social temperance movement emerged from the ground up and its members, working-class in the main, chose to abstain from alcohol of their own free will, rather than be 'told to do so' by the learned, or through tighter legislation. The Temperance Society therefore, encouraged the working classes to curtail their drinking habits, to act responsibly and to better their working and home life. Sobriety was also popular with the middle classes, who were shown that, through abstinence, they were no longer living as 'slaves to alcohol' with the evils of alcohol consumption behind them, they began to preach that society would move into a peaceful and respectable future.

The government, faced by these different calls, felt they had to respond, and Goulburn announced a number of new legislative powers and changes to tax under the Beer Act (1830). The Beer Act brought about two significant changes: reduction in the price of beer, and the opportunity for any taxpayer to brew and sell beer. Brewers and owners of licences were pleased, as reductions in the price of beer were seen as a way to change consumer behaviour, which could be done by offering cheaper beer in pubs that could now offer a full range of products from 'beer, to spirits (including gin), to cider. 'Full-Trade' licensed pubs could be opened by anyone, as the Beer Act also enabled any taxpayer to brew and sell beer. The 'free-trade' opportunity was seen as a way of encouraging entrepreneurship and, indeed, was seized upon very quickly, with 24,000 licences to sell alcohol taken up within the first six months of the Beer Act (Berridge 2005). The new licensed premises were known as 'beer shops', 'beer houses' or 'Tom and Jerry houses'. Tom and Jerry houses derived their name from the drinking and socializing activities of two popular characters; Jerry Hawthorn, Esq. and Corinthian Tom, serialized by Pierce Egan in *Life in London: Day and Night Scenes*.

Discussions around the success of the Beer Act lasted many years. Promoting entrepreneurial activities and commercial opportunities was in vogue, as the middle and working classes were encouraged to develop their own trading destinies. The 'free-trade' opportunities were seen as one of the useful ways to move Britain forward in the field of commerce. This was seen as a positive outcome of the Beer Act. Also, the Act gave entrepreneurs the opportunity to open their own business, without having to go through the corrupt network of licensing justices. Government also hoped that reduced taxes on beer, new pubs with consumerist landlords and a range of drinks available 'under one roof' would encourage the consumer to move from gin houses to ale houses. Unfortunately, 'free traders' could set up their own brewery and beer shop in their own home, leading to very poor quality drinks and outrageous promotions; no better than the gin houses offering 'free straw'. Increased supply of beer led to competitive price wars, which led to a rapid increase in beer consumption, subsequently leading to outbreaks of drunk and disorderly behaviour – again, showing no difference from the 'special offers' promoted in gin houses.

In all this, it must be remembered that in Victorian Britain, just as in Mesopotamia thousands of years before, beer (rather than spirits) was seen as a healthy element in a person's diet (McCrae 2004). Beer was regarded as a nutritious, healthy drink – unlike water, which often contained cholera inducing bacteria. Hence, school children were often given beer rather than water. However, this also occurred in the context of work regimes that were increasingly regulated and intensive, with 'to the second' start and finish times, complicated activities using heavy machinery and, often, long periods of strenuous labour. Therefore, 'hangovers' were causing labourers to shirk their duties, fall asleep, arrive late for work or not at all. Absenteeism or failure to work at full capacity due to a 'hangover' was not tolerated, and workers were often sacked instantly and replaced by an ever-increasing, readily available workforce.

Recorded absenteeism, instant dismissal and continuous recruitment drives added weight to the already heavily loaded argument that the working classes were upsetting productivity and drinking themselves into an early grave. In rural areas, such regimes were not as strict, and farm workers are often romanticised as 'sleeping off' their hangover in comfortable looking haystacks. The Beer Act, therefore, might have changed some consumer behaviour, but it did not help the 'Drink Problem'.

The next important event in the historical changes of alcohol consumption in the Victorian era happened in the 1860s. During this period, an even greater choice of alcohol products was made available, as Gladstone made a commercial agreement with France to import wine. Gladstone also provided legislation to allow 'off-license' sales of wine from any shop or grocer. This gave consumers further choices, such as drinking wine at home or with their meal in a restaurant. Whilst, at first glance, it seems that the government was giving people more products to sell and a greater number of outlets where beer or wine was available, they were again aiming to change behaviour. Beer and wines suggested 'lighter, healthier' options than spirits such as gin or whisky. Despite this, the perception of drunken, working-class behaviour still stood. Dostoevsky, for instance, commented upon this during 1862 when he visited London: 'On Saturday nights, a half-million workers flock into the city like a sea ... The people crowd into the open taverns and in the streets ... Here they eat and drink. The beer-houses are adorned like palaces ... They quickly hasten to get drunk to the point of insensibility' (Dostoevsky, cited in Minihan 1967: 223).

Government legislation might have aimed to increase commercial activities and change behaviour but the most immediate approach to the alcohol problem came from the Temperance Movement, which took many middle- and working-class consumers away from drunkenness into sobriety. The earliest Temperance supporters were not opposed to drinking beer, with total abstinence only becoming part of their teachings by the mid-1800s. They preached moderation and a life away from the gin 'epidemic'. The Anglican Church championed the Temperance Movement's stance regarding moderation in alcohol consumption. However, as the Temperance Movement focused more on abstinence, the Anglicans backed away. Teetotalism began to become a dominant feature of the Temperance Movement, as it slowly progressed from the fringes of society into the mainstream. As it became more mainstream, leaders, such as Joseph Livesey, radicalized and politicized the movement to extinguish alcohol from Britain and beyond. Lower-class men would 'sign the pledge' and be made to feel responsible for themselves and their families, feeling they could become a respectable member of society. The middle classes also turned away from alcohol and began to drink the new import of the day: coffee. To aid the acceptance of teetotalism, activists of the Temperance Movement began to provide 'temperance drinks' in addition to coffee, such as fruit juices. Eventually, even Coca-Cola was introduced as a 'temperance drink' (Babor *et al.* 2003), replacing the alcohol content of the popular European cocawine with a non-alcoholic syrup.

By the late 1830s, the Temperance Movement was becoming a major social phenomenon, reinforcing awareness of the addictive nature of alcohol and its effect on the nation's health, both social and physical. Alcohol as an addictive substance or 'disease of the will' (Valverde 1998) was a new concept, and one that the Temperance Movement used in the very first 'anti-drinking' campaigns. Prior to this period, alcohol had been seen in terms of its financial utility for the state; that is, used to raise money from tax, fines for drunken behaviour or incorrectly used legislated weights and measures.

Changing drinking habits during the World Wars

The First and Second World Wars were major catalysts for personal and social change, partly through major interventions by the state. Most industries had to contribute or change to support the war effort, and the alcohol industry was not exempt from this. During both wars, alcohol abuse was heavily criticized, both at home and in the rest of the world, as damaging the war effort. No doubt, the government was acutely embarrassed as international reports stated that Britain was a drunken nation (Gourvish and Wilson 1994). Absenteeism from work was rife, particularly during times when a disciplined, effective workforce was required. Therefore, Lloyd George, deemed to be an enthusiastic temperance campaigner (Plant and Plant 2006), made a number of changes during his wartime administration. He has often been remembered for his 'tough on alcohol' statements such as, 'We are fighting Germany, ... and drink' and 'Drink is doing more damage ... than all the German Submarines put together' (ADW 1919: 590). Despite the tough talk, initial legislation only tinkered with the availability of alcohol by banning credit (running up a tab) and empowering chief constables to close down public houses or reduce their permitted hours (Defence of the Realm Act 1914). Shortly after this period, the government announced it was to purchase the licensed liquor industry in its entirety. This was proposed in 1915 in order to cut down on absenteeism at work – it was not implemented. However, to help the war effort, it was essential that citizens worked at full capacity; therefore the announcement was made again in 1917. At this point in history, the government felt the need to purchase all of the foodstuffs and a substantial amount of beer to be able to feed the British population and the air force, navy and armies overseas. The brewing industry and government had many hours of discussion over the purchase of the liquor licensing industry; debating its viability, concessions and timing. The industry at this time was in a poor state. Limited licensing hours and the absence of 'men on the front-line' had severely cut the availability of beer and a large part of their target market. Additionally, no new pub licenses were being granted and many pubs became dilapidated due to lack of investment. Investment in the alcohol industry's own machinery and infrastructure was also poor. Business and government put self-interest behind them to work (they felt they needed to) together for national interest.

Social reformers were also arguing that absenteeism was caused by alcohol abuse. However, real evidence was lacking and, to address this, therefore, several researchers were employed to provide the factual evidence. As Turner (1980) commented, the researchers would have had to have 'supreme objectivity' to conclude that drink was the cause of citizens not working to full capacity. It must be noted here that heavy industry at that time was volatile, with many 'walk-outs', due to breakdowns in industrial relations.

The full-scale purchase of the liquor licensing trade did not occur, despite many discussion and proposals. There are many reasons for this. One could have been nervousness about over-regulation, making the industry unwieldy. There was also the possibility of having to stop breweries making beer, with fuel shortages on the horizon and more needy organizations, such as hospitals and schools, requiring the fuel (Greenaway 2003). The full reasons for the wholesale purchase could be debated for years to come. However, the state did eventually purchase the licensed liquor industry in Carlisle, then Bristol, Liverpool, Glasgow and so on. The purchase was made in cities where the workforces were specifically needed for the war effort, such as in the fields of shipbuilding and steel work. In some of these cities, the strength of the beer was reduced significantly, with the weak beer aptly referred to as 'munitions beer'.

By the end of the First World War and through the interwar years, the amount of alcohol drunk per capita had fallen and the government no doubt breathed a sigh of relief at their sober nation. The interwar years also brought great improvements in the physical space of the pub and the service of alcohol in general. The new environment consisted of pubs with gardens, family rooms, restaurants and meeting rooms. The first 'super pub' was introduced soon after the end of the First World War with Downham Taverns of South London having the capacity for 1,000 people, 36 lavatories, and even a hall that was the venue for Shakespearean plays. Restaurant spaces in pubs however, did not become mainstream until the 1970s, as they were still the place where working people met after work to socialize (Gourvish 1997). Opening hours did not change again until the 1970s, and it was not until 2005 that 24-hour licenses were made available. Beers were also being made at various strengths from 2 per cent alcohol by volume (ABV) to 5 per cent ABV. The amount of beer drunk per capita remained reasonably stable until the 1960s.

Conclusion

Even this brief history, focusing on the UK, resonates with the issues that surround alcohol today. The alcohol industry was seen as an important means of raising money. At the same time, alcohol abuse led to patterns of behaviour that negatively affected the well-being of the nation, especially in times of war. Control of alcohol consumption was important, with concerns about cheap drink and drink offers that are echoed today in discussions about regulating the price of alcohol, with off-sales from supermarkets deemed to be undercutting on-license sales to such a point that the licensed retail economy is under threat.

There is the same tension today between, order, community, health and well-being, enterprise and individual freedom. At the same time, the data surrounding judgements about the effect of alcohol and how these related to the practice of the industry were often far from clear or objective. Many of the anti-drink campaigns, not least the Temperance Movement, consciously polarized and politicized the issues, moving from temperance to abstinence, based in rhetoric. The contentious issues remain the same, as to how government is to respond to the problem of alcohol and how the alcohol industry is to define and take responsibility in these matters, not least in terms of the effects of marketing. Chapters 2 and 3 will focus on these issues, followed by a further discussion of the underlying issues of control, freedom and responsibility.

2
Social Responsibilities and the Alcohol Industry

Introduction

'... couldn't give XXXX for last orders? Vote Labour' was a text message sent to young people prior to the 2001 UK General Election. This suggests that the alcohol and licensing strategies, included in a party's manifesto, could aim to win over the hearts of voters.

Chapter 1 went through the changes in legislation, how the general public and the drinks industry helped to formulate policy – or rebelled against it, and how there was a change in the place and role of alcohol through the centuries. The election promise that opens this chapter was made to enable pubs, clubs and bars to choose when they close their doors and stop serving drinks. It was felt that the restriction to licensing hours imposed at the beginning of the twentieth century were no longer applicable to the twenty-first-century consumer. The licensed trade is often blamed for plying consumers with vast amounts of alcohol and yet the UK Labour government proposed in their manifesto that they were going to allow alcohol to be supplied 24 hours a day. Popular media at the time declared that additional drinking hours would encourage more 'binge drinking', more crime and serious long-term health problems. They also blamed the government for being irresponsible and 'assisting' drunken behaviour, adding to an already alcocentric environment. Of course, ultimately, consumers should make their own choices, know when they should stop drinking and go home quietly. This chapter looks at the global view of alcohol, demonstrating similar issues the world over. Facts, figures and commentary are shown, together with global, European and national strategies on how to cut down alcohol related harm. This chapter also includes details of some of the socially responsible initiatives taking place at global, national and local level to reduce crime and disorder in the night-time environment and under-age drinking.

A global view

It is clear that governments from most countries across the world, not only the UK, consider it to be their responsibility to shape their nation's drinking behaviour and to look after their health and well-being. Lobbyists from within countries, and 'global guidelines' produced by groups such as the World Health Organization (WHO), the European Commission for Alcohol and the Advisory Council of New Zealand, press governments to protect the weak, vulnerable and naive. Governments, therefore, demonstrate through legislation, taxes and educational programmes their duty as the 'providers' of safe and secure communities for their citizens. However, governments are in a dilemma. The taxes received from the sale of alcoholic drinks run into considerable amounts (see Figure 2.1, which shows HM Revenue and Customs revenue for 2007–08), but the cost of alcohol related harm is high.

Revenue from alcohol, as shown in Figure 2.1, is 1.8 per cent of the total revenue received by HM Revenue and Customs. This might seem to be a small percentage of the 'income' received by the government; nonetheless, it equates to £8,302 million.

Therefore, if the UK government were to minimize and control the supply and/or sale of alcohol through tax increases to the point that consumers could not afford to socialize in pubs, bars or clubs or buy from

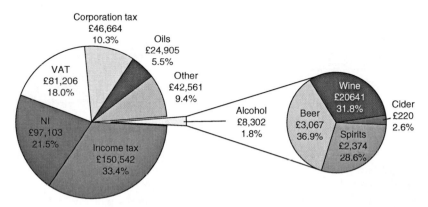

Figure 2.1   HM Revenue and Customs Revenue 2007–08 (£ million) (provisional)
Source: HMRC (Crown Copyright 2008).

off-licences, the income stream paid to governments might decrease considerably. Similarly, if the government encourages 'excessive' and/or 'harmful drinkers' to reduce their alcohol intake to 'safer levels', this would reduce the amount of taxes paid into the public purse. Governments, therefore, need to act ethically by putting strategies in place that will reduce harm to the person or society ... without losing the valuable revenue received from the sale of alcoholic drink. Social marketing initiatives to encourage responsible drinking are shown in Chapter 3.

The second issue that governments need to consider is the freedom of the individual to express themselves, their right to choose and their ability to voice their opinions without restraint. The Declaration of the Rights of Man (1789) states:

> Liberty consists in the freedom to do everything which injures no one else; hence the exercise of the natural rights of each man has no limits except those which assure to the other members of the society the enjoyment of the same rights. (Kreis 2004)

Governments are mindful of these rights, and consumers hold them dear. When strategies, rules and enforcement policies are debated or put in place, they can be seen to impinge on the rights of the individual to enjoy a full, pleasurable social life. Therefore, governments worldwide have to be able to demonstrate that their policies do not oppress the public, and that their decisions are just and fair. Justifications of coercion will be developed further in Chapter 5.

The World Health Organization is not the only source of global frameworks or agreements in this area. International trade and economic treaties were put in place following the Second World War. The World Trade Organization (WTO) monitors tariffs and trade across the globe, with over 100 countries subscribing to general agreements, accounting for over 90 per cent of world trade (Babor *et al*. 2003). The main aim of the World Trade Organization is to stabilize – but, at the same time, relax – international trade, with the goal of stimulating economic development and growth across borders. The World Trade Organization also acts as an inclusive platform where countries can discuss trading problems, settle disputes and reduce inter-state restrictions. It also resolves disputes through enforcement mechanisms. In terms of alcohol, domestic buyers and sellers will receive the same treatment as buyers and sellers from overseas. Therefore, internal taxes and regulations will apply equally over imported and 'home grown' goods. The percentage of VAT taken from a bottle of Duval beer imported from Belgium is the same as that taken from a bottle of Fullers London Pride beer brewed and bottled in the UK. Similarly, the law in the UK is that the alcohol percentage proof (often referred to as alcohol by volume (ABV)) must be shown on each bottle, whether is it imported or brewed and bottled in the UK. This means that, under the world trade agreements, governments cannot overly protect domestic production under the premise of 'fair and equal trade'. International trade agreements between countries are the backbone to effective and efficient global functioning. It is worth remembering William of Orange's (1689–1706) restriction of the outflow of British sterling to France; he taxed their wine and brandy so highly that retailers of alcohol moved to other cheaper UK alternatives to satisfy the needs of their consumers. Under the current trade regulations, that would not be acceptable.

All of these elements, the human rights of the consumer, international trade, the health and wellbeing of the nation, and the national economy are being juggled by governments across the globe. However, the 'top down' guidelines provide joined-up thought on many issues. The following sections show thinking and practice across the globe, and provide an outline of how governments present the overarching guidelines through social, ethical and/or legislative means. Enforcement to reduce the social, health and wealth risks that accompany alcohol will be explored, together with the inclusive, voluntary practices in action.

Is alcohol a burden on the world's population?

The World Health Organization directs and coordinates global health matters under the umbrella of the United Nations. Along with setting norms, standards and policy options for topics such as asthma, bioterrorism, pollution and tuberculosis, they place alcohol high on the agenda by providing a global account of the health and social risks it brings.

Naturally, the World Health Organization is concerned with the burden of illness that can be attributed to alcohol through intoxication (drunkenness), alcohol dependence (habitual, compulsive and long-term drinking) and other bio-chemical affects. Health issues are worldwide: 3.2 per cent of deaths (1.8 billion) and 4 per cent of disability adjusted life years (DALYs) (58.3 million) are from alcohol misuse. DALYs are a way of calculating the gap between the potential life-span of a person that has prematurely been cut short (YLL). A person's life could be 'hampered' through physical or mental disability or poor health, through an attribual illness. The number of years a person has physical or mental disability or poor health are known as 'years lost' (YLD).

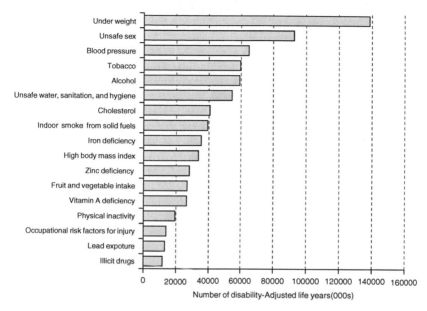

Figure 2.2 Burden of disease attributable to selected leading risk factors, DALYs in each sub-region (%), 2000
Source: World Health Organization (2002a).

As expected these statistics occur at different levels in different countries. Figure 2.2 shows that the two illnesses that effect people the world over are 'underweight and unsafe sex'. Interestingly, illness due to harmful alcohol and tobacco consumption shows a higher indication in developed countries. Vladimir Poznyak, Coordinator of the Management of Substance Abuse, Department of Mental Health and Substance Abuse at the World Health Organization, stated at the opening of a symposium on alcohol that, in 2002, 2,300,000 people throughout the world died because of alcohol related causes and that 64,975,000 DALYs were lost, again down to alcohol related causes. Poznyak, provided some statistics that all government officials must view with disbelief: 10–69 per cent of suicides are committed under the influence of alcohol, 80 per cent of homicides in Russia and 33 per cent of divorces in the UK are alcohol-related, and 5–14 per cent of parents in Japan that have alcohol disorders or a drinking problem abuse their children.

The DALYs attributable to alcohol can be drawn out and shown by country. Figure 2.3 maps how harmful drinking of alcohol is a burden on different countries.

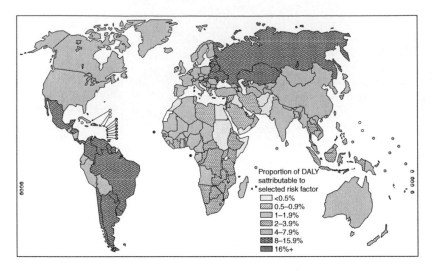

Figure 2.3   Burden of disease attributable to alcohol, various countries
Source: World Health Organization (2002b): 65.

The percentage of DALYs is low in Egypt, Morocco, Pakistan and Afghanistan, due to their religious views on alcohol consumption. However, there is continued concern over the amount of alcohol drunk throughout the world. As developing countries continue to take on West-ern influences and lifestyles, and global brands such as Carlsberg and Heineken are seeking new markets in countries such as Cambodia and China, the 'alcohol question' will continue to be asked. And, quite natu-rally with DALYs, deaths from alcohol (see Figure 2.4) or economic costs (see Figure 2.5), strategies and action will always be on the agenda.

The DALYs are now the most often quoted statistics when reporting the negative consequences of alcohol consumption. Deaths from alcohol in the world ranks ninth in terms of risk factors (see Figure 2.4). Does this mean that deaths from alcohol are less of a problem than DALYs, or does it point to a deeper toll on a nation's long-term health?

Of course, there is a heavy burden on the person who is disabled or in poor health as a consequence of harmful drinking, despite the fact that harmful or excessive drinkers might be exercising their human right to liberty and choice. However, there is also a burden on a harmful drinker's family, who suffer because they see the person they love in pain men-tally or physically. There is a burden on the health service to which the person is aligned, unemployment benefit payments might have to be made if the person can no longer work, there might be a 'cost' to the

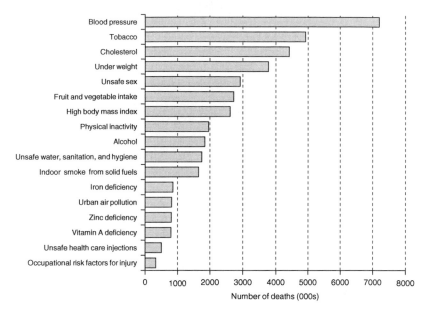

Figure 2.4 World deaths attributable to selected leading risk factors, 2000
Source: World Health Organization (2002a).

person's employer through lost 'man hours' and so on. The task of esti-
mating the cost in monetary terms is almost inconceivable. However,
the UK Cabinet Office commissioned research into the 'total cost' across
the functional areas that would be involved in alcohol related incidents.
Also, alcohol-related harm is not a matter for the individual alone, as
it includes family and friends, the individual's employer, the taxpaying
public and any citizen sharing the same societal space. The Cabinet Office
provides an overall economic cost of alcohol related harm. Figure 2.5
demonstrates a numerical cost in British pounds and also the number
of people that are affected by alcohol related harm. It also includes the
cost to the family and social networks – but because this is subjective
and emotional, it is unquantifiable in monetary terms.

Clearly, Figure 2.5 shows the cost is high in terms of disability and
poor health. Additionally, it signifies a breakdown of the economic costs
in the workplace, in the criminal justice system, crime and disorder,
chronic disease and so on. Governments, in the UK and overseas, find
facts and figures such as these useful as they crystallize the effect harmful drinking can have on the nation. Popular media often use these facts
and figures to criticize the public who drink alcohol, and blame them

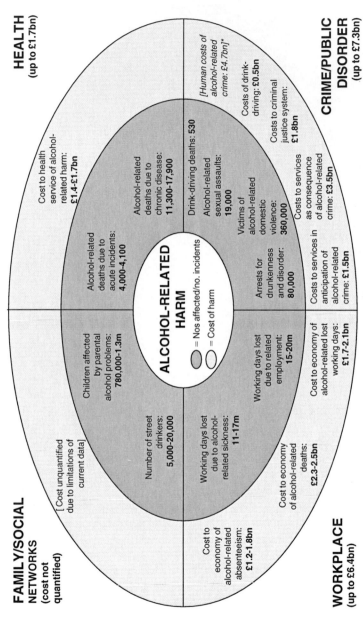

FAMILY/SOCIAL NETWORKS
(cost not quantified)

[Cost unquantified due to limitations of current data]

Children affected by parental alcohol problems: **780,000–1.3m**

Number of street drinkers: **5,000–20,000**

Working days lost due to alcohol-related sickness: **11–17m**

Cost to economy of alcohol-related deaths: **£2.3–2.5bn**

Cost to economy of alcohol-related absenteeism: **£1.2–1.8bn**

WORKPLACE
(up to £6.4bn)

Working days lost due to related employment: **15–20m**

Cost to economy of alcohol-related lost working days: **£1.7–2.1bn**

ALCOHOL-RELATED HARM

= Nos affected/no. incidents

= Cost of harm

HEALTH
(up to £1.7bn)

Cost to health service of alcohol-related harm: **£1.4–£1.7bn**

Alcohol-related deaths due to acute incidents: **4,000–4,100**

Alcohol-related deaths due to chronic disease: **11,300–17,900**

[Human costs of alcohol-related crime: £4.7bn]*

Drink-driving deaths: **530**

Alcohol-related sexual assaults: **19,000**

Victims of alcohol-related domestic violence: **360,000**

Costs to services in anticipation of alcohol-related crime: **£1.5bn**

Arrests for drunkenness and disorder: **80,000**

Costs to services as consequence of alcohol-related crime: **£3.5bn**

Costs of drink-driving: **£0.5bn**

Costs to criminal justice system: **£1.8bn**

CRIME/PUBLIC DISORDER
(up to £7.3bn)

*Note: All figures are annualised; *Human costs are those incurred as a consequence of the human and emotional impact suffered by victims of crime (e.g. attending victim support services); due to the lack of research in the field, equivalent costs have not been estimated for other alcohol-related harms. For this reason, human costs are not included in the crime/public disorder total figure.*

Figure 2.5   The numbers affected by alcohol-related harm and how much it costs
Source: Cabinet Office (2004): 14.

for growing crime figures or tensions within neighbourhoods. However, the issues themselves are not new. As Chapter 1 showed, previous governing bodies recognized alcohol-related harm, not least during the 'Gin Crazed' era. Facts and figures alone will neither help reduce alcohol-related incidents nor change behaviours. Strategies are needed to focus the way forward, rather than pure reflection on what has occurred. In recent years, the World Health Organization, the European Commission and individual states have worked together and agreed on strategies and general codes of practice. The strategies and codes have been disseminated to governments who have included those strategies in their manifestoes or introduced enforcement powers through legislation. This top down approach has many plus points and the World Health Organization has taken the lead in supporting and developing strategies, with governments, to set out a global ethical and just course of action.

The World Health Organization Expert Committee (January 2008) is certainly aware that reflecting on the past is important but does not provide the means to the end. They also realise that progress has been made, as they have been providing an umbrella alcohol harm reduction policy for a number of years and will continue to be the body that states can draw on to form their own strategies unique to their own countries. The current World Health Organization strategies, outlined in the 61st World Health Assembly on 20 March 2008, are summarized below:

Raising awareness and obtaining sustained commitment from member states

The World Health Organization would like to see commitment, in writing, from relevant partners. Commitment should come in the form of action plans detailing overall objectives and targets to reduce harmful use of alcohol. The World Health Organization also requests that partners build up regular reporting mechanisms internationally, nationally and at regional and local levels. The reporting mechanisms, it is hoped, will provide solid foundations for the building of awareness and continuity of effort. The UK government has provided many legislative powers to the police – such as penalty notices for disorder (PNDs) for persons who are deemed to be behaving in an unacceptable manner, and licensed premises closure orders where licensees have allowed drunkenness, under-age drinking, the supply of drugs and so on to take place in their premises (House of Commons Home Affairs Committee 2008).

Preventative measures and health sector response

The World Health Organization is keen for governments to include effective screening programmes, low cost interventions and effective treatment centres within a healthcare setting to aid and improve the individual and their families. They also aim to engage stakeholders in community action plans to reduce the harmful use of alcohol. Community based groups, due to their close relationship with citizens in their neighbourhood, have knowledge of 'unreported' alcohol consumption, children who are mistreated and 'hot spots' where drunkenness or violent behaviour occurs. Community based action should be encouraged to increase awareness of alcohol related incidents and harm at the local level. Many councils in England have their own community based action groups such as Street Angels in Calderdale or Night Wardens in Leeds. The community groups provide a service to the public. They keep a watchful eye on disturbances or injury and call the local police or ambulance services accordingly. Additionally, they help the general public with directions to restaurants and clubs, taxi services or food outlets.

Drink-driving

The World Health Organization recommends commitment by member states to provide consistent social messages on the dangers of consuming alcohol and driving. Similarly, the World Health Organization wishes to see greater use of police enforcement strategies such as selective breath-testing and random, targeted breath-testing.

Regulating the availability of alcohol

Different countries throughout the world have very different regulations for the supply of alcohol. The differences range from the available hours in which alcohol can be sold, the age of the person to whom it can be sold and the type of retail outlet that can sell alcohol. The key issue for developed countries is to ensure that availability does not put young or vulnerable people at risk. In developing countries, informal retail markets or outlets have few or no regulated controls in place for the sale of alcohol and it is in these countries that the World Health Organization would like to begin to regulate the supply of alcohol. Marketing of alcohol is covered in greater detail in Chapter 3. However, the World Health Organization is calling for tighter controls, bans and product placement to be considered to try to protect young or vulnerable people from feeling pressured to drink.

Fair pricing of alcoholic drinks

Chapter 1 gave some indications as to how taxes raised from alcohol sales has funded wars and been used in peace-making. Currently, in many developed countries the 'pile 'em high sell 'em cheap' philosophy has moved into the licensed trade, particularly off-trade such as supermarkets. Happy hours and the notion that some alcoholic drinks are cheaper than water is addressed in greater detail in Chapter 5, but the World Health Organization wishes governments and institutions to assess and evaluate pricing policies as part of their strategy to reduce alcohol related harm.

Reducing alcohol related harm

The World Health Organization encourages governments to develop effective strategies to reduce the negative consequences of harmful drinking in towns and cities. These strategies should include enforcement, prohibition of selling alcohol to intoxicated persons, policing the streets and reducing the availability of alcohol. These issues are constantly under review in the UK and many other developed nations who have their own night-time economy and alcohol reduction strategies (see Case 2.1 for details of initiatives that embrace the World Health Organization's recommendations).

Reducing the public health impact of illegally and informally produced alcohol

This plea from the World Health Organization is mainly directed at poor countries where illegal brewing is predominant. In countries such as Sudan and Kenya, illegal brewing is seriously harming those that drink it by causing poisoning and blindness.

Naturally, each country is ultimately responsible for defining and being accountable for the implementation of the aims that are applicable to them. Chapter 3 considers the policies specifically for advertising alcohol, whilst this chapter continues with the guidelines put in place to work for the central aims.

There is a positive feel about the strategies set out by the World Health Organization, especially where they have included a practical toolkit of advice, policy and marketing suggestions, to reduce drink-driving for example (see *Drinking and Driving – an international good practice manual* – World Health Organization 2007). Many countries use the practical manual and successfully reduce deaths through drink-driving, and it is hoped that the collective aims for the global alcohol strategy will also see positive results.

European alcohol strategy

The World Health Organization states that its members are ultimately responsible for developing policy and practice for their country/region.

Total recorded alcohol per capita consumption (15 yrs +) in litres of pure alcohol

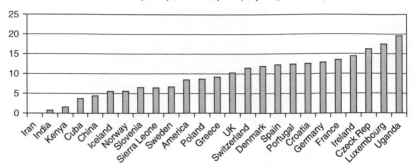

Figure 2.6 Per capita alcohol consumption in selected European and other countries (litres of pure alcohol per inhabitant) among adults from 15-years-old
Source: Adapted from World Health Organization (2004): 11, 12.

All members agree that an alcohol strategy is required. Figure 2.6 shows that different countries within Europe have varying degrees of alcohol consumption. This also includes some countries such as the USA and China, to give a worldview.

As long ago as 1992, the European Alcohol Action Plan provided European member states with policy outlines and implementation strategies, considering the initiatives such as protecting children and young people from feeling pressured to drink, reducing the risk of alcohol related problems, providing effective treatments that are easily accessible and ensuring there is a greater awareness of the harm that alcohol can cause (Saul and Colom 2001). By using the Global Strategy and progressing the European Alcohol Action Plan, the European Commission set out five priority themes and good practices in 2006:

- Protect young people, children and the unborn child
- Reduce injuries and death from alcohol-related road accidents
- Prevent alcohol-related harm among adults and reduce the negative impact on the workplace
- Inform, educate and raise awareness on the impact of harmful and hazardous alcohol consumption, and on appropriate consumption patterns
- Develop and maintain a common evidence base at EU level. (Eurocare 2007)

The themes are drawn down from the Global Strategy. In addition, the themes provided further guidance to member states within the European

Union on how to turn the priority themes into action, to the concern of the European Economic and Social Committee (EESC), who felt the priority themes and good practice are merely guidelines, and would have preferred a more legislative approach.

The European Alcohol policy themes are easily aligned to the World Health Organization's aims. Deciding on specific aims, drawn from earlier European Commission policies on alcohol, took between 2001 and 2006, when the policy themes were launched.

Priority theme 1 – Protect young people, children and the unborn child

Aim 1: To curb under-age drinking, reduce hazardous and harmful drinking among young people, in cooperation with all stakeholders
Aim 2: To reduce the harm suffered by children in families with alcohol problems
Aim 3: To reduce exposure to alcohol during pregnancy, thereby reducing the number of children born with foetal alcohol disorders.

Suggestions on how to move the themes and aims forward into practice included enforcement actions such as restrictions on sales and availability; local, community based actions to educate, inform and involve teachers, parents and young people; and the use of the media and training programmes to outline the consequences of harmful drinking. The European Alcohol Strategy also called on the producers and sellers of alcohol to join forces with these initiatives and play their part in education and community response.

Priority theme 2 – Reduce injuries and deaths from alcohol-related road traffic accidents

Aim 1: To contribute to reducing alcohol-related road fatalities and injuries.

Approximately one accident in four can be linked to alcohol consumption, and at least 10,000 people are killed in alcohol-related road accidents in the EU each year. The blood alcohol concentration limit (BAC) for driving within the legal limit varies from country to country around the world. It is considered that alcohol impairs judgement in the ability to drive a car safely. Moskowitz and Fiorentino (2000) suggest that 0.5 mg/ml or less would be acceptable. Action, be it frequent enforcement campaigns rather than only at peak periods such as Christmas, the New Year or national celebrations; systematic breath testing and, of course, education and awareness campaigns are now in the hands of the national governments. Table 2.1 shows the BAC limits in

Table 2.1 International BAC limits mg/ml

0.8	0.7	0.6	0.5	0.4	0.3	0.2	0.1	Zero
Canada	Bolivia	–	Argentina	Lithuania	India	Estonia	Albania	Armenia
Ireland	Ecuador		Australia		Japan	Norway	Algeria	Azerbaijan
Kenya	Honduras		Austria		Moldova	Poland		Colombia
Luxembourg			Belgium		Russia	Sweden		Czech Republic
Malaysia			Cambodia					Ethiopia
Mexico			China					Hungary
New Zealand			Denmark					Nepal
Singapore			Finland					Romania
UK			France					Slovak Republic
USA			Germany					Brazil
Zimbabwe			Iceland					Georgia
			Italy					
			Mauritius					
			Netherlands					
			Peru					
			Portugal					
			South Africa					
			Spain					
			Switzerland					
			Turkey					

Source: Adapted from ICAP (2007).

several countries, some of which are already complying with the suggested action. Some, however, might need to raise the issue in their own governments, and perhaps with the general public, to come into line with the European Policy suggestion. In addition to the general public, the European Commission also suggests additional attention should be given to young and new drivers, and commercial vehicle drivers.

Priority theme 3 – Prevent alcohol-related harm among adults and reduce the negative impact on the workplace

Aim 1: To decrease alcohol related chronic physical and mental disorders
Aim 2: To decrease the number of alcohol related deaths
Aim 3: To provide information to consumers so they can make informed choices
Aim 4: To contribute to the reduction of alcohol related harm at the workplace, and promote workplace related actions.

Currently, many member states have used improved enforcement practices and added to voluntary codes and standards to reduce the negative impact of harmful and hazardous alcohol consumption. This has occurred, in part, due to the devastating effects alcohol can have on a person's ability to work and the economic costs to the nation, as shown in Figures 2.3 and 2.5. Again, the Commission has recommended greater education and intervention in the workplace and within the public health services. Similarly, there has been a call for a reduction in marketing ploys such as 'happy hours' and '2 for the price of 1' offers, and an increase in infomercials regarding moderate and safer drinking, drink-driving and reduction in drinking whilst pregnant.

Priority theme 4 – Inform, educate and raise awareness on the impact of harmful and hazardous alcohol consumption, and on appropriate consumption patterns

Aim 1: To increase EU citizens' awareness of the impact of harmful and hazardous alcohol consumption on health, especially the impact of alcohol on the foetus, on under-age drinkers, on working and on driving performance.

Suggestions for putting this aim into action include making the consumer, particularly young persons and pregnant mothers, aware of the longer-term damage harmful drinking can have on their bodies, their unborn child and the ability to work in their adult life. Ensuring the consumer has all the facts should enable them to make their own lifestyle choices. This priority enables governments to use less legal enforcement. They might feel they have completed their ethical duties by fully informing their public through various mediums of the impact harmful and excessive drinking has on a person's physical and mental health, social and work-based lives, and the impacts on the wider community. The general public often begrudge legislation running their lives and shun a 'nanny state'. Therefore, education and awareness campaigns should be considered to enable consumers to understand the consequences of harmful and excessive drinking whilst being at liberty to make their own choices. In effect, this enables the development of socially responsible autonomy.

Priority theme 5 – Develop, support and maintain a common evidence base

Aim 1: To obtain comparable information on alcohol consumption, especially on young people, on definitions of harmful and hazardous consumption, on drinking patterns, on the social and health effects of alcohol, and information on the impact of alcohol policy measures and of alcohol consumption on productivity and economic development
Aim 2: To evaluate the impact of initiatives taken on the basis of this communication.

There are many differences in the alcohol guidelines, 'standard' strengths of alcoholic drinks (Table 2.3), the definition of 'binge drinking' and so on. Therefore, this policy theme aims to rationalize and provide standardized definitions so that data findings will be comparable across all areas. Similarly, evaluations of actions can then be debated and future strategies sought. Having said that, as pan-European legislation or campaigns have been dictated, it might seem difficult to compare success on a like-by-like basis, as some new member states might not have the resources to tackle each of the themed priorities.

Table 2.2 considers the 'standard unit' of alcohol. Consumers in each country are advised of a suggested guideline on how much they should consumer per day. For example, the guideline for an English woman is 2–3 units per day. Units in the UK are 8 gms of ethanol. The same English woman taking a holiday in Japan may receive 19.75 gms of ethanol per unit. Clearly, standard drinks are not standard throughout the world. Within Europe, the same pattern occurs. The amount of ethanol the English woman is given when ordering an alcoholic drink in Poland, Spain, France, Portugal and so on would be greater than that which she is given in England. If the evening's consumption is the

Table 2.2   Standard alcohol units, worldwide

Standard drink/unit size (in grams of ethanol)	Country
8.0	UK
9.9	Netherlands
10.0	Australia
	Hungary
	Ireland
	New Zealand
	Poland
	Spain
11.0	Finland
12.0	Denmark
	France
	Italy
	South Africa
13.6	Canada
14.0	Portugal
	United States

Source: International Center for Alcohol Policies 2007.

Table 2.3   Example of variation of ethanol units, by country

Country	Units	Total
England	3 units × 8.00gms ethanol	24.00gms ethanol
Spain	3 units × 10.00gms ethanol	30.00gms ethanol
Portugal	3 units × 12.00gms ethanol	36.00gms ethanol
Japan	3 units × 19.57gms ethanol	59.25gms ethanol

recommended 3 units, then the total is wildly different, as Table 2.3 shows.

Equally interesting is the term 'standard drink'. In the UK, a measure of vodka may be 25 ml, which equates to approximately one unit. The strength of most vodka spirit is 37.5 per cent ABV. However, some countries use 'free pour', so no precise amount of vodka is given, therefore, the consumer might receive 1.78 measures. Similarly, not all vodka is 37.5 per cent ABV. Vodka from Russia and Poland can have and ABV as high as 90 per cent. These are only limited examples of how difficult it can be to adhere to Theme 5, 'Develop, support and maintain a common

Table 2.4   EU beer duty rates

Country	Duty per HL at 5% abv*	Pence per pint**	VAT rate
Austria	25.03 Euro	9.7p	20.0%
Belgium	20.53 Euro	8.0p	21.0%
Denmark	345.75 Dkr	18.1p	25.0%
Finland	143.00 Euro	55.5p	22.0%
France	13.00 Euro	5.0p	19.6%
Germany	9.45 Euro	3.7p	16.0%
Greece	14.16 Euro	5.5p	18.0%
Ireland	99.36 Euro	38.5p	21.0%
Italy	16.80 Euro	6.5p	20.0%
Luxembourg	9.52 Euro	3.7p	15.0%
Netherlands	25.11 Euro	9.7p	17.5%
Portugal	15.52 Euro	5.9p	19.0%
Spain	8.87 Euro	3.4p	16.0%
Sweden	735 Skr	30.9p	25.0%
UK	61.10 £	34.7p	17.5%

*Either 5% abv or 12 degrees plato depending on system.
**Pence per pint equivalent (£1 = 1.465 Euro)
Sources: British Beer & Pub Association (2006) Eu Beer duty rates as at 11.10.2006 http://www.beerandpub.com/statistics_eubeerdutyrates.aspx [accessed 23rd December 2008].

evidence base', as 'standard' units or measures are anything but standard. It would not be an easy task to standardize these elements. The European Union has tried to harmonize alcohol excise duties for many years but, as Table 2.4 shows, VAT and excise duty on alcohol across Europe is far from equal.

It is interesting to see that some countries such as Spain, Germany, the Czech Republic and Cyprus do not place duty on their still wine. If harmonization were to take place, it would be very difficult to decide if all countries would bring duty charges to the highs of Norway and Iceland or to the lows of Spain or Cyprus.

Commentary on the European strategy

The European Economic and Social Committee criticized the Commission for not advising the public that the reason that alcohol causes harm is because it is a psychoactive drug, becoming a toxic substance when drunk excessively and, for some people, becoming an addictive substance. Public health specialist Peter Anderson, speaking through the press release by Eurocare, stated: 'The alcohol industry has lobbied to put their own profits above the needs of the European people, with Commission officials other than those directly involved with health issues surrendering to its pressure.' He went further by stating the European Commission's alcohol policy is 'much weaker than the first draft and has a much greater focus on education as the answer to solving the problems of alcohol, when the evidence shows that it does not work'. He called for 'better regulation of the product and its marketing (Eurocare 2007).

Similarly, the European Economic and Social Committee argued that the priority themes were without timelines or targets, therefore giving little impetus to the process, and a great deal of emphasis has been given to educating the public, a strategy that it was felt has little chance of success. These initial thoughts from the European Economic and Social Committee and Dr Anderson look to governments to leave less control in the hands of the consumer and provide a comprehensive set of directives.

Of course, each country in the European Union has a different view of alcohol in their society. Each recognizes the importance of subsidiarity; that is, each country taking responsibility for how any overall guidelines are implemented, and it is to one example of this, England, that we now turn.

Alcohol harm reduction strategy for England

Pubs have been at the heart of local communities for hundreds of years. More recently, they have appealed to men, women and families, increasingly becoming a social gathering place for people of all ages. Despite that, some parts of society are drinking harmful quantities of alcohol either socially in pubs, prior to going to pubs (known as 'pre-loading') or in their own homes. It is the excesses of drinking that have, in part, driven the UK government to provide an alcohol reduction strategy for England, whilst at the same time recognizing the social and economic good that alcohol brings to the country as a whole:

> They [pubs, clubs and bars] are also vital for the generation of new employment opportunities that breathe life into communities. Sales of alcohol of around £30 billion each year generate duty and VAT that buys our country's schools, roads, hospitals and puts policemen on our streets. (Department of Culture, Media and Sport 2002)

These are the words of Tessa Jowell, the Culture Secretary, as she addressed the Tenth Anniversary Conference of the Association of Licensed and Multiple Retailers in 2002. Tessa Jowell appreciated the contribution the licensed trade made in tax duty and VAT; she also announced that she was going to reform licensing legislation to encourage a 'European-style drinking cafe culture' and modernize hitherto Edwardian laws into twenty-first-century policies, and encourage families and friends to socialize in safe, friendly environments.

The main element being introduced was flexible opening hours. The new legislation would give pubs, clubs and bars the opportunity to open up to 24 hours a day, seven days a week. Licensed house managers were advised that their requests for longer opening hours would need to consider the impact their extensions would have on local residents. Additionally, there would be a seamless system for selling alcohol, providing entertainment and/or refreshment. To continue the reduction in bureaucracy, personal licences would be introduced instead of premises licences. This would make it much easier for licensees to move from managing and selling alcohol in one pub/bar to another without the requiring premises licences, thus bypassing a visit to the local Magistrates Court. This would be efficient in terms of cost and time. Also, the local authority would issue the personal licences rather than the Magistrates; this was deemed to be an improvement, as local authorities have a better understanding of their overall night-time economy. Finally, the Children's Certificate was abolished and, at the personal licence holders discretion, children could be allowed to have access to any part of the pub, bar or club (under supervision).

The improvements certainly enabled pubs, clubs and bars the opportunity to be more flexible and, also, they had the ability to alter their operating hours more simply. For example, many pubs, clubs and bars changed their closing hours from 11 pm on Monday to Saturday and 10.30 pm on Sunday to 2am on Monday to Sunday. Operationally they opened their doors until 12pm Monday to Sunday – but had the opportunity to extend their opening hours until 2 pm if a consumer was hosting a birthday party in the licence holder's premises or if it were the end of season Darts and Dominos party. The personal licence holder would not have to be granted a Special Licence from the Courts, as they had been required to do under previous legislation.

There were many positive elements to the promises made by Tessa Jowell. However, when the Alcohol Harm Reduction Strategy for England was published in 2004 many were worried about increases in crime, violence, sexual health and the strains on hospital and police services when pubs, bars and clubs could open 24 hours a day, 7 days a week. The popular media brandished phrases such as 'on the lash – permanently', 'excessive violence' and 'boozy Britain'. Indeed, newspaper commentators such as Chapman (2005) of the *Daily Mail* reported on the lunacy of 24-hour drinking, and judges and police warning that it would trigger a devastating explosion of violence. His colleague Nicholson (2005) reported, only a day earlier, that the change in the drinking laws would merely be, to consumers, an alcoholic 'free for all'. Sensationalist new phrases began to move into the popular language with *The Mirror* (2004); for instance, introducing us to 'Yob Squads' who were already spoiling cities and towns. Asthana (2005), of *The Observer*, reported that on an 'investigative night out' she was personally sold enough alcohol to kill a person, within three hours, within one bar. This led her to also consider the potential amounts of alcohol that consumers might be able to drink when extended opening hours came into play. And projecting the same message, but in a simpler way, Toynbee (2005) of *The Guardian* suggested that the 24-hour drinking proposal be scrapped as it was a 'foolhardy and [a] dangerous plan'. Health Ministers and Shadow Cabinet Ministers were also declaring their fears for the longer-term outlook.

Prime Minister Tony Blair and Tessa Jowell responded by stating they 'believed' that 24-hour drinking would create the European lifestyle, cut down disorder outside pubs, clubs and bars as consumers would not all be shepherded out of licensed premises at exactly the same moment, and would reduce 'binge drinking' as consumers would not feel 'rushed to cram in' an extra pint or two in the last 15 minutes before closing time. It would be difficult to substantiate these claims, and no research came forward as evidence to the claims. Further reactions to the press and media furore came in January 2005 as Tessa Jowell (Department of Culture, Media and Sport) and Hazel Blears (Home Office) tried to calm down the popular media. Jowell stated that the licensing reforms were written to simplify existing laws that were becoming unwieldy from the amendments made over the previous decades (Plant and Plant 2006). According to Jowell, however, a new type of woman had been born – known as a 'ladette'. The ladette is 'one of the boys', who probably does not have children or a mortgage, factors that might subconsciously moderate behaviour. The ladette aims to become intoxicated even before heading out for the evening. This phenomenon of 'pre-loading' is not new. Current research shows that drinking alcohol whilst getting ready to go out has been something women have been doing for some time. Suffice it to say, counter arguments were a daily occurrence as there was concern that 24-hour licensing would damage Britain's drinking culture beyond return, and the country waited with bated breath on 26 November 2005 – the first night that 24-hour drinking could take place.

The first night passed off without incident. Indeed, Inspector George Dawson of Merseyside Police said: 'I don't think it's been any busier than any other Friday night. There were no serious violent incidents related to drink' (*BBC News* 2005). The drunken debauchery and violence that had been predicted did not happen. In July 2007, the Home Office provided some statistics to review how the police and accident and emergency wards were coping with the predicted violent and licentious behaviour. The statistics compared information planning over two years – one year before the change in licensing hours and the year after the implementation of 24-hour drinking. Thirty police forces were reviewed and there was a 1 per cent decrease in incidents such as violence, criminal damage and harassment, and a 5 per cent fall in violent crime (Hough *et al.* 2008). However, it was not all positive news. Minor crimes at 3 am or later did increase, and the peak time for violent crimes moved forward by 30 minutes. Little of the positive statistics were reflected in the press.

Safe, sensible and secure

In 2008, the UK government and Alcohol Concern, provided an alcohol implementation toolkit entitled 'Safe, Sensible and Secure', the next steps in the National Alcohol Strategy. It provides a range of resources for local teams to set-up their own alcohol strategies for their cities and towns. The toolkit is for a range of teams including Crime and Disorder Reduction Partnerships, schools, probation staff, medical directors, emergency care, the alcohol industry, public house managers, the Door Supervisory Network and so on. The document tips its hat briefly to the positive role of alcohol in British society. The positive psychological benefits include the freedom for the individual to visit their local pubs, clubs and bars to relax, feel part of the community and meet new people (Kenyon 2009a). However, the main aim of the Safe, Sensible and Secure Toolkit is to enable citizens to enjoy alcohol whilst, at the same time, reducing the harm that is associated with alcohol through crime, violence, anti-social behaviour and poor mental or physical health. However, the alcohol industry, as shown in Chapter 1, contributes large sums of money to the late-night economy, the public purse and employment. It must be noted, also, that the election promise, brought into law in 2005, following the Licensing Act 2003, did not infer that all suppliers should make alcoholic drinks available 24 hours a day, 7 days a week. The choice of opening hours was left to the licensees to establish as they thought fit in terms of fulfilling their consumers' needs whilst remaining profitable. Hence, a good deal of responsibility was placed on the people on the ground. The Act also introduced a number of objectives, including cutting down binge drinking, and preventing crime and the disorderly conduct often associated with the fixed closing time.

The licensing objectives, introduced in 2005, have yet to be met fully and are regularly debated and reviewed. Popular media state that, since the introduction of 24-hour licensing laws, binge drinking, violence, billions of lost working hours, health and societal costs have not reduced, despite the good news presented regarding the crime figures. The government, licensed retailers and trade organizations are working together to tackle the irresponsible behaviour of the minority and to provide a safe, secure, controlled environment in which people can enjoy a drink or a meal with their friends and family.

The four objectives of the Licensing Act shown in the Safe Sensible and Social Toolkit are:

- the prevention of crime and disorder
- public safety
- the prevention of public nuisance
- the protection of children from harm.

The Licensing Act 2003 enabled flexible closing times, allowing for the possibility of premises to remain open for up to 24 hours. The actual hours of operation still vary from venue to venue, depending on the operator's wishes and the consideration of the views of people affected; for example, local residents and businesses. The operation of pubs, clubs and bars is transparent, as licensed house managers, as part of their application for a premises licence, are required to submit an operating schedule to the licensing authority that includes the proposed hours of operation. The general public, police and local authorities have the opportunity to view these documents at leisure. If no relevant counter representations are made in relation to the application, the licensing authority will grant the application.

The four licensing objectives are also in place to motivate town and city centres, pubs, clubs and bars and off-licence establishments, including supermarkets, to ensure they develop their own strategies to accomplish the objectives. Initiatives such as 'Challenge 21' are helping to achieve the aims to *protect children from harm* and to *prevent crime and disorder*. The Challenge 21 scheme is used by the sellers and suppliers of alcohol in pubs, clubs, bars, off-licensed premises and supermarkets. People buying alcohol who appear to be 21 or under are challenged about their age and are often asked to provide proof of age through passports, driving licences and so on. The Home Office found that the number of sales to people under 18years of age has gone down due to higher financial penalties and stricter enforcement. They stated that the Challenge 21 initiative is now becoming standard practice and is widely accepted, thus contributing to the decrease in sales of alcohol to those legally unable to purchase alcohol from licensed premises (Home Office 2007). Additionally, legislative powers have been given to the police in the UK to also help accomplish the objective *to prevent crime and disorder*. Police can issue on the spot fines of £80 if they find revellers urinating or being sick in shop doorways, or fighting in the streets. These initiatives are some of many that aim to change behaviours that are deemed unacceptable (see Box 2.1 for details of a voluntary initiative that is supported by over 80 locations across the UK).

Box 2.1   Best Bar None by Far

Greater Manchester Police had a number of issues concerning crime and disorder in their region. As part of the Manchester City Safe project and to achieve the four objectives set out in the Alcohol Strategy, the police, local pubs, clubs and bars, felt that to move forward they needed to work together, rather than follow different paths for the same goal. Therefore, a consensual approach was formed in order to make the night-time environment safe. Existing enforcement activities would still continue, but additional operations were also put in place to demonstrate that operators of licensed premises were also committed to improving town and city evening economies. To gain commitment by the licensees, a national awards scheme was put in place for those premises that showed their commitment. The scheme is called Best Bar None and was set up in 2007 by Greater Manchester Police, the Home Office and BII (the professional body for the licensed retail sector) awards. Licensees who join the scheme can demonstrate just how effectively they manage their premises with due diligence. Due diligence is shown under four categories; which are drawn out of the licensing objectives:

Section A: Prevention of crime and disorder

Capacity
Security
Drinks/drunkenness
Drugs

Thefts/burglary
Disorder.

Section B: Public safety

First aid
Public security
Event control
Glass
Fire
Building safety
Transport.

Section C: Prevention of public nuisance

Noise
Litter/waste.

Section D: Protection of children from harm

Underage policy
Under 18s policy.

Independently trained assessors visit each licensee. The assessments last between one and two hours as each of the categories needs to be discussed and evidence provided showing that staff training has taken place, capacity is monitored, anti-drugs policy is promoted, waste is disposed of effectively and so on. Following the assessment, those licensed premises that have been able to demonstrate good practice receive a plaque with the Best Bar None logo. The Best Bar None logo and scheme is becoming recognised, and Best Bar None administrators in local councils are approaching University Students Unions to promote pubs, clubs and bars that have the award so that students visit areas that are safe and secure. Additionally, some towns and cities are promoting pubs, clubs and bars that have the Best Bar None award on their tourism websites and brochures to demonstrate that their area is a safe place to visit for an enjoyable night out. In addition to working together with, and forming better relationships with, the police and local authorities, licensees are also demonstrating they are socially responsible citizens within the community.

Best Bar None is a voluntary scheme and it has a number of benefits:

1 It aids local council targets and demonstrates they have put a
  strategy in place to achieve the Alcohol Licensing Objectives;

2 It promotes the area and is contributing to a safer night-time environment;
3 It rewards good bars that are ethically and socially responsible;
4 It shows to the general public that a bar is serious about the type of consumer it does not want on the premises. Therefore, revellers who are drunk, disorderly, carry drugs and/or knives or are loud and/or abusive will not be accepted. The message is simple – we (Best Bar None licensees) do not want you here.

Conclusion

This chapter has reviewed the statistics on alcohol related harm. It has noted the framework of the World Health Organization and the European Strategy as key examples of global and inter-state responses. Whilst there are real differences in both recommendations and in national contexts, there is also a broad consensus about the need to deal with the problem and the importance of balancing individual freedom and government action. The response of the UK government with a strategy for England was also examined. The attempt to provide a positive framework for personal choice and responsible behaviour has left many questions. However, it has not led to the moral disintegration that some feared. On the contrary, such an approach, combined with careful local strategies, is beginning to develop a community of practice where the main European aims are being addressed, partly through reinforcing good and effective patterns of behaviour. In effect, this provides an example of subsidiarity, with international, national and local groupings each taking responsibility for different aspects, from broad framework and aims, to operating a community that is safe and hospitable.

We will further develop the ethical themes of freedom and intervention in Chapter 4. Before that we will examine the problem of alcohol marketing and advertising, a particularly contentious aspect of the alcohol industry.

3
Advertising and Marketing Alcohol

Introduction

Alcohol advertising is all around us. Whilst watching television we laugh with the young men playing practical jokes on their friends in the WKD advertisements; we linger over the imagery of Piper Heidsieck champagne as we flick through glossy magazines and we might even nod in appreciation at the band line-up shown on music festival t-shirts sponsored by Carling for nine consecutive years. Producers of alcohol beverage brands invite us to listen, look and even wear their messages. Some argue the promotion of alcohol brands should be totally banned to prevent young and vulnerable people being drawn into the hedonistic carefree lifestyles often depicted in alcohol advertising and sponsored events, which in turn could lead to physiological and psychological harm. The brewing industry and spirits manufacturers point out that they advertise primarily to protect market share and not to encourage alcohol drinking per se. And, of course, it is ultimately down to the consumer to negotiate between the 'upsides' depicted in promotional activity and the 'downsides' that excessive alcohol consumption has on their own physical and mental health.

This chapter will consider alcohol advertising, promotion and sponsorship, it will also discuss the rules and regulations that govern the messages depicted in them and evaluate how alcohol brands imbed themselves into our culture. The chapter has three separate sections. The first section will consider global regulations that surround alcohol advertising, and how European and UK communications fit within the international scene. It will also discuss the effects a total ban would have on industry and consumption. The second section will reflect on big-budget, high-profile television advertising, radio and press campaigns and alcohol brand sponsorship. This will include examples such as Guinness advertisements and Johnnie Walker Scotch whisky, sponsors of McLaren's Formula One racing team (based in Woking, England). Some fear that alcohol linked with the sport and leisure industry will encourage vulnerable consumers who feel the sponsors are inviting them into that world. Elite sports would be hit hard if the sponsorship money from the brewing industry and spirits manufacturers were to be banned, as finding new partners could take several years. The final section considers the advertising initiatives put in place by the organizations such as the Home Office and the National Health Service to encourage consumers to 'know their limits' and acknowledge the harm that alcohol can cause. There has often been criticism that advertisements and promotions encourage drinking. There are also a number of 'joint' communications put forward by alcohol manufacturers, departments of health and governments to educate the public about the social and physical harm of excessive drinking.

Alcohol advertising regulations across the world

The link between excessive, harmful drinking and health problems is a given. Alcohol producers and the World Health Organization (2008a) certainly agree on that. What they do not wholeheartedly agree on is a definition of what harmful drinking is, and whether alcohol advertising and marketing encourages consumers to drink or drink more, leading to the health problems frequently referred to throughout this book. Many countries have made, or are considering imposing, strict rules, regulations and legislation with regard to the promotion and advertising of alcohol. This is in response to pleas from the World Health Organization, Alcoholics Anonymous, law enforcement agencies, psychiatric services and so on. However, in 2002 the International Center for Alcohol Policies (ICAP) presented a report to the World Health Organization regarding the ethical position of the alcohol industry. They specifically reported on the ethical roles that beverage producers play whilst, at the same time, giving alcohol a 'space' within culture and society through advertising and marketing. The International Center for Alcohol Policies is an organization sponsored by international alcoholic drink producers including Allied Domecq PLC, Bacardi-Martini, Foster's Group Limited and South African Breweries PLC. Some would argue, then, that the report is not disinterested. However, alcohol producers clearly show their support to 'global group thinking' of how alcohol consumption affects health. It also shows they are prepared to review the effects that marketing and advertising have upon consumption levels, with the assurance that negative consequences will be acted on. This demonstrates their willingness to access and implement change where necessary, which, in turn, is an addition to each producer's ethical and corporate social responsibility (CSR) commitments. Bacardi-Martini, for example, state they adhere to the social responsibilities of both DISCUS (the Distilled Spirits Council for the United States – the main home for Bacardi) and the EFRD (European Forum for Responsible Drinking – European countries contributing to Bacardi-Martini's income) when marketing and advertising their range of alcoholic beverages. DISCUS states that alcoholic beverage consumption has been both an accepted practice and an important one in the forming of social and cultural traditions now and throughout history. Their voluntary codes, which were first published in 1934, provide clear guidance regarding the responsibilities to which beverage producers such as Bacardi should adhere. Codes are set in place so as not to include cartoon-like images, characters that would appeal to children, or images depicting sexual prowess and sexual success. Foster's Group Limited goes further in demonstrating worldwide social and ethical responsibility when marketing and advertising its alcoholic beverage range. Foster's Group Limited also states categorically that it will comply with the mandatory or voluntary rules and codes applicable to the country in which it is marketing its products. Additionally, if there are no guidelines, Fosters avow they will implement their own guidelines and, indeed, assist markets to develop their own voluntary code of practice (Fosters 2005). ❋

Recommendations from the industry sponsored report *Industry Views on Beverage Alcohol Advertising and Marketing, with Special Reference to Young People* (2002), prepared by the International Center for Alcohol Polices, did not state that worldwide enforcement policies should be implemented. They report that a total ban on alcohol marketing and advertising was not recommended, as their review did not show there was clear evidence of an association between adverting and levels/patterns of drinking. This concurs with Nelson's findings of 2001 and Ringhold's recent findings of 2008.

Nelson (2001) also states that, after a thorough investigation of published literature, the majority of scientific evidence does not show there to be a direct and material relationship between advertising and the level of alcohol abuse and alcohol consumption. Failure to find statistically significant evidence using advanced econometric methods, leads to the conclusion that there is no link between international bans and reduced alcohol consumption.

Overall, then, it could be argued that the data referred to in Chapter 2 about the economic and social costs of alcohol consumption cannot be simplistically connected to alcohol advertisements. The World Health Organization (2008b) has acknowledged this, accepting that alcohol is part of national cultures and celebrations, and turn their attention specifically to advertising that might influence children, those under the legal age limit for consuming/purchasing alcohol and 'other' vulnerable people. The World Health Organization goes on to say that alcohol producers will appeal to young people who have chosen to drink, because they are a profitable market. They understand that it is difficult to target young adults that want to drink without exposing those that do not wish to start drinking, as all share the same or similar media consumption patterns and leisure behaviour. However, the World Health Organization argues there is a need for controls and/or partial bans on advertising, the volume of advertisements, placements of alcoholic drinks within or around media, sponsorships and so on. They also recommend controls or partial bans on the content within advertisements (World Health Organization 2008b). This return to the notices that we are living in an alcocentric environment.

Interestingly, when the general public within the EU were asked 'To what extent do you agree or disagree with the following?: "Alcohol advertising targeting young people should be banned in all EU member states"', 76 per cent agreed to the banning of alcohol advertising targeted at young people. Every second respondent (50 per cent) said that they 'agree totally' with this idea. Figure 3.1 shows the findings, and Figure 3.2 shows the findings by country.

Of Slovakians, 93 per cent agreed with this statement, showing the strongest commitment to this statement. The Luxembourgers and the Danes are less committed, with 58 per cent and 59 per cent, respectively. It should be noted that this question could be misleading. The Eurobarometer is an excellent source of research regarding consumer perceptions and consumption of alcohol. However, the assumption behind the figures is that all respondents to the questionnaire have the same view of what young people are. The questions do not define young people in the minds of the respondent: they could be young people who choose to drink, young people who have just turned 18, young people who are under the legal age to consume alcohol on licensed premises or young people who are children and so on.

However, the need to follow specific ethical codes for marketing and advertising to young people is imperative and has already been demonstrated by Bacardi-Martini and the Foster Group. All global alcohol producers of repute also follow the recommendations provided by the World Health Organization to keep children and vulnerable people from harm. In countries such as Morocco, Jamaica and Kyrgyzstan (World Health Organization 2004), which have no minimum age for purchasing alcoholic beverages in licensed premises, self-regulatory codes set by the Alcohol Standards Association, International Center for Alcohol Policies, EGTA (2008), European Association of Television and Radio Sales

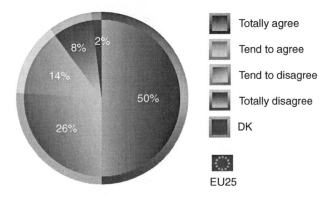

Figure 3.1   EU public response to the banning of alcohol advertising
Source: Eurobarometer (2007): 31.

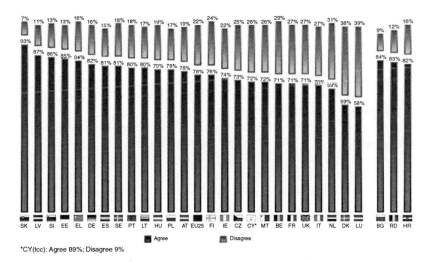

*CY(tcc): Agree 89%; Disagree 9%

Figure 3.2   Banning alcohol advertising, by country
Source: Eurobarometer (2007): 32.

Houses, the International Code of Advertising and so on, are crucial or they provide very detailed self-regulatory measures to ensure that alcoholic drinks are not promoted to consumers under the age of majority, as defined by that country.

Enforcement or self-regulation?

The World Health Organization has called upon each country not only to protect young people and vulnerable adults from harm, but also to reduce health problems: 'By the year 2015, the adverse health effects from the consumption of addictive substances such as tobacco, alcohol and psychoactive drugs should have been significantly reduced in all Member States' (World Health Organization 1998).

The World Health Organization is an important international non-governmental organization (NGO), but it has no legal basis. Therefore, it is down to each member state to provide codes, guidelines and policies to decrease the number of health related problems occurring within their borders. Many countries have enabled alcoholic beverage producers to 'self-regulate' alcohol advertising by actively embracing the International Code of Advertising brought together by the International Chamber of Commerce. The self-regulatory code conveys clear ethical messages for alcohol suppliers to follow, whether they are advertising on television, text messaging promotions or engaged in direct response marketing. The fundamental ethical implications are that advertisements must be decent, honest and truthful. With that in mind, the objectives are:

- to demonstrate responsibility and good practice in advertising and marketing communication across the world
- to enhance overall public confidence in marketing communication
- to respect privacy and consumer preferences
- to ensure special responsibility as regards marketing communication and children/young people
- to safeguard the freedom of expression of those engaged in marketing
- to enable effective communication (as embodied in Article 19 of the United Nations International Covenant of Civil and Political Rights)
- to provide practical and flexible solutions
- to minimize the need for detailed governmental and/or inter-governmental legislation or regulations. (International Chamber of Commerce 2006: 9).

Clearly, the International Chamber of Commerce suggests that all organizations promoting any product or service should take responsibility for communication. In essence, the International Code of Advertising is similar to DISCUS and the EFRD and, indeed, the many other international or country specific self-regulatory codes. The plethora of voluntary, self-administered, industry-driven and locally governed codes indicate that enforcement and legislation of alcohol advertising is not the preferred way forward for many. And, as stated above, banning alcohol advertising does not necessarily change the amount of alcohol drunk. ICAP (2008) goes on to say that many countries use voluntary codes and good practices but these are only a small step in tackling the wider problems excessive drinking has on health. Indeed, the World Health Organization's European Charter on Alcohol does not call for global enforcement *per se* but simply states:

> All children and adolescents have the right to grow up in an environment protected from the negative consequences of alcohol consumption and, to the extent possible, from the promotion of alcoholic beverages. (IAS 2003, 2)

Once again, this statement assumes that alcohol beverage producers are morally responsible for ensuring the environment is not dominated by hedonistic, fantasy filled promotional campaigns.

Out of these overarching statements and objectives, the Council of the European Union made specific recommendations in respect of alcohol beverages sold to or targeted at young people or children. The key recommendations in terms of alcohol advertising include omitting:

- the use of styles (such as characters, motifs or colours) associated with youth culture, featuring children, adolescents, or other young looking models, in promotion campaigns
- implications of social, sexual or sporting success
- encouragement of children and adolescents to drink, including low price selling to adolescents of alcoholic drinks. (Council Recommendations 2001/458/EC)

These recommendations clearly emerge from those made by the World Health Organization. It is evident, then, that advisory bodies are drawing from similar agendas to provide guidelines for member states in Europe and beyond. Despite the similarities in recommendations, there is bound to be a vast difference in interpretation and implementation of 'advertising policy' in countries that are often poles apart in their attitude towards alcohol. Some countries lean towards a temperance attitude to alcohol whilst others are more tolerant of a drinking culture. As there is no global formula, governments will have to make a decision as to whether to allow alcohol advertisers a free hand and or fully regulate every facet of the alcohol advertising industry.

In the 118 countries surveyed by ICAP, a wide variety of alcohol advertising policies came to light. For example, seven countries ban alcohol advertising completely, including Belarus and Ukraine. At the other end of the scale, there are 23 counties that have no controls on alcohol advertising. These 23 countries include Romania, Moldova, Georgia, Namibia and Laos. In 45 countries, alcohol advertising is specifically restricted through statutory legislation. Table 3.1 shows the alcohol advertising policies of France, Poland and the UK: all three countries have an openness about their drinking culture, and yet they have different views on alcohol adverting regulations.

As Table 3.1 shows, France enforces very strict legislation despite the fact that it is tolerant of a responsible drinking culture. France, as part of the Loi Evin (the French alcohol policy law passed in 1991 by Claude Evin), banned television and cinema advertising – at the same time, banning branded sponsorship of events. France also partly restricts alcohol advertising on the radio; it is only allowed between 5pm and midnight. They were keen to get rid of 'lifestyle' advertising, as this was often accused of encouraging consumers – particularly young people – to drink alcohol. However, the strict enforcement might change, as President Sarkozy has stated that wine is part of French tradition and the country's heritage and identity. He went on to say that he empathized with wine-makers who could not compete in a marketplace where some organizations (food, retail and so on) can advertise and wine-makers cannot. Sarkozy – who, incidentally, is teetotal – promised he would relax the ban on television and cinema advertising. Delphine Blanc, Director of Vin et Société, is still pressing Sarkozy to make good his promise (Kevany 2008).

Similar to France, Poland has complete restrictions with respect to the country's 'traditional' drink. It is not permitted to advertise spirits, such as vodka, in any form of medium. The Polish Unfair Competition Act (1993) states that it is unlawful to advertise alcohol, except beer. The restriction was put in place to combat alcoholism. Advertising beer and wine is allowed, provided that the adverts are not:

- performed on the basis of creating associations with sexual attractiveness, leisure, body fitness, science, professional activities, job or life success, health

Table 3.1 Alcohol advertising policies of France, Poland and the UK

	France			Poland			UK		
	Beer	Wine	Spirit	Beer	Wine	Spirit	Beer	Wine	Spirit
National TV	CR	CR	CR	PR	CR	CR	VR	VR	VR
Cable TV	CR	CR	CR	PR	CR	CR	VR	VR	VR
Satellite TV	–	–	–	PR	CR	CR	VR	VR	VR
National radio	PR	PR	PR	PR	CR	CR	VR	VR	VR
Internet	PR	PR	PR	PR	CR	CR	–	–	–
Printed newspapers and magazines	PR	PR	PR	PR	CR	CR	VR	VR	VR
Billboards	NR	NR	NR	PR	CR	CR	VR	VR	VR
Point of sale	PR	PR	PR	PR	PR	PR	VR	VR	VR
Cinema	CR	CR	CR	CR	CR	CR	VR	VR	VR
Rented videos	CR	CR	CR	VR	VR	VR	–	–	–
Product placement in TV shows and films	CR	CR	CR	PR	PR	CR	–	–	–
Sponsored events identified with brand name	CR	CR	CR	PR	PR	CR	–	–	–
Non-alcohol products identified with brand name	CR	CR	CR	CR	CR	CR	–	–	–

Notes: **CR** = Complete restriction; **PR** = Part restriction; **NR** = No restriction; **VR** = Voluntary agreement; – = Information not available/clear.
Source: Adapted from International Center for Alcohol Policies (2002): 23–30.

- conducted on television or radio, or in a cinema or theatre between 6 am and 8 pm, except for advertising performed by an organizer of a sporting event during that event. (Polish Investment and Foreign Investment Agency 2006)

Clearly, Poland has aligned its alcohol policy to the recommendations of the World Health Organization and the Council of the European Union. It should be noted that commercial advertising of alcohol in Poland did not exist before the early 1990s, due to television broadcasting being under the control of the Communist Party. Until 1992, many alcohol advertisements were shown, including advertisements for spirits. In 1992, the Ministry of Health banned all alcohol advertising due, in part, to an attempt to lead consumer behaviour away from alcohol consumption. However, the decision was changed in 2001, when the Complete and Part Restrictions shown in Table 3.1 came into force. In the early 1990s, beer was considered to be a drink that uneducated, poor, working-class Poles would choose. However, it was noted that young, educated and middle-class men, women and students were tending towards beer, rather than vodka, as their drink of choice. Beer advertisements in Poland now depict interesting lifestyles, such as students at parties, young women enjoying picnics or sharing an evening at a restaurant, or fun evenings for men in pubs and clubs (Rabikowska 2008). The sales of beer increased and the sales of vodka decreased, and this trend has continued with increases in the annual beer consumption similar to other European countries (PriceWaterhouseCoopers 2007). The change in the alcoholic drink chosen, however, is not necessarily accounted for by the fact that beer is the only alcoholic drink that can be advertised on television. There are many other factors that might have influenced the nation, including the economic growth of the country; exposure to new brands, with organizations such as Carlsberg investing in Poland; and the fact that many Poles travel internationally, which, in turn, exposes them to beer brands and culture in Belgium or the UK, for example.

It is clear that International and European organizations and commissions have similar agendas around health and well-being. Each organization, be it in an advisory capacity or in alcohol production, understands the affects of harmful drinking. As indicated, there are many ways to self-regulate or ban alcohol advertisements and promotions, and each country has its own policies ('Policies on Alcohol Advertising Restrictions Worldwide', in ICAP 2002). The following section reviews the UK government's range of restrictive policies and advisory bodies.

These would seem to be effective, despite the fact that Table 3.1 shows the UK to be self-regulatory.

Alcohol and advertising: government strategy for England and Wales

As outlined in Chapter 1, the UK government has attempted to ratio-nalize policy to offset the health problems created by the minority misuse of alcohol. In 2004, the government introduced the Alcohol Harm Reduction Strategy for England (AHRSE 2004). The strategy docu-ment was a long time in the making, as numerous consultations within the alcohol industry took place. Prime Minister Tony Blair's opening statement began: 'For the drinks industry, the priority is to end irre-sponsible promotions and advertising; to better ensure the safety of their staff and customers; and to limit the nuisance caused to local communities' (AHRSE 2004: 3). The strategy document confirmed that alcohol not only had many health benefits, but also the social benefits of enjoying an alcoholic drink with friends and family. Health problems, however, include coronary heart disease, ischemic stroke, peripheral vas-cular disease, diabetes, gallstones, cognitive functioning and dementia (IAS 2008). Generally, however, the 'nation' accepts responsible drink-ing as part of English society because of its benefits and its cultural heritage. But there has already been criticism of the strategy, per se, by scholars and practitioners alike (Alcohol Concern 2005, Drummond 2004, Luty 2005). The criticisms are mainly around the government delegating a large area of public policy to the commercial industry. There-fore, the key question remains: 'Will commercial, profit-led industries, which already reject policies that try to control alcohol consumption levels of whole populations, actively engage with the initiatives set out in AHRSE?' Even as we write, the alcohol industry is voluntarily developing a range of policies that align themselves to AHRSE, thus showing that the commercial giants, local brewers and spirits manufac-turers are all moving collectively in the same direction as governmental strategies.

As stated at the beginning of this chapter, the UK has opted for a self-regulatory system. The advertising codes are developed by the Com-mittees of Advertising Practice (broadcast and non-broadcast, BACP and CAP). The Advertising Standards Authority (ASA) acts as the indepen-dent regulator of the codes, and is the established means of dealing with complaints, recognized as such by the government and the courts. With respect to broadcasting, the ASA has co-regulatory responsibilities with the Office of Communications (Ofcom). Ofcom, however, is not involved in the day-to-day regulation of advertising; its focus, rather, is programme content, including product placement.

One example of a self-regulatory code for advertising is the British Code of Advertising Practice.

British Code of Advertising Practice

11.8.1 – Rules for all alcohol advertising

1) Advertisements must not suggest that alcohol can contribute to an individual's popularity or confidence, or that refusal is a sign of weakness. Nor may they suggest that alcohol can enhance personal qualities;
2) Advertisements must not suggest that the success of a social occasion depends on the presence or consumption of alcohol;
3) Advertisements must not link alcohol with daring, toughness, aggression or anti-social behaviour;
4) Advertisements must not link alcohol with sexual activity or success or imply that alcohol can enhance attractiveness;
5) Advertisements must not suggest that regular solitary drinking is acceptable or that drinking can overcome problems. (IAS 2005, Factsheet 7)

Such rules harness the aims and recommendations set out in the European Charter on Alcohol by the World Health Organization. In addition to the core self-regulatory structure, there are other organizations within the UK that contribute to good reflective practice. These include the Portman Group (an organization, sponsored by the main drinks industry, that has an industry code of practice for advertising) and the Drink Aware Trust (an organization, funded by the drinks industry and personal donations, that engages in educational campaigns and develops CSR campaigns).

The ASA has a dual role. First, the general public and the producers of alcoholic drink can make complaints using the easy to follow procedures provided on the ASA's website or their printed material, should they feel an alcohol advertisement does not accord with the codes. Second, the ASA monitors alcohol advertisements to ensure that, in their opinion, alcohol advertisers have not breached the advertising codes.

In the first ten months of 2008, the ASA received over 21,000 complaints; of these less than 2 per cent involved alcohol adverts. The

ASA investigated 142 complaints of about 24 of these adverts, upholding 20 complaints relating to 13 of them, which were found to be in breach of the code. Box 3.1 provides example adjudications.

Box 3.1   Complaints about alcohol advertisements

Southern Comfort

Brown-Forman Beverages Europe Ltd – 29 October 2008

A TV advertisement for Southern Comfort opened with an image of some glasses of Southern Comfort with ice. The advertisement then showed a group of friends entering a bar, greeting each other and posing for photographs. One of the friends said 'Yeah, Southern Comfort!' A young woman was shown carrying two glasses of Southern Comfort and placing them on a table. The friends then danced to music; on-screen text stated 'DRINKAWARE.CO.UK SOUTHERN-COMFORT.COM ...'. A bartender poured Southern Comfort into a shaker and said 'SoCo for everyone?'; the friends then raised their glasses in a toast while posing for a photograph. The scene froze and then morphed into one photograph of many stuck to a bulletin board. On-screen text stated 'FOR PICTURE PERFECT NIGHTS PLEASE DRINK RESPONSIBLY' and a bottle of Southern Comfort was shown. Energetic music played throughout the advertisement.

The full adjudication can be viewed on the ASA website at www.asa.org.uk

Comment

This advertisement received four complaints by the general public. Complainants felt the advertisement implied that, to have a successful social evening, alcohol was required, and it may encourage irresponsible consumption of alcohol and that alcohol would make an individual popular. The Advertising Standards Authority deemed the advert unacceptable on the grounds that it implied that successful social occasions needed the presence of alcohol (*breached BCAP TV Advertising Standards Code 11.8.1 (g) (2)). It was also deemed unacceptable because several 'rounds of drinks' were bought (*breached BCAP TV Advertising Standards Code 11.8.2). However, in terms of increasing popularity, the Advertising Standards Authority felt the advertisement did not suggest that alcohol had enabled the group of friends to become more popular as the advertisement implied that they were already friends (did *not* breach BCAP TV Advertising Standards Code 11.8.1(g)(3)).

Outcome

The advertisement could not be shown again in its original form.

Carling

Coors Brewers Ltd – 7 May 2008

This matter related to two TV advertisements and a poster advertisement for Carling beer.

TV advertisement 1

This TV advertisement depicted a group of male astronauts in spacesuits and helmets arriving in their spacecraft before a giant entity of light somewhere in space. The entity boomed, 'Do you seek the truth?' and one of the astronauts, with pronounced eyebrows, replied, in hushed tones, 'Yes.' 'Come forward', continued the entity. 'Hang on, are those trainers?' The camera panned to the feet of an astronaut who appeared to be wearing canvas loafers. 'Sorry, I don't make the rules', the entity continued. The astronaut in the trainers said, 'I thought they were quite smart.' 'The rest of you are all right', said the alien. 'Go on in without me', the trainer-wearing astronaut said. 'We're not leaving him!' exclaimed another. 'Actually mate', the astronaut with the pronounced eyebrows said to the entity, 'I think we're probably going to try somewhere else instead.' The trainer-wearing astronaut gave a grin. 'It looks rubbish anyway', said one of the others. Classical music played as the astronauts merged together into a group silhouette before the being of light and one of them gave a two-fingered victory sign. The text 'YOU KNOW WHO YOUR MATES ARE' appeared on-screen across the group of astronauts. This scene was replaced by a pint of Carling with the word 'BELONG' written across it in the Carling colours of black and red.

TV advertisement 2

This TV advertisement showed the same group of men lying down in a canvas tent that was flapping in a harsh Arctic wind. They were wearing furry hoods, woolly hats and blankets. Ice appeared in their beards and moustaches. 'The radio just died', said one. 'Are we going out then?', said another. 'Don't push it Dan', replied one of the others, who had a grey blanket pulled up over his head. 'Come on, it'll be fun', enjoined the party-goer. 'Go out there in the freezing wastes? You must be mad', the man in the blanket continued, 'We're not going are we?' Dan looked injured. 'We have to go out', he said, 'It's my birthday.' 'It is his birthday', one said. 'It is his birthday', emphasised another, as if just remembering. 'Well why didn't you say so', enjoined the blanket wearer. 'Of course we're going out.' 'Is it smart?', one asked. 'Smart casual, probably', said another. 'That's the spirit boys', said Dan. 'Let's give Dan the best birthday he'll ever remember', chimed the original nay-sayer, his gloom forgotten. The polar explorers helped each other up and moved as one out into the blizzard. 'It's brightening up', one commented. Elgar's Ninth Enigma Variation, 'Nimrod', played in the background as the explorers came together in silhouette against the frozen wastes in the falling snow. The words 'YOU KNOW WHO YOUR MATES ARE' appeared across them. The final screen shot depicted a pint of Carling with the word 'BELONG' imprinted on the glass.

Poster advertisement

A poster showed the silhouette of the astronauts that appeared at the end of TV advertisement 1 with the words 'YOU KNOW WHO YOUR MATES ARE' written across it. One of the astronauts was wearing trainers. The word 'BELONG' written in Carling colours appeared in the bottom right-hand corner.

The full adjudication can be viewed on the ASA website at www.asa.org.uk

Comment

Three complainants stated that the TV advertisements and the poster advertisement suggested that, to be able to socialise with a group of people, alcohol was integral to that friendship. These objections were not upheld, as the Advertising Standards Authority felt that, because the astronauts were not drinking, were not in a pub, club or bar environment, were not drunk and did not discuss or mention alcohol, the complaints were not substantiated (*see BCAP TV Advertising Standards Code 11.8.1 (a) (2) for the breach not upheld against the television advertisements and 56.11 for the breach not upheld against the printed media advertisement). The Advertising Standards Authority challenged whether the advertisements linked

alcohol with brave, tough and daring people and situations, and suggested alcohol could overcome problems. Again, this objection was
not upheld and no further action was required.

Outcome

The advertisements could be shown again in their original form.

Source: Advertising Standards Authority (2008), www.asa.org.uk
*Full copies of the relevant Code clauses can be seen in Appendix 3.1.

Whilst Table 3.1 suggests that the UK operates voluntary restrictions, it
is clear that the advertising system has strong regulation and monitoring. The ASA, in particular, has the power to ensure compliance and
ensures that the advertisements shown on behalf of alcohol producers
are acceptable. Input from regulatory bodies, such as the ASA, affords
a positive outcome, as it provides a forum for dialogue between alcohol producers, their advertising and the general public. This process also
underlines the point that no codes or rulings can be simply applied. All
need careful discussion and interpretation in the context of any particular complaint. The ASA provides an excellent independent forum for
that dialogue and interpretation.

Alcohol advertising spend

It is hard to imagine, with all the rules, regulations, legal conditions
and voluntary codes, that the alcohol advertising industry would continue to flourish; but flourish it does. The alcohol industry is big
business throughout the world and, in the UK, this means it accounts
for 77 per cent of the £54.13 billion drinks' market (Key Note 2008).
This means that consumers spend, on average, 5 per cent of their total
expenditure on alcohol (total expenditure includes food, clothing, mortgage payments, utilities and so on). Money spent on (all) alcoholic drink
advertising (at current prices) in 1995 was £174.8 million. In 2000, it
went up to £230.3 million; in 2005, it was £219.1 million; and, in 2007,
it came down to £197.6 million (James 2008). This shows, overall, that
the alcoholic drinks advertising spend has increased by 13 per cent since
1995; the peak in alcohol advertising expenditure in the year 2000 is
likely to be attributed to the pre- and post-millennium celebrations.

It has also been suggested that the amendments to the ASA codes introduced in 2005, see Table 3.2, have made it more difficult for alcohol

Table 3.2 Alcohol Advertising Standard Codes Amendments, 2005

1 Alcohol producers must not make it implicit in their advertisement that drinking alcohol is an essential element to the success of a social occasion.
2 Alcohol advertisements must not suggest an implicit link between alcohol and sex.
3 Alcohol advertisement and producers must not use any element that would link specifically with youth culture, as this may appeal to people under 18 years of age.
4 Within the message of the alcohol advertisement the alcohol itself must be handled and served responsibly.

Source: Adapted from Mintel (2007).

advertisers to be creative, innovative and appealing, which might have contributed to the decline in advertising spend (Mintel 2007).

In addition to the changes in alcohol advertising codes of practice, there might have been several other social and economic factors that have compelled advertisers to reduce alcohol advertising spend, not least the credit crunch of 2008. However, alcohol advertising across many different media remains in a healthy state. Alcohol producers often use a range of advertising media, including, television, cinema, outdoor media, sponsorship and on-licence promotional kits. Naturally, advertising has greatest impact if 'seen' at the point of purchase, particularly as many consumers do not know which branded drink they will choose, up to the point of purchase. Therefore, millions of pounds and hours of creative thought are injected into point of purchase advertising so that the promotion can stimulate brand switching or impulse purchases. Heavyweight advertisers (for example, Baileys, Smirnoff or WKD) often provide licensees in pubs, clubs and bars with promotional kits, which include items such as branded glasses, clocks, mirrors and staff uniforms in addition to bar towels, beer mats and posters. More recently, the outdoor media are also being used very creatively by WKD, VK (Vodka Kick) and Strongbow cider. Outdoor media include large billboard or advertising hoardings, advertising on buses or taxis, and tube/train station advertising boards. Advertisements viewed in the homes of consumers or at the point of purchase are to help inform, remind and possibly encourage consumers to switch brands.

As stated earlier in this chapter, there is no conclusive evidence that high amounts of alcohol advertising induce high levels of alcohol consumption. Box 3.2 gives a brief outline of some of the advertising campaigns with which Guinness have been involved. Highlighted in the case study are promotional campaigns that would no longer be acceptable, based on the current voluntary code of advertising practice.

Box 3.2   Alcohol advertising winning awards and our hearts

One such company that has a long history in advertising, across a range of media, is Guinness. Guinness is an Irish stout that is well known throughout the world and it has been on the scene since 1862 when they branded the drink with the Brian Boru harp logo.

During the 1930s and 1940s, Guinness became synonymous with phrases that John Gilroy turned into Guinness slogans, which, in turn, found their way into everyday speech. John Gilroy was the advertising artist that introduced the slogans and very quickly his style of artwork became hugely popular. Some of Gilroy's phrases were 'Lovely day for a Guinness', 'Guinness gives you strength' and 'A Guinness a day!' The artwork presented animal characters and consumers were introduced to the now famous Guinness Toucan; seals, lions and ostriches were added to the advertising campaigns, which provided material for use in licensed premises and outdoor advertising.

The light-heartedness of the Gilmore period came to an end during the 1980s, when new symbolism was introduced with the 'Pure Genius' campaign. The 'Pure Genius' campaign played on Guinness' distinctive black body and white creamy head – one of the dominant messages of this period. Rutger Hauer, an eccentric yet edgy iconic actor, fitted this colour scheme as he always dressed in black but has light blond hair, pale skin and pale blue eyes, matching the colours of a pint of Guinness. The loveable toucan and seals were replaced with Rutger Hauer to encourage consumers to the cool, sophisticated and contemplative world of Guinness. The campaign made Rutger Hauer even more famous than his career in films and he stayed in the role for seven years, delivering over 20 advertisements. The only downside to Guinness was the fact that it took such a long time to pour that pub goers tired of waiting for their drink while their cider- or vodka-drinking friends had received theirs.

In true advertising fashion, the downside was turned into a positive and, at the beginning of 1994, the 'Anticipation' campaign was launched. Guinness introduced the two-part pour during this campaign. A man danced crazily waiting for his pint of Guinness to be poured, settle and then 'topped-up' in the two-part pour process.

During this advertisement, consumers were being 'trained' to wait patiently for their Guinness. Prior to the television advertising, Guinness had filmed the two-part pour process in O'Neill's Irish Bar in Huddersfield, West Yorkshire to be released as a training video. Steve Kenyon (licensee) and his staff provided a training rider for use in Europe; it demonstrated how to pour the perfect pint of Guinness. Clearly, with the amount of money Guinness were ploughing into television advertising, they wanted to ensure that all licensees had the knowledge of how to complete the two-part pour. Consumers in Ireland enjoyed the advertisement so much that the music 'Guaglione' by Perez Prado reached the number one slot in the music charts; it also reached number two in the UK.

The next campaign from Guinness stunned the advertising industry because of its creative direction and captured the hearts of the consumer. The campaign was 'Surfers'. Again, Guinness played on the ideas that their stout is worth waiting for. Indeed, Guinness began introducing the slogan 'good things come to those who wait' and heavily pushed the fact that it takes 119.5 seconds to pour the perfect pint. The 'Surfers' advertisement depicts a man with a group of friends waiting in anticipation for the 'ultimate wave'. The advertisement is shot in black and white, reflecting the colours of a pint of Guinness and referring back to the Rutger Hauer advertisements. As the 'ultimate wave' arrives on the horizon, the surfers dash into the water and ride the waves on their surfboards. The froth of the sea churns up around them, suggesting the perfect pint is being poured. Four white horses emerge from the waves and seem to be galloping alongside the surfers. At the end of the advertisement, the sea is calm, representing a pint of Guinness that has settled to become a perfect pint.

The voice-over for the advertisement was:

He waits; that's what he does.
And I tell you what: tick followed tock followed tick followed tock followed tick ...
Ahab says, 'I don't care who you are, here's to your dream.'
Here's to you, Ahab.
And the fat drummer hit the beat with all his heart.
Here's to waiting.

This, of course, is signalling to the consumer that the anticipation, the wait and the final result are all worthwhile.

The advertisement won the hearts of the General Public who, in 2001, voted it as number 1 in the *Sunday Times* and Channel 4's 100 Greatest Television Advertisements. The 'Surfer' advertisement was also awarded for its creative execution and innovative style, and won a gold award for Creative Direction and a further gold award for TV and Cinema Advertising at the British Design and Art Direction Awards.

This case shows how advertising can be viewed as more than 30 seconds of information that tells the audience about new products. Alcohol advertisements might be admired by the audience and the industry. The Guinness advertisements could also change the perception of Europeans (and perhaps across the world) as to whether it is worth waiting 119.5 seconds for the perfect pint of Guinness. In many respects, the Guinness advertisements were aesthetically pleasing. They also highlighted pleasure in alcohol that was focused in an ethos of reflection and responsibility.

Alcohol brands are striving, through advertising, to persuade consumers to choose their brand over their competitors'. This shift in alcoholic drink choice because of advertising might have occurred due to a number of dramatic changes in the consumption of alcohol type in recent years in terms of wine and cider.

The total amount of alcohol advertising spend, broken down into alcohol product type (beer, spirits, wine, cider and so on), shows that UK advertising spend on wine and cider has grown by 248 per cent and 484 per cent, respectively (Key Note 2008). However, taking inflation into account, total expenditure on alcohol advertising has actually decreased by 19 per cent. Some brewers and spirits manufacturers are big spenders on advertising. During 2004, £202.5 million was spent on alcohol advertising (*The Drink Pocket Book* 2006). Tables 3.3 and 3.4 break down the advertising spend and sales by value, respectively.

The facts contained in Tables 3.3 and 3.4 are interesting in their own right, but do not support the argument that high advertising spend

Table 3.3 Advertising spend, 2004

	Advertising spend (£m)	%
Beer	110.5	56.3
Cider/perry	5.4	2.75
Wines	18.2	9.27
Spirits	51.0	25.98
Alcopops	11.2	5.71
Other	Not comparable	

Table 3.4   Sales by value, 2004

	Sales by value %
Beer	44.15
Wines*	27.27
Spirits and liqueurs	19.48
Alcopops	Not comparable
Other**	9.09

Notes: ** includes cider, ready-to-drink (alcopops) spirits, fortified wines and other alcohol; * includes still, light wines (table) and sparkling wines/champagne.
Source: Adapted from *The Drink Pocket Book* (2006).

encourages consumers to drink alcohol. As highlighted earlier in this chapter, this question itself is unanswerable, as there are many reasons alcohol consumption levels change. The more important question is, therefore 'Do consumers drive alcohol producers to invest more money in the alcoholic drinks they are enjoying now, or is it the alcohol drink advertisements that encourage consumers to try out new products that they are showing on television, in the press, on the radio and so on?' Fashion trends in alcoholic drink choice have occurred many times. Alcopops, which appeared in the 1990s, have recently dropped out of favour in terms of sales on-trade and advertising spend. In 2004, approximately 20 per cent of consumers stated they had consumed a Bacardi Breezer in the last month. This figure dropped to 11 per cent during 2007 (Mintel 2007). Over the same period in 2004, Bacardi-Martini spent £1.9 million pounds on advertising and only £0.6 million during 2006 (Mintel 2007). Therefore, did the lack of advertising stop consumers choosing Bacardi Breezer as their drink of choice? Or was it new alcoholic drinks launched on the market, such as Magners cider, that captured the consumers' imagination? Or, perhaps the popular press tarnished the image of alcopops as a children's drink, thus turning the more mature consumer away from an alcoholic drink that had such negative connotations associated with it. Whatever the reason, only WKD and Smirnoff Ice currently use television, cinema and press advertising of alcopops; it will be interesting to know whether advertising campaigns for these products cease altogether as consumers seek alternative products.

New product launches in the cocktail market have been increasing recently. One of the reasons cocktails are becoming popular is because they are reminiscent of the past or fantasized holidays in far off places.

Table 3.5   Magners' advertising spend

	Outdoor	Press	Radio	TV	Total
Magners – Original Irish Cider	1,583,914	467,263	561,474	5,621,733	8,234,384

Source: Mintel (2006).

Indeed, Barcardi-Martini have changed their television advertising spend away from Bacardi Breezer to their traditional white rum with the recent introduction of a television advertisement entitled 'Bacardi: Born in the Sun'. Smirnoff has also been encouraging consumers by means of a range of television, press and billboard advertising to drink a cocktail known as a Moscow Mule, which uses Smirnoff vodka as the alcohol base. Smirnoff also provide kits, so that consumers can also make their cocktails as home if they are unable to visit a 'mixologist' in their local cocktail bar. In total, the Moscow Mule campaign cost £4 million, including television and print advertising, digital and outdoor advertising, as well as supporting the off-trade with in-store promotional kits. Interestingly, Smirnoff marketed a 'ready to drink' (alcopop) named Moscow Mule in the early 1990s. Perhaps Smirnoff feel that the consumer experience gained from having a cocktail made before their eyes is more appealing than a ready-made alcopop with its negative connotations as a children's drink. Therefore, did consumer behaviour in choosing cocktails influence the giant corporation machines of Barcardi-Martini or Smirnoff (Diageo) to advertise their core spirit range, or did the advertising influence the consumer to consider cocktails as the latest 'must have' alcoholic drink?

Ciders received little in the way of advertising spend during the early part of the twenty-first century (see Table 3.3). However, advertising spend in 2006 moved up to £16.4 million, which equates to 1 per cent of total alcohol sales (Mintel 2006). The main reason for this is that two cider brands, Bulmers and Magners, went head to head in the battle to gain the highest share of the cider markets. Sales in cider had increased at a phenomenal rate as consumers, again, switched brands and added cider to their repertoire. Table 3.5 shows how the total advertising spend for Magners cider was almost double that of all other cider producers put together (see Table 3.3).

One of the interesting elements to the Magners advertising campaign was the suggestion that consumers should pour their cider over ice. Enabling consumers to buy their bottle of cider from the bar, receive

a branded Magners glass, be provided with ice up to the brim is completely different from the 'traditional' way of receiving a pint of cider. At
will, the consumer proceeds to top up their own glass as they continue to
drink their cider. This 'new process' engages the consumer in the process
of 'delivering' the drink, which, in turn, makes them feel involved in the
drink before it is consumed. Also, could this in any way be viewed as the
company showing responsibility for engaging the consumer in drinking
the product diluted by melted ice, thereby encouraging a more relaxed
and responsible drinking style? Many alcohol producers note that their
advertising campaigns are to increase or maintain brand share. Magners
advertising campaigns are attractive, with the viewer shown contented
social scenes of community spirit, such as a party or collecting apples for
the harvest. That, alongside the involvement in pouring the drink and
replenishing it at will from the bottle purchased at the bar, gave cider a
new image, so consumers may have changed their 'drink of choice' in
order to take part in the current trend. Despite the cider phenomenon,
it did not last. This bears no reflection on the product – whose sales are
acceptable – but two cold, wet and windy British summers 'ruined' the
cider over ice experience. The experience of cider advertising reinforces
the argument that there is no simple correlation between advertising
and alcohol misuse. Its major effect was on the share of the market, and
the ethos that it portrayed was amusing, thoughtful or positive, with no
inducement to irresponsible behaviour.

Sponsorship

Just as television, press, outdoor media and so on have an extensive array
of 'industry watchers' and regulations, alcohol producers that sponsor
sporting, music or other social events also have rules, regulations and
associations. Though sponsorship seems to be a new phenomenon, it
dates back to Ancient Greece over 2000 years ago, focused then in sport
(Masterman 2007). Sports sponsorship is one of the most high-profile
areas, with alcohol producers providing 11.5 per cent of the sponsorship
market. This takes second place behind financial services organizations,
which account for 19.2 per cent of all sports sponsorship funds (Key
Note 2007). Big business alcohol producers sponsor many events, such
as the Johnnie Walker Championship at Gleneagles, the Carling Football Premiership League (which ended in 2007), the Guinness Rugby
Union Final, and also the 29th Heineken Regatta. Even small family-
run beverage businesses such as the Travellers Rest Inn, Upper Hopton,
West Yorkshire sponsor their local cricket teams to provide helpful funds.

Alcohol producers also sponsor music festivals. Carling sponsored the Leeds and Reading Music Festival, Tenants sponsored T in the Park and Heineken sponsored Oxygen.

The money pledged to the sporting teams or the arts has been heavily criticized as being another way to target young people and encourage under-age or binge drinking. Professor Ian Gilmore, President of the Royal College of Physicians and Chair of the UK Alcohol Health Alliance refers to one study, undertaken in a country with a similar sports and drinking culture to our own, as giving 'stark messages that hazardous drinking, common in sport, is seen more when the individual or club is sponsored by the drinks industry' (Cuthbertson 2008: 1). On the basis of this, Gilmore argues for a ban on alcohol related sponsors. However, the research to which he refers does not show a direct link between sponsorship and the drinking behaviour of sport watchers, not least because the research was conducted with sports stars.

Anderson and Baumberg (2006) have published an influential report, *Alcohol in Europe*, which discusses the increase in alcohol consumption in Europe over the last fifty years and specifically outlines recommendations to cut down the binge drinking culture, including a ban on sponsorship by alcohol companies and alcohol brands throughout Europe. The statistics relating to the effect of alcohol on different areas of society are impressive. However, once more, there is no connection empirically established between alcohol advertising, sponsorship and the binge drinking culture. Rowley and Williams (2008) conclude that there is very little research that even attempts to establish these connections. The links are simply assumed. At the very least, research would need to consider the complexity of the sporting culture, what core values that culture communicates, and how those values relate to the product, any advertising and to the values of any other sponsors involved in that situation. The culture of modern sport stresses health, well-being and discipline, and inclusivity – values that directly oppose binge drinking, exemplified by the English Football Association Respect Campaign.

Government information advertisements

Alcohol advertising and sponsorship has been under a great deal of pressure to be responsible, abiding by the voluntary codes, whilst creating images that protect brand share and encourage only brand switching. Berridge (2005) argues that there are no public messages that suggest other drinking options, such as abstinence. This is still the case, but the

UK Home Office and the National Health Service (NHS) have funded high profile television, radio and press advertising to inform consumers of the potential consequences of drinking. This ethical policy of educating the consumer shows how various arms of society feel responsible for the emotional and physical health of the individual. The Home Office, which deploys the Police Force, and the NHS see the brunt of alcohol excesses through the accident and emergency wards on Friday and Saturday nights or through chronic liver disease, have felt compelled to provide messages for consumers to consider alongside the advertising messages that promote alcohol brands.

One of the most objective, educational messages has come from the 'When it comes to alcohol – know your limits' campaign. Alcohol unit awareness has grown and many consumers know the recommended daily guidelines are 3–4 units a day for a man and 2–3 units a day for a woman. However, education must continue because all consumers are not aware of the daily recommended limits, neither are they always aware of the number of units in each alcoholic drink that they choose. Therefore, in May 2008 the 'Know your limits' campaign began. The campaign, which cost £10 million, uses television, billboards, press and radio, alongside websites, giving the public the opportunity to test their knowledge and calculate the number of units they have drunk.

The reason for this campaign is partly due to research showing that 77 per cent of people do not know how many units there are in a glass of wine (NHS 2008: 1). Therefore, consumers might be drinking more at home or in pubs, clubs or restaurants than they thought. For example, there are 1.25 units of alcohol present in a 125ml glass of 10 per cent ABV white wine. However, wine served in pubs, clubs and restaurants is often served in a standard measure of 175ml, where the white wine is 13 per cent ABV. This means that one standard glass of wine equals 2.3 units. The size of the glass/measure and percentage ABV is often different from pub to pub, and is certainly measured differently at home; therefore, consumers can easily lose track of how much alcohol they have consumed. The same can happen with bottled beers and lager brands, or cocktails and spirits that are 'free poured', so it is difficult to ascertain exactly what measure of alcohol is in each drink. The Public Health Minister, Dawn Primarolo, and Chief Medical Officer, Sir Liam Donaldson, stated that they were keen to inform people of the number of alcohol units in their favourite drinks so that consumers could become more aware of the amount they were drinking. This advertising campaign educates the public and gives them the opportunity to be aware and take responsibility for their own behaviour.

Two further nationwide advertisements have considered the more short-term consequences of an alcohol-fuelled night out. The advertising campaign strap line is, 'You wouldn't want to start a night like this so why end it that way'. There is a creative treatment for men and also one for women. The storyboard hinges on some of the degrading consequences of drinking too much (Box 3.3).

Box 3.3   You wouldn't want to start a night like this so why end it that way (male version)

The story begins with a young man getting ready for a night out. He then moves to the kitchen, open the door of the fridge and smears what looks like a takeaway curry down the front of his shirt.

He then goes to the bathroom and urinates over his shoes, reaches to his ear and rips out his earring, puts on his leather jacket, tears off the sleeve and, as he leaves for his night out, he kicks his stereo player down the hallway. The creative treatment concludes with the strap line: 'You wouldn't want to start a night like this, so why end it that way'.

Logos for the Home Office and Alcohol Know Your Limits are shown as the treatment ends.

Recent research regarding this advertisement is mixed but generally very favourable (Kenyon 2009b). However, participants stated that the television advertisement is very good, but soon forgotten, and suggested the very familiar 'Alcohol – Know Your Limits' logo should be present on beer pump heads to give consumers a 'self-check' at the point of sale.

Conclusion

This chapter has shown the worldwide perspective on alcohol advertising. It has also shown that the issues surrounding the advertising of alcohol are complex, and that empirical research has not established the connection between negative alcohol culture and advertising. For the most part, advertising is about competition for the market share. It also noted that, in the UK, alcohol producers must adhere to a self- regulatory code of practice for advertising or sponsorship. Regulation is provided by organizations such as Ofcom and the ASA to ensure that the codes are not breached. The process is transparent. Consumers and non-consumers have the right to complain if they feel that advertisements have broken guidelines. In addition the monitoring by these bodies, provides a context within which codes can be interpreted. Importantly, codes cannot be simply applied, they always have to be interpreted, and this demands that a body is given the task of interpretation in any conflict situation. Within that conversation, there are many different approaches to alcohol advertising, some of which are recognized as having aesthetic merit. Some also begin to focus on values, such as patience, that are quite contrary to the speed drinking culture, and this will be developed in the next chapter.

Also, the NHS and the Home Office have begun working together to encourage consumers to drink responsibly by providing educational advertisements to enable consumers to recognize their limits when it comes to alcohol. This illustrates the ways in which different agencies in this situation can aim to influence consumers. These are not mutually exclusive. On the contrary, providing different perspectives – from the framework of a positive culture of celebration, to careful reflection on the negative consequences of inappropriate drinking – can be mutually reinforcing. Indeed, placed together, the two approaches might be important in developing personal responsibility. It is personal responsibility, however, that tends to be absent from discussions about alcohol advertising. Indeed, many of the contributions focus solely on a deterministic view of the culture of the effects of alcohol advertising, as if there were no personal responsibility involved. Following chapters will look more closely at how personal responsibility relates to the wider responsibilities of government and the industry.

Appendix 3.1

BCAP TV Advertising Standard Code (correct as at December 2008 – for full and up-to-date version see www.cap.org.uk)

Guidance notes for the television alcohol advertising rules

> Rule 11.8.2(a)
> (1) Advertisements for alcoholic drinks must not be likely to appeal strongly to people under 18, in particular by reflecting or being associated with youth culture.

Guidance note:

The purpose of this rule is to prevent advertisements that might encourage those under 18 to drink, or think they should drink, alcohol. Thus, themes that are likely to appeal strongly to those under 18 are unacceptable.

It is not possible to produce an exhaustive list of possible infringements to this rule, but, as a guide, particular caution should be exercised as follows:

a) Personalities. Avoid those who are likely to have a strong appeal to the young; for example, pop stars, sportsmen and sportswomen who command particular admiration of the young, television personalities, youth-orientated performers and any person who is likely to have strong influence on the behaviour of the young.
b) Avoid themes that are associated with youth culture; for example, disregard for authority or social norms, teenage rebelliousness, mocking or outwitting authority be it parental or otherwise, immature, adolescent or childish behaviour or practical jokes and any behaviour that seeks to set those under 18 apart from those of an older age group.
c) Teenage fashion or clothing mostly associated with those under 18.
d) Avoid music or dance that is likely to appeal strongly to under 18s. But an advertisement that, for example, features an old recording that, perhaps as a result of its use in the advertisement, becomes popular with the young once again, will not necessarily be challenged. Announcements of alcohol-sponsored events may be made but the emphasis must be on the event, not the alcohol.
e) Language commonly used by the young but rarely by an older generation; for example, slang or novel words.
f) Cartoons, rhymes or animation. Avoid those likely to have strong appeal to children and teenagers. Mature themes are likely to be acceptable.
g) Caution is needed in the use of all sports. In addition, certain sports have a strong appeal to the young, for example, skateboarding or 'extreme sports'; they should be avoided.
h) Avoid puppets or cute lovable animals that are likely to inspire strong affection in the young.

Humorous treatments cannot be used to circumvent the rule and, in any case, immature, adolescent or childish humour must be avoided.

This rule requires particularly sensitive judgements. If they have any doubts about an advertising idea, advertisers or agencies are strongly advised to consult the BACC (or broadcaster compliance team) at the earliest stage of script development.

Rule 11.8.1 (g)
(1) Advertisements must not show, imply or encourage immoderate drinking. This applies both to the amount of drink and to the way drinking is portrayed.

Guidance note:

This rule is intended to prevent viewers thinking that immoderate consumption of alcohol is acceptable. It would therefore rule out, for example, scenarios such as drinking sessions, drinking games, downing drinks in one swallow or excessively quickly and pub or club 'crawls'.

Advertisements must not show or suggest an excessive amount of alcohol dispensed per person. Depictions of well-stocked bars or guests arriving carrying alcohol are acceptable provided that nothing implies that immoderate consumption has taken or will take place.

In considering what would constitute an excessive amount of alcohol, please apply the Department of Health's Recommended Daily Amounts of alcohol.

(See also Rule 11.8.2 (c)).
(2) References to, or suggestions of, buying repeat rounds of drinks are not acceptable. (Note: This does not prevent, for example, someone buying a drink for each of a group of friends. It does, however, prevent any suggestion that other members of the group will buy any further rounds.)

Guidance note:

Advertisements may show a person buying a drink for friends but must not suggest that a pattern of round buying is to be, or has been, established. The use of the word 'round' or similar is unacceptable.

Advertisements must not suggest peer pressure on individuals to drink alcohol. (Note: Rules 11.8.1(g)(1) and 11.8.1(g)(2) do not apply to advertising for low alcohol drinks).

http://www.asa.org.uk/asa/codes/tv_code/Guidance_Notes/Guidance+notes+for+the+TV+alcohol+advertising+rules.htm

The British Code of Advertising, Sales Promotion and Direct Marketing (The CAP Code)(Correct as at December 2008 – for full and up-to-date version see www.cap.org.uk)

56.11 Marketing communications should not suggest that drinking alcohol is a reason for the success of any personal relationship or social event. A brand preference may be promoted as a mark of, for example, the drinker's good taste and discernment.

4
Ethics and Alcohol

The problem that alcohol presents was set out at the beginning of this book and, thus far, we have explored several aspects of the ethics and responsibility of government and the industry. This chapter will begin to focus on the underlying ethical theory, initially through reflection on the perspective of public policy. It will first examine the 2007 report by the Nuffield Centre for Bioethics on Public Health Policy. It will then argue for a broader approach that focuses the ethical debate on social responsibility and the theme of shared responsibility. Through this, we will return to corporate responsibility and the responsibility of the industry as a whole. We conclude that the debate around self-regulation still has some way to go, and that the essential focus of this debate should be around shared responsibility and how this can best be negotiated in practice.

The ethics of public policy

The recent report of the Nuffield Centre for Bioethics (2007) focuses on alcohol as a part of a wider concern for public heath policy. It begins with an exploration of core ethical issues. At the heart of these, from a public policy perspective, is the debate about the relationships between the state and the individual. At one extreme is the libertarian position, which argues for minimal natural rights: life, liberty and property (Nozick 1968). The task of the state, in this view, is to ensure that these are protected. Any interference with the health of people has to be only in furtherance of that protection. The individual themselves must thus decide how they will maintain their health, putting individual responsibility at the heart of this (see Deacon 2002: 31ff.).

At the other extreme are collectivist views. These focus on equal health care provision and enabling a high level of health amongst all people.

Basic rights in these views do not provide grounds against state intervention but, rather, are about provision of what is best for the people and for the community as a whole. The theoretical backdrop for these arguments tends to be utilitarian, working out the greatest good for the greatest number, or one of social contract, the idea that intervention reflects the will of the people as a whole.

The report suggests (Nuffield Centre for Bioethics 2007: 14) that between these two positions is a variety of views, summed up in the liberal position. This affirms the importance of individual freedom, but acknowledges that some intervention might be necessary. Such intervention has to be justified, on the basis perhaps of the vulnerability of some disadvantaged members of society, or even on the basis of enabling autonomy. The libertarian position sees autonomy in terms of the freedom to choose or govern, something that has to be defended. Berlin (1969) refers to this as negative freedom, or freedom from oppression or intrusion. A liberal position looks to develop more positive freedom that would both enable the person to have the information about possible options that would enable authentic autonomy and the resources that would enable choice to be fulfilled. This means making education and health provision available to all on the basis of need. This is justifiable precisely because education and health are basic human values (ibid.: 15). Some writers, such as Browning (2006), would see these as pre-moral values, values that are needed to fulfil the very idea of what it means to be human. This would involve the person as agent, interdependent and with a nature that is both physical and psychological, requiring health to sustain that nature.

In trying to resolve the tension between the autonomy of the individual and the right of the state to intervene in health matters, the report turns first to Mill. Mill's essay on liberty argues that 'the only purpose for which power can be rightfully exercised over any member of a civilised community, against his will, is to prevent harm to others' (Mill 1989: 13). The good of the person, physical or moral, is not sufficient to intervene. Hence, we might remonstrate with the person whose health is being affected by his or her own actions, but we cannot force them to alter their behaviour. Mill concludes 'Over himself, over his own body and mind, the individual is sovereign' (ibid.).

At first sight, Mill's position seems simplistic. However, he offers four qualifications to his principle of harm:

1 The principle only applies to those who have mature 'faculties', who are able to exercise rational decision-making. Hence, it would be

reasonable to intervene to protect children or vulnerable adults, such as severely mentally disabled.

2 Mill accepts that public services can be supplied for all, necessary for the joint working of society, including the provision of clean water and regulation for working hours.

3 Mill stresses the importance of education for all. This is focused on education that would persuade and advise, not coerce, people into behaviour that is healthy.

4 Mill argues that whatever is done must protect the individuality of the person; this is very much about the person being responsible for the conduct of their own life. This would provide a framework for public health that cares for the vulnerable and the environmental context of health, and provides education around health care.

The report usefully compares public health ethics with bioethics around the issues of freedom and consent. Consent is key to bioethics, and the respect for the freedom of the individual person around a discrete intervention in health care or medicine. However, there are situations where the harm principle requires intervention regardless of consent; for example, in the case of dealing with highly infectious diseases. In cases of less extreme harm to others, the report argues that democratic procedures and clear accountability for reasonableness are sufficient. In other words, the case has to be made in a context of accountability.

The report goes on to suggest that a simple liberal position is not sufficient. Other values than freedom are of importance, including equality and community. Equality is a complex concept, including equality of respect, outcomes, resources and opportunity. All these aspects have some relevance to health. It is multidimensional, not least because, where there appears to be health care inequality, it would seem to be connected both to personal responsibility, and poor physical and social environment, including inadequate educational resources (DHSS 1980). This would seem to indicate the importance of a diverse response, involving a mixture of approaches, stressing the limitations of a simple informed consent approach. An example of this is the provision and use of seat belts. A simple information approach was unsuccessful. To cut down on the harm to individual motorists and to those directly or indirectly affected by this demanded a change of attitude and behaviour. To change attitudes and behaviour requires the individual taking responsibility for this. The solution was to make the non-wearing of seat belts illegal, something that encourages drivers to own their own behaviour and be accountable.

The report then argues that a further key value is that of community. The report's expression of this still focuses on benefits, not least the way in which being part of a community that provides health care for all brings benefit to all, not only to the individual. At the heart of that is the idea that 'each person's welfare and that of the whole community matters to everyone' (Nuffield Centre for Bioethics 2007: 23). This suggests that the liberal approach is simply too individualistic, and has to be modified to accommodate focus not simply on the community, but on the very fact that public health cannot be simply about how the state relates to the individual. The individual exists in interdependent relationships, and the health of an individual is tied into the health and well-being of the rest of the community. Such considerations lead the report to argue for a revised liberal framework: the stewardship model. This expresses the idea of the liberal state acting as stewards to individuals in particular need and the population as a whole.

The stewardship model

This revised liberal framework centres on the classical harm principle, with additional focus on care for the vulnerable, providing health information, with the provision of key services 'through which risks are minimised', and help to change behaviour (ibid: 27).

Public health programmes, then, should aim to:

- reduce the risks of ill health that people might impose on each other
- reduce causes of ill health by regulations that ensure environmental conditions that sustain good health, such as the provision of clean air and water, safe food and decent housing
- pay special attention to the health of children and other vulnerable people
- promote health not only by information and advice, but also with programmes to help people to overcome addictions and other unhealthy behaviours
- ensure that it is easy for people to lead a healthy life; for example, by providing convenient and safe opportunities for exercise
- ensure that people have appropriate access to medical services; and
- reduce unfair health inequalities. (Nuffield Centre for Bioethics 2007)

There would remain liberal constraints including that such programmes would:

- not attempt to coerce adults to live unhealthy lives
- minimize interventions that are introduced without the individual
  consent of those affected, or without procedural justice arrangements (such as democratic decision-making procedures) which
  provide adequate mandate
- seek to minimize interventions that are perceived as unduly intru-
  sive and in conflict with important personal values.

As noted earlier, the harms and costs associated with alcohol are
massive and are experienced across society. The wider effect on life
chances, relationships and social networks is not quantifiable; however,
it is estimated that parental alcohol problems affect between 780,000 to
1.3 million children in the United Kingdom. This clearly makes alcohol
abuse a social, not merely an individual problem. In this respect, alcohol directly parallels the seat belt case in the UK. Wearing a seat belt is
not simply a matter of individual choice. Not wearing a seat belt can
lead to potential great damage to the individual if involved in a crash.
It also leads to a greater cost to the family of the person involved and
to the health services. If this is multiplied across the community, then
the cost becomes significant. This case was instructive because, despite
the attempts to encourage people to belt up, there was little immediate success. It was necessary to provide the legal framework in which
drivers could be empowered. In all this, the ethical perspective shifts
from simple ideas about freedom to issues of care, responsibility and,
even, justice. First, the person is part of a community and has to be
aware of his effect on that community. Second, the person is responsible
for more than himself. This is something we will return to later in greater
detail. This points not simply to personal responsibility but, rather, to
familial and civic responsibility. Third, it raises issues of justice. If a person is responsible for the alcohol abuse and negative effects on others, or
refuses to change his or her behaviour, should the health service at least
have the option of not treating him or her? The report argues against
such penalizing for several reasons:

- The aetiology of alcohol dependence is complex and occurs often
  over a long period. It is not a simple act, such as putting on a seat
  belt. Whatever the initial responsibility, and this is considered in the
  chapter on alcoholism, once the person is dependent then the lack of
  will is precisely part of the problem.

- It is argued that this would lead to unfair stigmatization of those dependent upon alcohol.
- There is a danger that it would begin to erode the basic values of equality of health care, with treatment based on need rather than merit.

However, there is a moral position somewhere between penalizing and treating the patient. In effect, this position looks to set up a contract with the patient. The term 'contract' might refer to a written or unwritten agreement. The health service will aim to treat the patient, provided that he or she takes responsibility for their behaviour. This might make treatment itself conditional upon behavioural change. A liver transplant, for instance, might be conditional upon the patient accepting an alcohol dependency treatment programme. The report argues that the ethical ground for this is not about penalizing the patient but, rather, about how this action would improve the clinical effectiveness of the treatment. A second moral argument is that this would enable the person to take responsibility. It provides the incentive for the person to take responsibility and a framework to enable that development. This is not a matter of legal incentives effecting change. It is, rather, focused in the medical contract. The medical contract provides a way of developing the responsibility of the patient. Robinson (2001) argues that the contract can enable the development of moral meaning, from shared expectations of behaviour through to responsibility in relation to treatment. The report argues that it is reasonable to make treatment conditional on action on the part of the patient, with the NHS providing the means of change. The guidelines for such an approach are already in place in the UK (Department of Health 2005), requiring, for instance, abstention from alcohol for six month before a liver transplant. Transplant is also deemed questionable in cases where the person is unlikely to cut down on excessive drinking.

Business

The report argues the responsibility of business is also important in this issue. First, it is in the interest of business as a whole to do something about alcohol. It is estimated that over £6 billion pounds are lost annually through absenteeism related to alcohol (Nuffield Centre for Bioethics 2007: 110). This raises a general issue about alcohol at work. For most firms, it makes sense to have a code of conduct that restricts the use of alcohol. In some cases, this is central to health and safety, as in the operation of machines or driving. Once more, this is about establishing a local contract or focusing a broader, national contract into the local context.

The social responsibility of the alcohol industry itself is more problematic. As we have noted, this involves major questions about how the industry relates to the advertising and access. Marketing aims to create customers and this involves convincing the potential customer that they have a need for this product. As Babor *et al.* (2003) note, alcohol is not an ordinary commodity. Establishing a need for alcohol can lead to dependency. Need is most often established through enabling the person to identify with the practice, in this case of drinking. This involves, in turn, the development of a sense of worth or well-being associated with the product. Ideally, for marketing in general, this would involve associating the product with status, thus making the status in some sense conditional upon the use of the product. In the case of alcohol, this means that advertising is likely to create the context within which vulnerable people might form a dependency relationship with alcohol. To counter this, there is a need to ensure that those under age are not given easy access to the product – either in terms of access or price. The report reaffirms the position of the ASA in providing tight guidelines for alcohol advertising, as has been noted above.

Government

Babor *et al.* (2003) argue for a coercive approach from the state to the public problem of alcohol. They found that evidence pointed to the greater effectiveness of increasing taxes, and restricting times of sale and the number of retail points that sell alcohol. There was also some evidence that banning alcohol advertising might help in reducing the negative effects of the product.

The stewardship model would allow the government to follow such coercive approaches and the Nuffield Report recommends all of them, with particular stress on an increase in taxes on alcoholic beverages, and on a careful analysis of the effect of extended opening hours on levels of consumption and anti-social behaviour.

The vulnerable

How business and government protect the vulnerable, especially children and young people, is at the heart of the Report's work on alcohol. It stresses the need for state and business to work together in the stewardship model, and their duty to prevent harm to health. In particular, it stresses the need to develop ways of enabling people to make better choices, and therefore looks to make clear in any packaging both the dangers of alcohol and the need to drink responsibly.

Critique and development

The Nuffield Report is an important contribution to the ethical debate about alcohol, providing some justification for coercive activities, supported by a BMA report (http://www.bma.org.uk/ap.nsf/Content/HubAlcohol). In particular, the concept of stewardship takes the debate away from potentially narrow philosophical considerations into a focus on shared responsibilities. However, it has several limitations. The first is that it stays very much within a conventional ethical debate around issues such as harm prevention and autonomy. The stress on prevention is mirrored in their concern to 'protect' the vulnerable and reduce the harmful effects of alcohol consumption. As such, the debate does not take this beyond a slightly altered liberal position, with a soft sense of paternalism. As Ikonomidis and Singer (1999) note, there are many different views of paternalism that have some liberal elements. Hence, so called 'soft paternalism' aims to include the best interest of the person or the group. The idea of best interest takes us beyond simple harm prevention to looking for the best outcome for all involved in the situation. This is not something that can be worked through simply in terms of looking at what interventions are permissible. It demands more radical attention to creative work across the community, and how these areas can work together for positive outcomes. In terms of any underlying view of freedom that moves beyond negative freedom, from coercion to positive freedom (Berlin 1969), the latter involves resources that enable the person to exercise decisions and actions. It also involves moral freedom (Novak 1990), which looks at the social context of freedom and any responsibilities or obligations this might involve. Positive and moral freedom both demand a development of autonomy away from simply freedom of choice to something relating to the capacity to make decisions in the context of a plural community where many different narratives concerning worth are competing. This, in turn, involves the development of character in relation to community, and the support and development of personal responsibility. The Nuffield Report stops short of moving into that depth.

The second, related problem is that the concept of stewardship that the Report sets out is thin. It does try to point to some sense of shared responsibility. However, underlying the negative freedom is a narrow anthropology that sees humanity as involving isolated individuals. Underlying positive and moral freedom is a view of humanity that involves interdependence with the social and physical environments. The history of the so-called 'stewardship model', of course, involves a much stronger idea. It originates in theology, across the Abrahamic faiths, and focuses on the idea that the social and physical environments are not 'owned' by anyone other than the creator. The created world is a gift for all, and all have to steward those resources. This is not only about being stewards to individuals or the population as a whole, it is about recognizing a shared environment that transcends particular interests, that has limitations as well as resources, and that therefore needs effective stewardship. The key to the theological base to this is God's call for a free and willing response of humanity to be co-creators (Gülen 2004). In many ways, the secular analogue of this is the view of Jonas (1984), who argues for global responsibility based on the interdependent nature of the social and physical environment. All this points to a view of community that is much more active, and a related view of responsibility that cannot be summed up in legislation or 'responsibility messages'. This moves us into a view of health care that goes beyond provision and looks at how to engage a community and its members actively in response. Titmuss (1973) began to explore this in his idea of the gift relationship. The theory had problems, not least a paucity of examples at the time of what might constitute gift in health care. However, the broad argument looked to take welfare and health care beyond the welfare state and into the welfare society. This involves a consciousness of shared responsibility and an imperative to find ways of fulfilling that and serving the community. Again, the Report does not begin to explore this.

Third, and related, the Report does not begin to work through the issues of autonomy in a pluralist society. This is nowhere more evident than in its view of vulnerability. Simply to say that children or young people are vulnerable avoids many different issues. Is vulnerability simply diminished autonomy or a lack of judgement? The problem with that view is precisely its relativity. Autonomy, if it is about the capacity to reflect and make judgements, is something that is always developing, never fully worked out. Such autonomy is also worked out in terms of plural communities. The person develops the capacity to govern the self in relation to, and in dialogue with, different communities. The different communities all want to assert a view of value and responsibility, some of which is shared, some of which is different. The capacity to govern the self involves developing ways of handling these different demands and, thus, developing criteria for judging between them. Simply to display messages about responsible drinking does not help persons at any age to develop that level of autonomy. Such autonomy is only developed through enabling reflection on the different communities and the way in which responsibility is worked out in those communities.

All of these points suggest the need to go beyond the thin stewardship model and develop a stronger stewardship model. Given the point about the plurality of society and communities, we would argue that a strong stewardship perspective actually strengthens any view of autonomy. Such a model would include many of the Nuffield Report's recommendations, but focus far more on the way in which responsibility is played out day to day through the different stakeholders working together. It would also lead to the need to take the issue of alcohol beyond that narrow focus on to the more fundamental issue of how responsibility is modelled and developed. To explore this, we will focus first on the example of corporate responsibility, one aspect of the responsibility of the wider alcohol industry. Our initial focus is on the case of Brown-Forman (see Box 4.1).

Box 4.1   Brown-Forman

The Brown-Forman corporation is one of the largest American companies producing spirits and wine. Brown-Forman embraces the issue of responsibility as central to the marketing, not as an afterthought. Hence, they see marketing as an exercise in marketing responsible drinking, and see the need to reflect on and develop the ways of fulfilling their corporate responsibility continually, as a matter of course. In their Corporate Social Responsibility Report (2007–08), they accept certain basic guidelines, and these are in some respects even more precise than those of the ASA, including:

- Adverts should not feature children, cartoon figures of anything that appeals to primarily to persons below the [legal age limit]
- There should be no suggestion that alcohol use represents a 'rite of passage' to adulthood
- There should be no suggestion that alcohol is a means to attain success
- Adverts should not depict situations in which beverage alcohol is consumed excessively or irresponsibly
- Models and actors must be a minimum of 25 years old
- There must be prominent responsibility statements in all advertising initiatives. (Brown-Forman 2008)

From the word go, then, marketing does not associate alcohol with any of the major issues that might occur in personal development. It is not a means to any end, especially achieving maturity or success, or a condition for acceptance. In all, it sets up the parameters of a community that is quite different from the child or youth communities. There is no suggestion of child play (cartoons), the actors are older, and responsible drinking is embodied.

However, with responsibility as a central part of the brand itself, not an afterthought, the company then begins to fill in, through particular advertising, what responsibility might look like. They include some examples of the 'responsibility messages':

'Keep your judgment pure. Drink responsibly.' – *Finlandia*
'Drink it, love it, know when to stop.' – *Virgin Vines*
'We make our wine responsibly, please enjoy it responsibly.' – *Fetzer*
'Please be as mature as our Estates Rums. Drink responsibly.' – *Appleton Estate*
'Responsible drinking is always in style.' – *Little Black Dress*
'Celebrate responsibly.' – *Korbel*

Two points are worthy of note here. First, some of the messages include clear affirmation of core virtues, including good judgement and maturity. This begins to spell out what responsibility might actually mean. One of the dangers about the simple tag line 'Drink responsibly' is that it does not explain what responsibility looks like. Hence, the more that indications of this that can be given, however brief, the better. Second, tag lines such as 'Drink responsibly' can easily be seen as 'bolt-on', and not central to the marketing message. However, what makes such tag lines most marginal is precisely their incongruity with what is communicated in the advertisement. If the images, narrative or context of the advertisement stress a different message, then that will take precedence over the exhortation to drink responsibly. Hence, even overt 'messages' need to be congruent with the whole presentation (as one section of Brown-Forman found in a negative judgement from the ASA noted in Chapter 3, p. 61). With ideas such as 'celebration', the messages also aim to get across a sense of community ethos. This begins to embrace the positive view of moderate drinking in the context of a community. Alcohol is seen as part of a community of celebration, it is associated with good values and good experiences of the community – not with loss of self-control, hedonism or negative motivations. In effect, Brown-Forman aims to set up not simply a positive view of alcohol but, rather, a normative view of community in which alcohol is drunk. In terms of autonomy and plurality, it sets up an alternative to, for instance, the popular view of student drinking culture or binge drinking culture. Sketching an alternative community is much more effective than simply saying 'Drink responsibly.'

Brown-Forman, however, (through their Jack Daniels product) go one step further and also directly sponsor part of a sporting activity, specifically a car in the National Association for Stock Car Auto Racing (NASCAR). On the face, it this breaks two cardinal rules of alcohol marketing: the ASA's injunction not to associate alcohol with sport, and the danger of associating drink with driving. Brown-Forman tackle this problem head on and argue, in effect, that the association of alcohol with sport and driving is not, per se, wrong. It would be wrong to associate uncontrolled drinking with these activities or to imply that success in sport was only possible through drinking alcohol. However, they aim to associate the sport with responsible drinking. Once again, this stresses control and judgement, with the tag line on the cars, 'Pace Yourself, Drink Responsibly': the message will be seen by those who are under 18, but it is not one that appeals to a youth culture. On the contrary, it sets out a cultural meaning to which they might aspire. To reinforce this, the Jack Daniel's team was the first to restrict the sale of team merchandise to 21-year-olds or above. In moral terms, this is not about reduction of harm; it is more about setting out a positive moral message. It is also, again, a moral message that stresses the virtues. 'Pace yourself' involves control, maturity and good judgement. The idea is directly against the instant gratification that is associated with excessive drinking. Moreover, virtues such as these are also essential for success in professional driving. This sets up a framework of integrity, using the same virtues in relation to the use of alcohol. It is precisely such congruence that gets the message across to the consumer. In consumer research, Brown-Forman have noted that Jack Daniels leads all other brands in being perceived as a product that encourages responsible drinking (Brown-Forman 2008: 13).

It would be foolish to suggest that such an approach is, of itself, sufficient. It needs reinforcement in other contexts. It also needs continued reflection on value and practice to enable responsive and effective development in this area, and Brown-Forman sees it as part of its responsibility to review practice and respond to criticism. One example of this is in the sale of flavoured malt beverages. These have been criticized, in that the mixture of spirits with sweet drinks (often termed 'alcopops') and the colourful presentation make them appealing to young people. How-ever, using the same responsible marketing techniques for these 'Country Cocktails', market research suggests that the primary consumers are between 30–49-years-old. Despite this, Brown-Forman has changed the colours of the liquids and the bottles, in case the original bright colours might attract under-age drinkers. The group remains open to review and challenge.

Brown-Forman is also continually reviewing its advertisement place-ments. The US code advocates that adverts should be placed in context where 70 per cent of people are over 21 years of age. A group of US State Attorneys General campaigned for alcohol advertising that would reach an audience comprising at least 85 per cent adults. After several discussions, Brown-Forman agreed to aim for this higher figure.

Finally, Brown-Forman sees itself as heavily involved in confronting the harmful effects of alcohol and in working with others to develop public policy in this area. This has involved work with the Century Council, an industry association that aims to reduce under-age drink-ing and drink-driving. This council works with other partners, such as the NGO Mothers Against Drunk Driving. This has led to a focus on education, gathering support for zero tolerance legislation, lobbying for better enforcement of existing laws, and helping to develop multilingual programmes. In addition, Brown-Forman has developed networks across America and Europe, and become involved in community activities around education and healing projects. Brown-Forman is also involved directly in debate around major issues of public policy. Issues include arguing for equivalent taxation between different forms of alcohol, argu-ing for a level commercial playing field in terms of local taxes and opening hours, and arguing for the continuation of self-regulation in the industry. Brown-Forman recognize that it is difficult to argue for any of these factors if it, and the industry as a whole, is not demonstrating responsible practice.

Responsibility

In recounting the Brown-Forman case, this is not a simple support of the alcohol industry; the case illustrates several levels of responsibility working together. Responsibility has been thoroughly, but not exhaus-tively debated in business ethics and governance for the past two decades. Schweiker (1995) notes three interrelated modes of this concept, each of which can apply to the individual and to the corporation: imputability, accountability and liability. These categories are examined more closely in the context of personal responsibility in Chapter 7, but also have relevance to the responsibility of the corporation.

Imputability

Actions can be attributed to a corporation. Hence, the corporation can be seen as having been responsible for those actions and the decisions that led to them. Such decision-making forms the basis of developing corporate identity. Responsibility needs to be carefully worked out by a corporation in relation to its particular practice. It is not sufficient to develop a code and simply follow that. The corporation needs to take responsibility for articulating and reflecting on values and practice, and for developing that practice through dialogue. In other words, the corporation needs to be responsible for its own values and responses. In Brown-Forman, this is well illustrated by the use of the racing car and its team. The working through and owning of responsibility is precisely seen in the way that it questions the received wisdom of regulatory bodies. Brown-Forman could simply have followed such guidelines without really engaging the moral responsibility in this issue. Instead, it chose to found its response in the central idea of marketing responsible drinking, rather than marketing drinking and then encouraging responsibility. The result is that it looks to communicate the values and virtues that are around community and maturity. Part of any sense of agency is about how we challenge community myths and received wisdom. In squarely entering the debate about public policy, the corporation is also looking to assert its own position on justice in the marketplace. Both of these actions could be seen as simple self-interest. However, whilst these actions might be in the interest of the group, the point is that it has set out the values that underlie its practice and is making itself accountable for both.

Accountability

The corporation is responsible or answerable *to* someone. The basis of this, most often, is the development of a contract in a narrow and a broad sense. Contracts involve narrow expectations and targets, but also broader expectations about how one relates to the other in the relationship. Any contract can be modified and developed by the parties and, thus, contracts between shareholders and executives need not be confined to a single purpose. Brown-Forman is clearly accountable to those involved in ownership of the corporation. However, its accountability relationship is focused in the relation of the company as a whole to society. Hence, accountability is focused in identity and relationship. In effect, this moves into the idea of corporate citizenship, working through the wider societal and civic responsibilities of the firm, as well as the responsibility to the consumer.

Liability

The person or growth is responsible *for* something or someone. Liability (as distinguished from legal liability) goes beyond accountability, into the idea of caring for others, a sense of wider shared liability for projects, persons or groups. Each profession has to work these out in context, without an explicit contract. Working that out demands an awareness of the limitations of the organization, avoiding taking too much responsibility, and a capacity to work together with others to share and negotiate responsibility. This is responsibility *for* people and projects in the past, present and future. Once again, this can have a strictly legal sense or a wider moral one that encompasses the broadest possible view of stakeholders, from those directly affected by any business or project to the social and natural environment in which these operate. The Brown-Forman approach recognizes liability at various levels, for the vulnerable in society – especially the young, but also liability for ethical meaning. This is summed up in the meaning associated with responsible drinking already noted (p. 88). This involves playing a part in ethical leadership in wider society, through setting out the ethical parameters of practice and the underlying values. It accepts shared responsibilities and, through creative attempts to embody those, is providing shared leadership in society.

In all this, Brown-Forman illustrates that the debate has moved from simple reflection around the reduction of harm and when one might begin to intervene in this issue. This is not to devalue those concerns but, rather, argues that, in addition, there needs to be focus on the working through of responsibility. This moves the ethical debate away from a simple argument on concepts and consequences, to one about virtues and how they can develop responsible engagement. In Chapter 7, we will look at how the virtues are at the centre of the development of personal responsibility in therapy. However, the virtues can also be used in terms of corporate activity.

Corporate virtues

Brown (2005) argues that virtues are critical to responsible leadership of the corporation. He argues that the core collection of virtues is integrity. Much of the focus in business on branding raises the question as to whether this reflects image or integrity. Image is an instrumental concept, getting across something positive about the company in order to sell the product. However, image without integrity runs the risk of losing market credibility and, ultimately, consumer or client trust.

Corporate integrity is characterized by the same elements as individual integrity:

Integral thinking

This is the integration of the different parts of the company, decision-making, ethos and so on, and enables the development of greater awareness of the company identity and its role in the community.

Consistency

This refers to the consistency of character and operation between value and practice; past, present and future; and in different situations and contexts. The behaviours will not necessarily be the same in each situation, but will be consistent with the ethical identity of the agent. Closely related to consistency is the idea of transparency in the corporation. This involves ensuring that values and practice are open to scrutiny and reflection. This demands involvement in terms of perspectives from groups outside any particular project or institution.

Relational awareness

Identity is not individualistic but, rather, is based on a plurality of relationships; these include: cultural, interpersonal, organizational, social, and natural (Brown 2005). Hence, the corporation has to be aware of, and responsive to, this plurality. This plurality is evident inside and outside the corporation, and involves working with very different responsibilities, often attached to roles. Brown (2005) notes, for instance, that the corporation has to attend to civic and personal responsibility inside the corporation, allowing employees the time to fulfil volunteer or family activities. Hence, space for fulfilling parental responsibilities to a new child, for instance, is recognized by law. At the same time, the civic responsibility of the corporation itself has to receive attention. The corporation is part of an interdependent network of relationships in its community. The corporation is also part of, and shares responsibility for, the wider environment, local and global.

Learning and self-criticism

Absolute integrity is impossible to attain. In this light, integrity becomes a learning concept. It is revealed through how the company responds to crises, dilemmas, challenges and ongoing engagement with the community. Central to this is the corporate capacity to reflect, to evaluate practice and be self-critical, to be able to cope with criticism and to alter practice appropriately. This capacity to learn means that integrity should not be seen as simply maintaining values and ethical practice.

Brown (2005) also stresses the importance of purpose to integrity, one that can be seen to be worthy, and that can be seen to connect to practice. The worth of a purpose is always a matter of debate. The important thing is that the corporation should be able to declare that purpose, defend it clearly and rationally, and embody it in practice.

Responsibility is, in turn, key to integrity. The development of imputability and agency are core to integrity and depend on the corporation being responsible for its own reflection on purpose and action, awareness of the social and physical environment, and responsiveness to that environment, through creative and imaginative action. Accountability and liability are at the heart of relational awareness. This demands that the corporation give an account of its reflections and activities to stakeholders and wider society.

A good example of integrity is the case of Brown-Forman and *Blender* magazine. *Blender* ran one of Brown-Forman's advertisements with a picture of Hilary Duff (a young celebrity) on the front cover next to the headline 'HILARY DUFF, Good girls don't ... but she does'. The contract with Brown-Forman stipulated that *Blender* should not run any Brown-Forman advertisements if the cover included people who were under the legal drinking age. As a result, even though the readership involves more than 70 per cent of those over the legal drinking age, Brown-Forman cancelled the contract. This exemplifies continual review, a broad awareness of responsibility, a capacity to change course, and a capacity to move beyond what might be seen as simple self-interest.

All this begins to offer a more developed view of responsibility based in the character and virtues of the corporation. It does not suggest a quick fix, but does point to the need to develop ways of operating that exercise responsibility in practice, demanding continual reflection and dialogue. However, can this approach be easily applied to a unique product such as alcohol and to an industry that is diverse and has many stakeholders?

No ordinary commodity?

The issue of moral liability has a direct input to the debate on the nature of alcohol as a product. As noted above, Babor *et al.* (2003) argue that alcohol is a very distinctive product, both in terms of its potentially addictive nature and in terms of its negative effect on society. It is most often associated with tobacco in this respect (Palazzo and Richter 2005). It might be argued that tobacco is more dangerous, given its addictive nature and direct negative effect on health. However, these two are far from alone in being associated with negative effects. The marketing of the food industry and, in particular, the chocolate industry is in some sense responsible for the increase in obesity and for the development of illnesses such as diabetes (BBC 2004). It could be argued that, in different ways, this is also the case with many other industries, including mining, oil, motor vehicles and computer games. At the very least, such industries need to be aware of the possible effects of their products. In one sense, then, alcohol is not dissimilar from many other products. Indeed, it could be argued that all firms need to develop this level of awareness about the effects of their products, and how they respond to such issues.

This raises a more general issue of the relationships between marketing and the public. Perhaps the important point is that all marketing is clearly aimed at influencing and changing the behaviour of the potential consumer. So, in one sense, none of the relationships is value neutral at all. The key question is, rather, how advertising actually affects the other and just what response the firm aims to elicit. The full spectrum of this ranges from firms who aim to change the behaviour of their customers to respond to environmental issues, such as Interface Inc. (http://www.interfaceinc.com/goals/sustainability_overview.html), to firms simply aiming to the change behaviours in terms of purchase choice. Given the nature of alcohol, the need to use it responsibly, and the argument that responsibility is shared, not discrete, than part of the task of the alcohol industry is, with others, to enable consumers to develop and exercise their responsibility.

The alcohol industry and conflict of interest

Cook (2006), however, argues that it is impossible for the alcohol industry to attain integrity. It has an inherent conflict of interest between selling a product and thus aiming for increased sales, and the aim of harm reduction. The industry looks to espouse both but, by definition cannot, and hence the argument seems to suggest that the alcohol industry must take some responsibility, in the sense of culpability, for the level of harm. Critical to Cook's argument is the evidence, put forward by Babor *et al.* (2003), of the 'prevention paradox'. This suggests that, though heavy drinkers are at most risk of harm, they involve the minority of harm cases. Those who drink less are less subject to harm but more numerous. It is

they who account for most of the cases of alcohol related harm. The conclusion is that the alcohol consumption of the whole population should
be addressed. If the alcohol consumption of the whole population needs
to be reduced, then this would certainly suggest that there is a major conflict of interest for the alcohol industry. Given such a conflict of interest,
it is easy to view the work of the alcohol industry around social responsibility as, at best, cosmetic – the CSR equivalent of green washing. This
has led to heated arguments about the alcohol industry trying to influence public policy. Room *et al.* (2002) suggest that the reason why the
UK government did not go down the line advocated by the World Health
Organization report is because they were influenced by the alcohol industry. The alcohol industry, worldwide, has set up education and research
groups, and it is alleged that these are aimed at 'rubbishing' the findings
of the various World Health Organization reports (Cook 2006: 33).

There are various difficulties with this line of argument. First, a great
deal of it is precisely based in allegations. Cook, for instance, refers three
times to different allegations in the space of two paragraphs (2006: 32ff.),
as if these had the force of empirical evidence. Ironically, one of the allegations is that the industry sought to induce academics to write reviews
that are critical of the World Health Organization reports. By implication,
this would involve the loss of academic integrity. The implication of this
is to deny the possibility that the World Health Organization data can
be questioned critically or that it might be interpreted in a different way.
It would seem that Cook is denying the possibility of academic freedom
and integrity to any groups or persons related – or, indeed, unrelated – to
the industry. It is hard, in this light, to know what the basis for 'neutral'
debate might be. In any case, the data in Chapter 3 suggests that there is
no simple causal connection between alcohol advertising and the negative effects of alcohol. Hence, even if the paradox were proven, it would
still be difficult to conclude, for instance, that all advertising should
be banned, or that the industry was responsible for all the effects of
alcohol.

Second, and connected, this sets up a debate about the dynamics of
dialogue in the corporate world that has been replicated across many
trans-national corporation cases. A good example of this is the Nestlé
controversy (Robinson 2002), where there was a presumption made by
the various NGOs that Nestlé was wrong either to market breast milk substitute or to do it in the way that it did. The debate about data became
intractable, with the underlying polarized dynamic affecting the interpretation on both sides. Entine (2002) and Robinson (2002) argue that
this is about the politics of research, and that a balanced appreciation of

data cannot be arrived at without the different parties working together. In the Nestlé case, this led to the most successful phase when all agreed to work with the independent Muskie Commission, whose task was to police the marketing practice. The important basis of this was both the recognition of shared criteria, and that both sides placed their trust in the Commission. As the Commission developed its work, so the criteria for judging practice were further developed. The work of the ASA in advertising provides a close parallel. By extension, we would argue that shared data gathering is a moral imperative, not least because, without working through these issues together, there is little chance of agreeing a shared view of the truth or a sense of shared responsibility. Hence, it becomes difficult to negotiate how responsibility is to be fulfilled and to work through to a creative ethical conclusion.

Third, this still leaves the issue of whether there is a direct conflict of interest. If the data is open to debate, and if the so-called paradox is based on that data, then it is not clear that such a paradox has been established. Moreover, widespread drinking and related incidents of harm cannot be seen as directly caused by the alcohol industry. The consumption of alcohol might have contributed to that harm, but the harm was ultimately caused by possibly many other factors, including lack of judgement and discipline on the part of the persons involved, or factors unrelated to the alcohol consumed. This differs from tobacco, where use of the product directly causes harm, and where, despite Palazzo and Richter's (2005) argument that the tobacco industry can have a second-level social responsibility policy, it is hard to not to see a direct conflict of interest.

Sustained responsible drinking, including not drinking and driving, would lessen the figures of harm dramatically. In the light of that, it is in the interest of the alcohol industry as a whole to work hard with other agencies at effectively reinforcing such patterns of drinking. As Brown-Forman suggest, this would be long-term perspective, not a short-term share value led approach. However, ultimately, the trust established with customers, and the association of the product with well-being, is in the interest of the company. This suggests that simply to polarize self-interest of the industry against the interest of wider society is erroneous. There is an area of shared interest. However, the more creative perspective is in terms of shared or mutual responsibility. This looks to working through the different ways in which this can be fulfilled together. In the light of this, it is clear that self-interest does not necessarily set up a conflict of interest.

None of this is meant as a knock down ethical argument about conflict of interest. The argument, rather, is that effective social ethics is quite a different enterprise than such arguments, demanding a long-term commitment to work together through shared responsibility, something we shall return to in Chapter 8.

The responsibility of the alcohol industry

This argument reinforces the idea that responsibility is essentially shared. Hence, whilst responsibility is often described in terms of roles or organizations, such as professional or corporate responsibility, these do not represent a view of discrete responsibilities. Rather, they represent how the different areas work out a shared responsibility in practice. Hence, alcohol corporations can develop the practice of good responsibility, but there is still the issue of the wider shared responsibility of the industry itself, built up of producers, retailers and so on. In a report for the Joseph Rowntree Foundation, Baggott (2006) acknowledges the great efforts made by many of the alcohol firms in the UK to develop and maintain their corporate responsibility. However, he notes the difficulties of self-regulation of the wider industry (ibid.: 34). First, the alcohol market remains competitive. At one level, this suggests that firms can only work together in a limited way. Perhaps more damaging is openness of the market to new firms, many of which are perceived not to adhere to any code of social responsibility. This would suggest the need to reinforce some form of overall regulation.

Second, and related, self-regulation does not offer any means of policing the efforts of the industry or of providing any necessary sanctions.

Third, any regulation of a whole industry requires a body that is genuinely independent. The Portman Group in the UK has worked hard to achieve this. It includes an independent complaints body. Nonetheless, it is still perceived by many to be too involved in the industry.

Fourth, there are too many codes in operation, from industry-wide (including organizations such as the Portman Group; Trade Associations, such as the Scotch Whisky Association; and bodies such as the ASA) to specific business codes. This creates two potential problems. There is a proliferation of different demands, making the coherent response of business difficult. The different codes can also lead to contradictory demands.

Fifth, whilst there is, in particular firms, some excellent monitoring and accounting of practice, such as the CSR policy of Diageo, there is no effective monitoring of the industry as a whole. If there is to be a sense of the responsibility of the industry, such a mechanism should be in place. In turn, such a process should be independently audited.

Dialogue about this situation is ongoing, with the UK government being heavily involved – proposing, for instance, the replacement of the Portman Group with a central independent body. In this, it is becoming clear that the issue is less about either self-regulation or central regulation but, rather, a judicious and mutually supportive combination of the two. The issues behind this are not unique to the drinks industry. Even in the area of the codes of ethics for the professions, such as engineering, there are similar issues relating to the proliferation of professional codes, the need to develop coherence between them, and the need to develop effective compliance (see Robinson *et al.* 2007). This raises a question about the nature of the responsibility of the drinks industry as a whole. In some respects, it parallels the nature of professional responsibility. Any professional person or group, for instance, has a responsibility to maintain the 'integrity of the profession as a whole' (Robinson and Dixon 1997). In other words, lapses in good practice affect the reputation of the profession as a whole and, thus, affect the trust that is critical to the continued work of that profession. Core to this, again, is a sense of the shared and mutual responsibility. In the medical profession, such responsibility and related trust is maintained by practice being related to registration and, thus, the ultimate sanction of deregistration, something that the engineering profession does not yet have in the UK. The drinks industry has similar concerns. Whatever one firm does will affect the industry and its relationship with customers and other agents. However, the industry does not have the power to regulate such practice. It might eject a member from the voluntary association, and even try to name and shame them. However, the 'rogue' firm – be that producer or retailer – can still operate, and might even use naming and shaming to its advantage, focusing on a risky lifestyle and non-compliance as a marketing tool.

In this light, some degree of overall regulation would seem essential in order to reinforce the shared responsibility of the industry, as well as the good practice of particular firms. This would apply especially to marketing strategies in bars and supermarkets. It would reinforce the identity of the industry, with a positive effect on the trust of customers and related agencies. It would also reinforce in this the three modes of responsibility: immutability (developing a sense of the agency of the industry as a whole), accountability (through accounting for the practice across the industry), and liability (through dialogues between industry and firms and between industry and related agencies, including government, and ensuring a stress on the responsibility of the consumer).

Baggott notes the example of Scotland's attempts to develop statutory provision to underpin self-regulatory activities in such areas as training in the industry. This could be developed in other ways, such as 'clarifying the position on competition law with regard to socially responsible practice in areas such as point of sale promotions and other efforts to improve standards down the supply chain' (2006: 44). This would involve a careful analysis of the present codes and development of how they can effectively relate to regulation, including licensing laws. It would also, as Baggott suggests, involve a good deal more nuanced research around the practice and effectiveness of codes.

At the heart of this, however, is a development beyond a simplistic view of ethics, either as based largely in terms of harm reduction or in terms of conventional corporate responsibility. The concern for the responsibility of the industry as a whole reinforces the point that the identity of any drinks firm is plural. The firm not only has a responsibility as a firm, but also as member of the industry. In turn, this relates to the civic responsibility of the firm, and to the responsibility of other related agencies that have a concern for alcohol and the effects of its consumption. At the core of such an approach to ethics are constant questions about shared responsibility and about the negotiation of that responsibility.

All of this demands the development of trust, so that genuine dialogue can take place. This process takes much longer, and suggests that the ethical response is found in the development of relationships over time, in such a way that the responsibility of all involved can be engaged, as much as in the developing in any arguments about ethical meaning. The nature of such dialogue can be summed up in the idea that responsibility itself is precisely developed through the practice of it.

- First, it enables the development of agency. It demands articulation of value and practice, which clarifies both what we think and do. Articulation, the development of narrative, becomes essential for reflection and learning. It will enable the corporation and stakeholders to see just how values and practice relate, leading to learning.
- Second, dialogue demands the development of commitment to the self and others. It is not possible to pursue dialogue without giving space and time for it to develop, and this, in turn, demands a non-judgemental attitude. Commitment to the self and others is also essential if the potential critique of values and practice is to emerge from articulation and reflection.
- Third, dialogue enables listening and, with that, empathy, appreciation and responsiveness. We learn about others, as well as ourselves, only if we are open to both.

- Fourth, dialogue enables the development of a more realistic and truthful assessment of the data in any situation, as noted (pp. 96–7).
- Fifth, dialogue itself sets up a continued accountability with those involved. This is partly because it sets up a contract, formal or informal, that establishes expectations that are continually tested.
- Sixth, dialogue enables the development of shared liability, not simply the recognition of shared interests. This leads to the negotiation of responsibility.
- Seventh, dialogue extends the imagination and develops creativity. It shows what is possible, especially where responsibility is shared, and so increases the capacity to respond.
- Finally, doing all of this enables real partnerships, and everyone involved, to engage personal as well as group responsibility.

Such a dialogue has to go beyond the usual stakeholders: health care providers, the alcohol industry, the suppliers of alcohol and so on. At one level, this requires identification of wider stakeholders. A good example of this is the responsibility of the media in general. The UK Ofcom code, for instance, stipulates that television and radio programmes should not 'condone encourage or glamorize' alcohol misuse before the watershed (9 pm, in the UK). Recent research (news.bbc.co.uk/1/hi/health/7598288.stm) has noted that, during the period late 2007 and early 2008, there were over 700 comments that encouraged excessive drinking. The research focused on several radio stations that were aimed at young people. Of those comments, 244 had been made by presenters. The comments typically suggested that alcohol was necessary for a good weekend, and that a hangover was the mark of a successful evening. The presenters, then, were reinforcing not only excessive use of alcohol, but also a set of values that saw alcohol and excessive use as good. Hence, drunkenness was seen as an achievement. It is reasonable, in that context, to stress the responsibility of the presenter. Many listeners will directly identify with presenters, and this could lead to unhealthy alcohol consumption being reinforced.

Conclusion

This chapter has suggested that the issue of harm avoidance is important but insufficient as the focus for an adequate ethical response to the problem of alcohol and its industry. Also important, but insufficient, is the tension between individual freedom and government control. We argued that the Nuffield Report's development of this was useful, but does not really develop the idea of stewardship – a concept that is based in responsibility. The development of shared responsibility through negotiation becomes an important way in which all involved parties can be engaged and exercise such responsibility. Whilst there have been several good efforts in developing such responsibility, this engagement has not been fully realized; partly because the debate has been polarized, partly because it has had a narrow ethical framework, and partly because there has not been sufficient, effective, trust-building dialogue. What is argued for here is a model of ethical engagement argued that is proactive and creative, rather than simply about the establishment of reactive codes. Possible developments in shared responsibility will be examined in Chapter 8. Wider regulation, if used creatively, connecting to the developments in shared responsibility, including the personal responsibility of the consumer, can help to support such practice.

5
Young People, Social Scene and Popular Culture

Introduction

Teenagers and young adults experience physical and psychological changes as a part of ordinary growth and development. In addition, they take their meaning and identity from relating positively and negatively to different groups, including school, family, interest and peer groups. This used to be seen as a linear development, with the teenager gradually going through the stages of maturity and letting go of the family in exchange for a new family and so on. Post-modern times (Connor 1989) suggest two things. First, there have been many social changes, including greater mobility and increasing breakdown of traditional social patterns, such as the nuclear family. Second, there has been an increase in ethical, social and cultural pluralism. This has led to questioning of the meta-narratives that seemed to give direction to social and moral meaning up to the middle of the twentieth century. For the developing child, this sets up a potentially confusing set of expectations and experiences. The issue of acceptable alcohol consumption emerges for the young person in such a social context, requiring both clear social frameworks for practice and the development of mature moral reflection that begin to handle the many different social messages.

There are minimum age regulations in European countries for when young people can buy alcohol from a licensed venue. For example, purchasing beer or wine off-premises in the UK this is generally 18-years-old, in Germany it is 16-years-old end in Denmark it is 15 (World Health Organization 2004). However, there are many subconscious signals sent to young people about the social acceptability of alcohol consumption, the 'rights of passage' and the rituals of alcohol consumption. Therefore, young people receive many messages that indicate, both socially

103

and psychologically, it is acceptable to consume alcohol is a part of growing up. However, global problems are increasing. These do not necessarily involve more young people drinking. Indeed, the number of 16–24-year-olds and 11–15-year-olds consuming alcohol in Great Britain is decreasing (Office for National Statistics 2006). The major problem, as reported by governments, social and health campaigners, is that the amount of alcohol drunk on each occasion by young people who do drink is increasing. Because of this, the terms 'binge drinking' and 'extreme drinking' have entered our vocabulary.

This chapter will be split into two sections. The first section will consider European drinking lifestyles, The European Youth Forum (YFJ) Positional Paper and the UK's drinking behaviour. Many young people are subconsciously and consciously motivated to take up drinking, as they want to feel part of their community, enjoy alcohol at social gatherings, meet new people and relax (Kenyon 2009a). What they drink and how often they drink it differs from country to country, and this will be discussed. Additionally, there are many other motivations for drinking, and these will also be evaluated towards the end of this chapter. Drinking more on each occasion and drinking beyond 'acceptable limits' has led to an increased amount of research, and a raft of shocking statistics. To address these, it is argued that young people need to develop their understanding of alcohol, so that it can be part of their lives in a positive way rather than in a way that causes harm socially or to their long-term health. This chapter, therefore, presents the many educationally driven strategies aimed at young people. It will also consider the role of the family in helping to establish the right balance between freedom and health risks associated with 'risky drinking'. Running through the chapter are references to the World Health Organization's report on alcohol strategies, the European strategies and local initiatives for alcohol related education. All of these strategies or initiatives have the same goal – to protect young people from alcohol related harm.

The second section will discuss how alcohol is part of a young person's social scene, their 'right of passage' into adulthood, their motivations and the camaraderie, felt when taking part in recreational drinking. Youth, teenagers, adolescents, whatever name is given, have always pushed boundaries, of themselves and those around them. Heavy and episodic drinking has been 'the norm' on and off throughout history for a minority, as shown in Chapter 1. Therefore, are young people only conforming to this norm? Or, have 24-hour news, a better understanding of psychological issues and addictive tendencies, and a greater knowledge of the long-term consequences of drinking over the 'acceptable limit' begun to define and assert behavioural boundaries? This section will discuss in greater detail 'binge drinking', 'drinking to get drunk' and 'extreme drinking' as these social issues make headline news on a regular basis – all of which promote the alcocentric environment. It will also debate the reasons for the increased growth in these areas, including details of economic factors, changes in lifestyle and social freedoms. Interestingly, in face of the extensive coverage and debate of additional drinking on each occasion, young people in the UK do not necessarily consider alcohol and drinking to be a problem. Issues that are a problem to them are knives, gun crime, teenage pregnancy and drugs (Department for Children, Schools and Families 2008). The chapter will conclude by drawing together the initiatives that are in place to enable the young consumer to make their own choices based on the educational programmes, and social and family networks. For the purposes of this chapter, young people are defined as being between 10 and 24 years, mirroring the age range of the many studies in this area.

Europe

The YFJ presented a provisional paper in 2006 that discussed how it would provide a holistic approach to promoting and improving the 'relationship' between young people and alcohol. They also investigated and developed policies to reduce alcohol-related harm. This might sound little different from the World Health Organization's message, or the items on the agenda of many governments. However, the YFJ is different from many other global and national organizations because it is made up of national youth councils and international non-governmental youth organizations and, most importantly, it is run by young people for young people. The concerns of the YFJ also include the 'usual' long-term health problems, violent behaviour by the young person and being 'caught up in' violent behaviour in public places or in the home. Importantly, their key aim is to empower young people to look after themselves responsibly and to make healthy choices. The onus, therefore, is on the individual young person making decisions, rather than top-down government enforcement initiatives, compulsory ID cards or fines for 'drinking on the streets'. This sends a clear message that, ultimately, it is the person that makes responsible decisions, not legislation. The YFJ argues that empowering such responsible decision-making demands, firstly, more education about alcohol, and secondly the need to create or provide alternative ways of spending leisure time. As with the first point, this is not particularly radical, but it does go back to the idea that the young person should have before them alternative possibilities and communities around leisure-time activities, and that an important part of developing responsibility is being able to handle the choices that arise from relationships with different groups. Thirdly, the Forum stresses the need to help young people develop strong self-esteem. This final recommendation suggests that beneath the loud and brash picture painted of young drinkers there is in fact an uncertainty about values and, thus, about self-esteem and the criteria for self-esteem. Cooper (2008) supports this recommendation, recognizing new pressures experienced by many young people. These include the breakdown of family networks, teenagers perceiving relationships as transient, and the decrease in the long-term commitment of marriage.

Many national or cross-national surveys have been conducted in and between countries with regards to adolescent drinking, drunkenness and more recently, binge drinking. Ahlström and Österberg (2004/05) state that the highest consumption of alcohol, by young people, takes place in countries with established economic wealth such as Europe and North America. In Africa, eastern Mediterranean countries where Muslim values predominate, Asia or the Indian subcontinent, alcohol is drunk less by young people. It is important to note, however, that a general statement such as this does not mean that 'everyone' in Europe or North America consumes alcohol excessively. In fact, only a small proportion of people, within a country, consume the majority of alcohol drunk. For example, 20 per cent of people who are 'drinkers' in America consume 90 per cent of the alcohol drunk (Greenfield and Rogers 1999). The problem, however, is that young people (aged 11–15 years) are drinking more on each occasion (Home Office 2008), and more young men are drinking to the point of intoxication (Babor *et al.* 2003). Consequently, young people the world over, particularly in developing countries (Room *et al.* 2002) are becoming part of the 'drinkers'. Without doubt, young people in some European countries are less likely to drink alcohol due to their religious values. For example, over two thirds of 15–16-year-olds abstain from consuming alcohol in Turkey, whilst only 5 per cent of 15–16-year-olds in Czech Republic and Denmark abstain (Hibell *et al.* 2004). This reflects the idea that, as young people learn social behaviour from other members in their close communities, family, friends, their wider community and the culture within their nationality, their own drinking behaviour complies with the social norms. Taking this idea further, it is interesting to consider whether young people align themselves to consumer alcohol products that are associated with their country, as it would seem natural to assume that young people from southern European wine-producing countries would drink wine and those from beer-producing countries would drink beer. Generally this is the case, but there are some anomalies. Culturally, the French and Italians let their children and adolescents join them for 'highly diluted' wine around the family dinner table, and this is considered to be part of family life. Despite that, Andersson *et al.* (2007) suggest that 24 per cent of Italian students aged 17–18-years-old had drunk less than 10 times in their lifetime, and only 28 per cent of 17–18-year-old students' in France consume wine. With regard to beer-producing nations, such as Denmark, UK and Ireland, young people from these countries are less likely (necessarily) to drink with the family: they drink regularly outside the home and do not drink moderately. Returning to Andersson *et al.* (2007), four-fifths of Polish students aged 17–18 had drunk beer in the last 30 days, thus demonstrating young people are shifting their 'drink of choice' away from the 'vodka belt' of Eastern Europe to a more modern, Western European drink.

The individual economic power of a young person also has an effect on whether young people drink alcohol or not. A longitudinal study in Finland stated that 14-year-olds who were working were more able to afford alcohol when their country and family enjoyed buoyant, economic times. However, when adult unemployment was higher, their opportunity for part-time work and their pocket money reduced, due to a reduced family income. Therefore, alcohol consumption levels also reduced (Lintonen *et al.* 2004/2005). This is not always the case. A similar study in Spain showed that the amount of pocket money received did not necessarily equate to whether the young person consumed low or high amounts of alcohol (Ariza-Cardenal and Nebot-Adell 2000). Rowan (2007), Director of the Rutland Centre in Dublin, suggests that young people will 'find money' to drink alcohol even though UK alcoholic drink in pubs, clubs and bars is a highly taxed item. Van Hoof *et al.* (2008) also investigated whether discounted drinks 'happy hours' would enable 14–17-year-olds in the Netherlands to 'go out more often', with their money stretching further in cafés that offered 'happy hours'. Their conclusions were that 'alcohol discounts … do not attract adolescents to visit particular cafés and/or to spend more money when going out' (van Hoof *et al.* 2008: 340). In the UK, Kenyon (2009b) found that 16–17-year-olds who were regular drinkers (went out of the home and consumed alcohol more than once a week) drink until they had 'run out of money' or had 'spent up', aligning drinking to economic buoyancy. These facts give interesting information about the types of alcoholic drinks consumed in different countries and whether economic factors, such the young person's purchasing power, influence a person's ability to drink. However, they do not necessarily give the full picture as to the age ranges, locations where the research took place and the comparability of the national drinking cultures are disparate. However, research undertaken on a worldwide basis shows that harmful drinking has a wide range of negative social consequences including crime, violent acts by and against young people, unemployment and absenteeism from school and/or work (World Health Organization 2008).

Alcohol in the mind and in the body

Behind many of the statistics and the related, often sensationalist, headlines are key issues about the mind and body of young people. The 'grey matter' or cortical and also sub-cortical regions of the brain changes dramatically, both structurally and functionally during the teenage years. This area of the brain processes emotional stimuli and aversive stimuli (such as pain), but also relates to goal-orientated, goal-directed and goal decision-making. Many parents notice dramatic changes in their children as they develop through their teenage years, both physically as their bodies move through puberty, and also behaviourally as the young person becomes more independent and begins to take control of decision-making. At the same time, their prefrontal cortex develops and young people begin to act impulsively, often ignoring the negative consequences that the irrational and/or spontaneous behaviour may bring (Winters 2008). Additionally, the intensity and speed that excitement, arousal and rewards bring is greater during teenage years than when people become adults. Spear (2002) also reports that adolescents subjectively 'lose their inhibitions', to a greater extent than adults, due to their environment and circumstances when consuming alcohol, and this is considered to be a direct result of the developing cortex.

Excessive drinking and early exposure to alcohol during the cortex changes is considered by some to lay down a predisposition to become addicted. This is a highly contentious claim, as some researches concluded that early drinking is merely a point in the young person's life cycle when they choose to drink (McGue *et al.* 2001). Others argue that there is a causal effect and that early consumption will lead to later alcohol abuse (Hawkins *et al.* 1997). It is not clear whether any empirical research could confirm such a hypothesis, not least because of the number of variables; hence, this debate will continue. However, Alcohol Concern (2007) has noted that the following health risks can be associated with excessive drinking, suggesting that early drinking will bring these health risks to a person sooner in their life cycle. Health risks associated with excessive drinking include: liver cirrhosis, gastritis, cancers, fertility problems, coronary heart disease, impotence, high blood pressure, strokes, mental health problems and neurological disorders. The question remains as to whether such data would actually influence young people, who, for whatever reason, have begun to drink excessively.

Communicating with young people

Unfortunately, when presented with these types of health risks a teenager or young adult would not necessarily consider that this applies to him or her. Alcohol Concern (2007) goes on to argue that more immediate risks might get their attention. These involve personal risks such as unsafe sex, sex they regretted, and not knowing if they had had sex the night before. For young people, such risks raise not only the problem of dealing with regrettable consequences, but also of the loss of control in their lives demonstrated by such actions. By losing control through excessive drinking, the young person is opening him- or herself up to actions of which they are not fully aware. Ironically, it is happening at the moment when many believe that they are asserting their independence. This dynamic was central to the concern of thinkers such as Aquinas (see Chapter 6, 130–1), in arguing that the person who knowingly drinks to excess is responsible for any bad actions committed whilst under the influence of alcohol.

The National Health Service (2008) notes chronic long-term illnesses related to alcohol abuse. As do Alcohol Concern, which also points to possible short-term or immediate consequences that might happen to a young person due to excessive alcohol consumption. These include impotence, losing consciousness and the increased chance of the young person having an accident or causing injury to themselves or others. They also include longer-term effects to a person's self-esteem, such as decrease in genital size, lower sperm count, loss of body hair, irregular periods and lower fertility, damage to an unborn child, weight gain from alcohol's high calorie content and skin problems.

Alcohol Concern and the National Health Service have excellent knowledge, building websites that give crucial information, from understanding the alcohol strength found in many beers, wines, and spirits, to advice for women, to fact sheets about alcohol and mental health, to details about alcohol and crime. Whilst laudable, some argue that these are 'too mature', too concept driven for young people, particularly early teenagers. Therefore, education about the potential harm that alcohol can bring additionally needs face-to-face education and discussion forums being part of the national curriculum in UK schools.

The National Curriculum requires some form of education regarding alcohol (and drugs) be included in day-to-day teaching within either science classes, or personal, health and social education (PHSE) (see Box 5.1 for an additional source). They have also presented a number of suggestions on the depth of information that needs to be shared with young people at different ages. It is felt by the UK Government and Wired for Health (an educational arm that guides teaching in schools) that, because approximately one-fifth of boys aged 11–15 years and approximately one-seventh of girls aged 11–15 years will drink alcohol every week (Wired for Health 2008), education in primary schools is now essential. One of the reasons for this is to give young people knowledge, including

---

Box 5.1   Talk to Frank

Talk to Frank is a mechanism in the UK for young people to discover information and advice about alcohol and drugs. Advertising campaigns on television and radio, and in popular print media, have made young people aware of the advice they can receive – confidentially.

Talk to Frank is actually sponsored by the Home Office, yet, as a consumer of the advice network, this is not noticeable. Perceptually, this is a strategy, as the Home Office could be viewed as a law enforcement agency rather than a pastoral or advisory service.

Young people can gain a great deal of knowledge about the types of alcoholic drinks and drugs available, and their consequences. One of the most interesting features of the site is the opportunity for any young person to provide a 'story'. Stories are written by young people, for young people and reflect actual, real-life experiences. Stories can be uploaded from any PC and viewed by visitors to the site. A poignant story regarding alcohol and its effects currently on the web shows that alcohol can turn you 'inside out'. The storyteller gives a brief account of how alcohol became their 'best friend' as it took away all their worries, and how this led to a loss of freedom to one of dependency. The use of stories enables reflection, openness and honesty, and communicates emotional as well as conceptual content. Hence, visitors are more likely to Talk to Frank identify with the storyteller and listen to any advice. Any young person can also telephone or e-mail for help and guidance. Pseudonyms can also be given to ratify the confidential promise given in the advertising campaigns.

an understanding of the effects that alcohol has on friends, family and wider groups: each child should therefore receive education at various ages throughout their life at school. Materials to help and support the child's education are provided by Wired for Health. Support materials are also available for teachers. Early education will help young people gain an understanding of alcohol in an environment where they regularly discuss issues such as healthy eating, diets, sex, relationships and so on. This brings alcohol out into the open, as opposed to leaving it as a taboo subject. Additionally, it is the discussions that young people have with each other at lunch or break-times that will enable them to speak even more freely with teachers or parents. The web materials available through Wired for Health provide clear advice. Additionally, there are many links to other sites, such as www.need2know.co.uk which provides information for young people about alcohol, careers, keeping fit, mental heath, careers and so on. There are also many click-throughs to www.talktofrank.co.uk, a website specifically designed to give 'all you need to know' information about drugs from A to Z. Two websites, www.need2know.co.uk and www.talktofrank.co.uk, clearly understand the needs of young people: the information is not patronizing and it uses highly targeted messages and language appropriate for a young audience. Therefore, young people in the UK have access to a wealth of information to advise them that alcohol is often part of their social scene and national culture. But, all of the organizations present their case for alcohol consumption as something that is acceptable in moderation, and provide guidance to help young people understand where a fun night stops and an unattractive, unhealthy night begins.

Help and advice from the young person's family is also vital. Young people understand the norms of behaviour from the first day they are born from members of their own family. And as children grow older, the knowledge of the unwritten rules and regulations of family life develop, and discussions and 'negotiations' to stay up late, get the latest mobile phone or go to the cinema begin. Running parallel to that, young people will soon discover how alcohol is used and viewed within their family circle at Christmas or at the dinner table. Recent research projects in understanding the relationship between the discussions, or their absence, between parents and children about alcohol have found that good relationships within the family, regular communication about alcohol and mechanisms for 'give and take' reduce dependence on alcohol and reduce the levels of alcohol drunk by young people. Unfortunately, young people are more likely to drink irresponsibly if they live within a family unit where they received high levels of criticism and harsh conflict

---

Box 5.2   BII Schools project – how the UK alcohol industry gets involved

In addition to Government run education, the alcohol industry also is involved in helping young people to understand the nature of alcohol and how it can be included in their daily lives. The BII is one of the main organisations that enable the on- and off-licensed trade to gain the National Certificate for Personal Licence Holders. All purveyors of alcohol must gain this certificate. Therefore, the BII have a vested interest in keeping the pub, club, bar, restaurant and off-trade business alive. At the same time, they actively seek the chance to engage with initiatives that help young people to understand the licensed trade and how they can enjoy alcohol responsibly. One of the projects they have become engaged in is the Schools Project. Teachers are supplied with materials such as case studies and quizzes to help pupils aged 11–15 understand alcohol, alcohol and law, how people can consume alcohol responsibly and what happens if people misuse it. When pupils complete the short programme of study as part of their PHSE (Personal, Social and Health Education), for example, they can take an exam. Upon successful completion of the exam, pupils are awarded the BIIAB Level 1 Certificate in Alcohol Awareness.

The BII is an organization of charitable status that works with a variety of industry partners to support and fund the Schools Project. The industry partners include Marstons PLC (pub company), Mitchells & Butlers (licensed retail and brewers), Plymouth Gin (distillers), Butlins (holiday resort), The New Inn, Hereford (coaching inn).

This initiative deserves recognition as it looks to form a community of young people, a charitable organisation that can supply the industry with recognised accreditation to young people who engage in understanding alcohol and the alcohol brewers, licensees, licensed retailers and distillers. The community's objective, it seems, is to share knowledge of what alcohol is and how to consume it responsibly.

---

over their behaviour, or parents that have a laissez-faire or totally passive, permissive attitude (Hayes *et al.* 2003, Highet 2004). This concurs with previous studies, where it was found that moderate levels of parental control and a supporting role, one that promotes sensible drinking, lead to acceptable drinking behaviour in young people (Foxcroft *et al.* 1997). Kenyon (2008) goes on to argue that 'It is better to let them have a drink in a safe environment with parents. If you don't – they'll find some [alcohol] and drink it on the streets in an environment that isn't always safe; especially if they don't know the strength of drinks or how many units are in a measure.' Additionally, research with young people in Edinburgh highlighted that 13–15-year-olds believe their parents prefer it if they are having a drink under their watchful eye, rather than on the street (Highet 2004). It seems, therefore, that young people who have a good supporting network with their families, and who have had the opportunity to consume alcohol within a safe, nurturing environment, drink responsibly in future years. Young people who come across conflict, perhaps through their own 'drunken' behaviour, or do not have parents that discuss sensible use and misuse of alcohol may become more dependant and/or irresponsible drinkers.

However, in many ways this does not give a full picture. In Europe, the UK in particular, there is an increasing breakdown of the traditional 'nuclear family', leading in many cases to major crises and changes in relationships, with young people having to find frameworks of meaning and support from other groups. This means that younger and younger people use their social network and peers as their 'core group' (Cooper 2008). Additional social networks such as youtube.com, currently showing 128 videos entitled 'Alcohol, my only friend' inspired by a song from Start Trouble, which may also be used by young people to seek knowledge and guidance. However, the question is raised as to whether peers of virtual groups have the same monitoring and moderational affects that the family has over their children/teenagers (Wood *et al.* 2004).

Binge drinking, drinking to get drunk and extreme drinking

Binge drinking is a relatively new phrase but the activity of excessive, heavy drinking, going on 'a bender' or having an all-day session (ADS) has been a cultural activity for millennia. We have already noted Bede's (eighth-century) reference to 'oceanic' consumption and Dostoevsky's (nineteenth-century) drinking to the point of 'insensibility'. The International Center for Alcohol Policies stated over 10 years ago that whilst it occurred, there was difficulty in discussing heavy episodic drinking, as there was no definition that could be agreed upon worldwide. Unfortunately, this makes it difficult to draw comparisons between research projects within a country and across countries. However, some progress has been made in defining binge and extreme drinking.

The two earliest definitions of binge drinking, if we are to use this phrase, came from Bloomfield *et al.* (1999) who stated it to be 10 or more alcoholic drinks in one session. In this case, one drink is equivalent to one standard unit, which equates to approximately 8g of ethanol (see www.knowyourlimits.co.uk to assess the number of units found in alcoholic drinks in the UK). In real terms, one unit equates approximately to one 25 ml measure of vodka, if the ABV is 40 per cent. One pint of lager, which has an ABV of 5 per cent, will, however, equate to 2.8 units. Therefore, a binge is 10 vodkas or virtually three-and-a-half pints of lager (three-and-a-half pints of lager = 9.8 units). In the same year, Raistrick *et al.* (1999) differentiated the amount drunk by men and women, and stated that a binge was 10 units for men and 7 units for women. The reasons Raistrick *et al.* (1999) suggested for this differentiation are numerous. One reason is that women have a higher proportion of body fat and less water in their bodies than men. Hence, alcohol is less diluted, producing a stronger and more speedy effect. Also, a woman's liver does not break down alcohol in the same way that the liver in a man's body does. This is because a woman's liver produce has less dehydrogenase, the enzyme the body uses to break down alcohol.

Nevertheless, defining binge drinking using standard units can be very difficult for young people to understand, as the percentage ABV varies from one bottle of wine to another, and different types of beers and lagers have different percentage ABVs. This can actually be said for many spirits, ciders, pre-packaged drinks (such as alcopops) and made-to-order cocktails. Despite academia and researchers not working from a standardized definition for binge drinking, and alcoholic drinks with various ABVs, in 2004 the UK Cabinet Office provided a raft of statistics detailing the problems of young people binge drinking (Cabinet Office 2004). The Cabinet Office provided two new definitions to enable the general public to understand what constitutes binge drinking, together with a definition for chronic drinking. Binge drinkers, the Cabinet Office argued, included people ' who drank above double the recommended daily guidelines on at least one occasion in the last week' (ibid.: 11). Chronic drinkers were considered to be those who regularly drank large amounts. This definition did not satisfy the general public or the media, as it suggested that if men drank between 3–3$\frac{1}{2}$ pints of lager or 8 vodkas and women drank more than 2–2$\frac{1}{2}$ pints of lager or 6 vodkas in the last week (using the same percentage ABV lager and vodka shown in the previous example above) they could be considered to be binge drinkers. It was noted at the time that the definition involved drinking less than the definition in 1999 had indicated. The unit-based definitions also place all young people under one head, when some might take their drinks over several hours and others drink them within an hour. The *Journal of Studies on Alcohol and Drugs* (2008), guidance to authors submitting a document to their journal containing the term 'binge drinking', is to use the term only if referring to extended alcohol intake for periods of time, two days or more. Additionally, the journal argues that 'binge drinking' refers to a person who continues alcohol intake to the point of intoxication, and that the normal activities of the man or woman are set aside in order to continue to drink alcohol. This definition provides clearer guidelines regarding when and for how long drinking takes place and has a definite outcome: intoxication.

Martinic and Measham (2008) have proposed 'extreme drinking' as a term to describe the activities that young people engage in, with known motivations and outcomes. To ensure clarity, this sets out five key criteria: intoxication, motivation, process, outcomes and alcohol experience. All of these must be involved for drinking to be 'extreme'. Intoxication must occur within a short period of time, involving a high number of alcoholic drinks, such that high levels of alcohol in the blood of the young person can be measured. The motivations of extreme drinking are specifically to lose control or 'controlled loss of control' (Measham 2002), to go drinking to get drunk, to take risks and push boundaries, and to go further than acceptable social levels would allow. The process that takes place during extreme drinking does not happen alone. Martinic and Measham (2008) state that extreme drinking is a social activity, where peers encourage each other to behave in that way. Because the activity is with friends, the camaraderie is heightened and the experience is all about shared pleasure, hedonism and engendering a positive attitude. One of the main outcomes is drunkenness. When drunkenness is associated with disorderly behaviour, there are negative consequences to society at large but, if contained within the social group, disorderly behaviour might be self-policed. A further negative outcome could also be severe reduction in finances and, possibly, time off work due to the 'morning after' effect. The final key aspect of extreme drinking is the alcohol experience. When a group of friends and/or peers engage in this type of activity, they demonstrate they can 'handle their beer'. Extreme drinking associated with the rituals of sports teams, initiation ceremonies, or stag and hen nights is seen as extreme but acceptable. For the most part, these are not regular activities. In the context of sport, for instance, there is an increasing awareness of the negative effect of alcohol on sport performance. Also, they occur, for the most part, within the boundaries of a community. Perhaps most importantly, they are focused in a purpose that goes beyond the consumption of alcohol. The purpose of binge and extreme drinking is excessive drinking. At one level, this requires a careful social management to ensure that the negative effects of this behaviour are contained. At another level, it asks major questions of wider culture and of the moral development of young people, and whether behaviour is a consequence of an alcocentric environment.

Popular culture and celebrities

Newspaper and magazines moguls, the paparazzi and talk-show hosts provide the consumer with endless stories of celebrities falling out of taxis drunk. Prince William and Prince Harry photographed enjoying drinks with friends, sells magazines. Ewan, the son of Tony Blair, the former prime minister, made headline news for being found drunk in Leicester Square in 2000 after celebrating his final GCSEs. Photographs of Cristiano Ronaldo, Wayne Rooney, Carloz Tevez and Gary Neville after this year's Manchester United Christmas Party are posted on the sporting web pages of the *Mirror* (2008). The media interest is ambivalent. For some, it involves a process of identifying with the celebrities. This reinforces the positive view of alcohol and community that the media develops in soap operas such as *Coronation Street, Emmerdale, Neighbours* and *Eastenders*. None of these idealize alcohol. All have moral dilemmas being worked out as part of their ongoing story lines, such that many schools have used these to help pupils reflect on ethical decision-making. All of this reinforces the important role of youth-centred fictional media in helping young people to reflect on values, practice and relationships. It also reinforces the need for schools to continue education about alcohol within the broader development of ethics and responsibility.

Other headlines are more judgemental, focusing on the shame of some celebrities. Amy Winehouse and Britney Spears are women that have made their fortunes in the music industry. They are well-known icons for many young people but have filled more newspapers on their exploits of wild nights out and boozy exploits than their music. Further headlines reveal how many times Lindsay Lohan went to alcohol and drug rehabilitation before the age of 22, or that Drew Barrymore was in rehabilitation twice before her sixteenth birthday partly because she began drinking alcohol and partying by the time she was 11-years-old.

Articles in magazines and newspapers have shown young people that terrible consequences can befall even the rich and famous when they drink excessively. However, such headlines can also encourage a voyeuristic enjoyment in the downfall of the idol in question, focusing on censure rather than active reflection about what was wrong and why it was wrong. Moreover, such cases even deliver mixed messages that wish both to condemn and reinforce the value of celebrity.

These different signals from the media add to the many voices that young people have to handle. They ask questions about which of these messages they can believe and what criteria they might use to judge between them. As such, they focus directly on the moral development of the young person.

Moral development

The study of moral development is too broad and complex to sum up here. However, it is worth noting five areas that work on moral development. First, the work of Kohlberg (1984) argues that development involves working through stages, from early ones that focus conforming to the moral meaning of the groups or community, to later ones that can handle being part of several groups and focus on the person taking responsibility for articulating and justifying their values and how they relate to practice. The critiques of Kohlberg from writers such as Gilligan (1982) warn not to see such stages as rigid, but still focus on the need to takes responsibility for how the person responds to different groups and their needs, a slightly more relational approach.

Second, much of moral development is focused in the development of identity, and this requires the opportunity to identify with others and test out how that relates to our identity. This has a strong affective as well as conceptual element and is best enabled, as noted, through stories of individuals and communities.

Third, moral development requires a capacity to reflect critically on the self and on values that give meaning to the self, as an individual or part of a community. Unquestioned values actually discourage taking responsibility (Bauman 1989).

Fourth, moral development requires reflection on underlying narratives of meaning, not simply moral concepts. In particular, this focuses on the purpose of the person or group. Being able to appreciate the value of one's purpose, in relational or role terms, and thus identify with the positive effects of this purpose, directly builds positive identity and contributes to the esteem of the self and group (Mustakova-Possardt 2004, Robinson 2007).

Finally, such development is facilitated through dialogue and critical conversation that enables the self or group to relate to others, including other cultures. Such dialogue of difference enables people to engage with these critical questions, and invites the person to take responsibility for assessing his or her own values and those of others.

All this would suggest that, in addition to a clear legal framework for young people and the important information about alcohol and the consequences of extreme drinking, education, across the board, should further develop the focus on moral development and the practice of responsibility. One example of this in higher education is the development of Personal Development Profile Modules on Responsible Engagement (Leeds Metropolitan University, School of Applied Global Ethics). In the first-year modules, this approach focuses on the role and purpose of the student, of higher education and of the University itself, connecting these to learning skills. In the second year, the approach focuses on professional and community responsibility, connecting to the skills and virtues of employability. The final year draws all this together under 'global responsibility', connecting this to the skills and virtues of leadership. In each case, the story of learning, the professions and leadership is developed, and the issue of alcohol fits easily into such reflection.

Conclusion

This chapter has considered the biomedical, physical and social changes that young people experience, and the pressures they have to handle in relation to alcohol. Education is critical in enabling young people to develop a good relationship with alcohol and, whilst many families are fragmented, advice and educational opportunities are present in schools and other communities, and through the Internet, e-mail or telephone. Binge and extreme drinking, nonetheless, remains a major problem with young people, requiring a mixed response, including clear legal frameworks, the reinforcement of these by the alcohol industry, and greater focus on the development of moral responsibility at all levels of education. Ultimately, this takes us back to the cry from the YFJ to provide responses to the problem that will focus not only on control, but also on well-being, self-esteem and identity. Chapter 6 will focus further on the ethical identity of religious communities in relation to alcohol.

6
Religion and Alcohol

Religion is often seen as having a negative response to alcohol. It is associated by many with the temperance movement, which argued for abstinence, viewing alcohol as evil. In this chapter, we will argue that the response of religion to alcohol is much more complex and diverse. We will begin with the Judeo-Christian tradition, noting that wine was very much part of the culture, and that any negative view of wine was around drunkenness. We will then briefly note how views have developed since Biblical times, leading to the plurality of perspectives now held.

We will then examine the Islamic response to alcohol, noting that, whilst there is a diversity of practice around different cultures, there is a strong negative view of alcohol, not least because it affects the relationship with God. Hence, Islam stresses the need to abstain. We will finally glance briefly at the worship of wine in the person of Bacchus, and then conclude with some comments on the importance of taking worldviews, including those of religions, into account.

Background

Despite some debate about the translation of *yayin* and *oinos* (terms in the Septuagint – the Koine Greek version of the Hebrew Bible – that translate most of the Hebrew words for wine) there is broad agreement that these refer to alcoholic beverages. Initially, in the times of the Hebrew scriptures wine was usually drunk without water. Hence, wine mixed with water was viewed negatively, exemplified by its use as an Old Testament metaphor for corruption (Isaiah 1: 22). Following Alexander the Great's conquest of Palestine, the Greek practice of mixing wine with water took hold.

The practice of wine making is referred to in several passages. Palestine was well suited to viticulture, with references to this practice in Canaan before the Hebrew invasion (Genesis 14: 18; Numbers 13: 20, 24). Wine was a valuable commodity in the local and regional marketplace. Hence, vineyards were protected from robbers and animals by high walls and manned watchtowers. Rituals surrounded the production process, not least at the time of the grape harvest. Most of the harvest went to the wine press for the men and boys to trample, often accompanied by music. What remained was either eaten or matured into raisins. The process of fermentation began soon after pressing, and the must (freshly pressed grapes) was usually left in a vat for the first stage of fermentation. At the completion of the fermentation process, the wine was either stored in large earthenware jars or sold in wine skins.

Judaism and Christianity

Judaism and Christianity developed in cultures where alcohol was a part of everyday life. It was associated with community well-being and celebration, and was central to many major rituals.

Celebration

In the context of general nourishment and feasts, the Bible associates alcohol with joy. In the context of one parable, about who should rule over the trees, the vine answers, 'What, leave my new wine, which gladdens gods and men, and go to hold sway over the trees' (Judges 9: 12–13). Psalm 4: 7 compares the effect of alcohol to the joy of a loving relationship, 'But you have put into my heart greater happiness, even than that had from grain and wine in plenty'. In Psalm 104:14ff., wine is connected to the fecundity of creation, and a sustainable planet:

> You make grass grow for the cattle, and plants for the use of mortals,
> Producing grain from the earth,
> Food to sustain their strength,
> Wine to gladden the hearts of the people,
> And oil to make their faces shine.

Ecclesiastes 9: 7, from the pragmatic Wisdom literature, links alcohol-centred celebration to God's favour:

> Go then eat your food and enjoy it, and drink your wine with a cheerful heart, for God has already accepted what you have done.

A little later comes the aphorism:

The table has it pleasures and wine makes for a cheerful life. (Ecclesiastes 10: 19)

Zechariah (9: 17), in reflecting on the people of the Lord, notes:

What wealth is theirs, what beauty,
Grain to strengthen young men and new wine for maidens.

The joy of the people is compared to the experience of drinking wine:

So the Ephraimites will be like warriors,
With their hearts gladdened as if by wine.
Their children will see and be glad: their hearts will rejoice in the Lord.
(Zechariah 10: 7)

Ecclesiastes, another example of the Wisdom School, uses the image
of wine in several places. In the context of moderate consumption it
emphasises joy and wisdom:

Wine is very life to man, if taken in moderation.
Does he really live who lacks the wine that was created for his joy?
(31: 27)

Ecclesiastes then goes on to suggest that alcohol has to be consumed
in a disciplined fashion, both at the right time (community celebration)
and in the right frame of mind, not whilst dominated by anger or anxiety:

Joy of heart, good cheer and merriment are wine drunk freely at the
proper time.
Headache, bitterness and disgrace is wine drunk amid anger and
strife. (31: 28)

The implicit ethical injunction is to avoid using wine negatively or in
any attempt to ameliorate emotional problems. We will return to this
theme in greater detail later, but it is worth briefly pointing out that
this suggests that there is a responsible decision involved before wine
is consumed and that to consume it for the wrong reasons could lead
to not facing up to the underlying problems, turning to alcohol as the

short-term answer to those problems, and thus eventually to the disgrace referred to in the text.

Consumed in the right way, wine is compared several times to intimate love (The Song of Solomon 1: 4; 4: 10; 7: 6–9). Similarly, God's kingdom is compared to a vine or vineyard (Genesis 14: 18 and Hebrews 7: 1). Wine is also associated with blessing, and with abundance of resources that goes with the keeping of God's commandments, and of maintaining the covenant. Hence, Melchizedek blesses Abram's army with bread and wine (Genesis 14: 18ff.), and Isaac, and then Jacob, bless their sons with reference to an abundance of grain and new wine (Genesis 27: 28). Israel was promised an abundance of wine as well as rain and oil, if they kept the convent with God (Deuteronomy 7: 13; 11: 14). Israel would also be cursed with the taking away of its wine, if it failed to keep the covenant, hence:

> You will plant vineyards and cultivate them, but you will not gather the grapes, for the grub will eat them. (Deuteronomy 28: 39)

However, as the community looks towards the coming of the Messiah, the Day of Judgement, with Israel drawn together, wine is associated with renewals and celebration. It is spoken of in terms of 'fresh wine' running down the hills and mountains (Amos 9: 13). The planting of vineyards and drinking of wine is associated with the reclamation of the city communities, as the Israelites return to their land (Amos 9: 14). With Isaiah, this develops into the full-blown eschatological feast that will be inclusive of all peoples:

> On this mountain the Lord of Hosts will prepare
> A banquet of rich fare for all the peoples
> A banquet of wines well matured
> Richest fare and well-matured wines stained clear. (25: 6)

Alcohol, then, was not simply a core part of culture and commerce, it was also central to the theology of community, covenant and creation that had, at its heart, material and communal well-being as much as, indeed as a part of, spiritual well-being (Forrester and Skene 1988). Spirituality was not about a dualism of airy spirit and material body, but was itself physical and relational. Hence, the sign of God's favour had a material expression and the disfavour was expressed in allowing Israel to experience oppression and exile. This experience of the Israelites inevitably led to their focus on the return to the Holy Land, and to the ideal community, focused in their old arrangements, that had alcohol very much at the centre.

Perhaps the important point about all this is that alcohol is not viewed in terms of the individual but, rather, in terms of the community, and the health of the community as a whole. Hence, the use of wine is tied to the belief and value systems of the community, and is perceived as something negative in so far as it goes against that community or is used by the individual for wrong ends. In this light, it is not surprising that such a positive view should be expressed in the rituals of the community.

Ritual

From the earliest times, wine is associated with an offering to God. Libation, a ritual pouring for the wine, was seen as a form of sacrifice. Hence, when Jacob set up the pillar in the place where he had spoken to God, he first poured a drink offering, and then one of oil (Genesis 35: 14). Isaiah uses such libation as a metaphor for the sacrifice of the Suffering Servant (53: 12), seen in the Christian faith as a prophetic indication of Jesus.

Wine was prescribed for feasts and sacrificial rituals. In particular, newly fermented wine was presented daily as a drink offering (Exodus 29: 38–41), as part of the offerings of the first fruits (Leviticus 23: 9–14) and in a variety of lesser offerings (Numbers 15: 1–11). First fruits were tithed and offered at the festival of this name. The tithe was eventually limited to seven traditional agricultural products (wheat, barley, figs, pomegranates, dates, olives as oil, and grapes as wine). The festival and associated tithe is set down in Exodus 23: 16–19. The festival of Succoth (booths) had agricultural and historical roots. In effect, it was the harvest thanksgiving, 'after you have gathered in from your threshing floor and from your wine press' (Deuteronomy 16: 13). The reference to booths (temporary huts) is to the only dwellings the Hebrews had in their time in the wilderness. Hence, such booths were built in gardens and synagogues, decorated with garlands and fruit, reminding the community of the need to trust in God's protection (see Isaiah 1: 8). This also links into the experience of the nation cast out of its material and physical environment, and looking forward to the return. Wine is part of that whole culture and the experience that the Hebrews longed for.

The Christian Eucharist

Wine is central to the celebration of the Christian service of the mass or Eucharist. The term 'Eucharist' means 'thanksgiving'. The service itself is based on the Jewish festival of the Passover. This commemorates a critical part of Jewish history, the liberation from Egypt. At the heart of the Passover celebration was bread (unleavened to recall the hasty escape of the Hebrews) and wine symbolizing the sharing of the covenant community. It was such a meal that formed the last supper of Jesus on the evening before his death and which, in turn, he asked his disciples to repeat in remembrance of him (Luke 22: 17–19, Mark 14: 22–5; Matthew 26: 26–9). For Christians, this focuses on the ultimate act of sacrifice: that the Son of God, Jesus, should give up his life for all. The Eucharist takes the idea of a lived out story, the rehearsal of a crucial moment in the salvation history, to the level of a sacrament. A sacrament is a ritual involving an outward sign that conveys or lives out an inward spiritual presence or grace, in this case the underlying truth about the nature of Jesus, and his sacrifice. Some theologians argue that this is, in effect, a dramatized identification with Christ in the moments before his sacrifice, helping the worshippers to empathize fully with his decision and the final moments of his life. Other theologies go as far as to view the bread and wine as becoming the body and blood of Christ, the idea of transubstantiation. The act of blessing at the centre of the rite sanctifies the activity and experience. Most theologies view some sense of the presence of Christ in the narrative and ritual of the Eucharist.

If wine is associated with the festival at the heart of the Eucharist – and thus with liberation, sacrifice and salvation – it is also, by extension, associated with the very end of time. Passover had two functions; the remembrance of the deliverance of the Jews from Egypt, and looking forward to the coming of the Messiah. Jesus locks into this perspective as he looks forward to sharing the Passover in the Kingdom of God (Luke 22: 18). The two perspectives come together in one prayer of thanksgiving over the elements of bread and wine of the Anglican Eucharist (Silk 1986):

> Holy God,
> As the grain once scattered in the fields
> And the grapes once dispersed on the hillside
> Are now reunited on this table in bread and wine,
> So, Lord, may your whole Church soon be gathered together
> From the corners of the earth into your kingdom,
> *All*   Amen.

None of this means that the nature of alcohol is holy. It does mean that alcohol is used as an important symbol of the action of the divine, and as part of a ritual that helps those who participate to identify with the action of God in the person of Christ. This, in turn, connects to the historical narrative of Hebrew faith, and then looks forward to the end of time.

In broader terms, the New Testament accepts the positive view of wine held by the community in general, from celebratory to medicinal, as part of creation and community. At the wedding of Cana (John 2: 10), Jesus enables the guests to enjoy great quantities of extra wine miraculously changed from water. As wedding celebrations drew on, when the guests were inebriated, it was the tradition that they were then served the less good wine. The wine given after the miracle was the very best. Some see this as an eschatological theme played out through an enacted parable rather than an actual miracle (Barrett 1978), with the good wine pointing to what Jesus has to offer at the end of time. Others see the story as focusing on the humour and care of Jesus, with a sense of community at its heart.

Alcohol was also used for medicinal purposes. Many commentators argue that it was used as an anaesthetic, which is why Jesus was offered the wine at his crucifixion (Matthew 27: 34, 38). In the parable of the Good Samaritan, the Samaritan assists the injured man partly by pouring oil and wine onto his wounds (Luke 10: 34), commonly thought to cleanse wounds. Meanwhile, in I Timothy (5: 23) there is advice to drink wine as well as water, for the sake of the stomach and frequent infirmities. This might have been to purify water, or for direct medicinal purposes.

Drunkenness

Within the positive context of alcohol, there was a negative view of wine, associated largely with drunkenness. This term is referred to over seventy times in the Old and New Testaments. It is often associated by the prophets with the wealthy, but is not exclusive to them. It is seen in itself as moral failure, focusing on the responsibility of the individual. For the Hebrew Scriptures, such a failure is once more seen in terms of the covenant relationship between God and Israel. Hence, the breakdown in moral responsibility involves a breakdown in accountability to God, leading the person or group away from the covenant. This ties in with the broader point about the covenant and the Hebrew nation as a whole. At one level, this turning away from God is evidenced in physical and moral breakdown:

> Wine is an insolent fellow, strong drink a brawler; and no one addicted to their company grows wise. (Proverbs 20: 1)

Do not keep company with the drunkards or those who are greedy for the fleshpots, the drunkard and the glutton will end in poverty, in a state of stupor they are rescued to rags (Proverbs 23: 20).

Whose is the misery?
Whose is the remorse?
Whose are the quarrels and the anxiety?
Who gets the bruises without knowing why?
Whose eyes are bloodshot?
Those who linger late over wine,
Those always sampling some new spiced liquor. (Proverbs 23: 29f)

Focused in the pragmatic reasoning of the Wisdom School these verses in some ways parallel the public information advertisements of the twenty-first century, helping the reader to reflect on the consequences of drunkenness. First, it leads to a loss of wisdom. The fact that alcohol abuse can lead to the loss of wisdom makes it wise to avoid such practice. Second, it leads to the loss of prosperity and the onset of poverty. The description of Proverbs 23: 29 is that of habitual drunkenness and alcohol addiction. Third, drunkenness seems to be part of a broader moral breakdown, focused in the vice of intemperance, associating drunkenness with gluttony. The description of such a moral breakdown once more makes drunkenness a matter of personal moral responsibility. Again, this is set in the framework of the covenant with God. The scene is one of the person moving away from a community into an individual and lonely world where meaning is lost. Hence, Isaiah sets intemperance into the context of not responding to the deeds and presence of the Lord:

Woe betide those who rise early in the morning that they may follow strong drink, who sit late into the night inflamed with wine! At whose feasts there are harps and lutes, tabors and pipes and wine:
Yet for the work of the Lord they have never a thought,
No regard for what he has done. (Isaiah 5: 11–12)

As noted, in Ecclesiastes 31: 25–31 the moral responsibility for allowing this to happen goes back to the person. If the person is not in the right frame of mind, this will lead to the abuse of alcohol. There is also the implication that apart from the vice of intemperance, drunkenness allies itself with other vices that might already exist in the person – not least, folly.

Prophetic thinking extends the moral issues further, to the moral responsibility of those who are in power, and the people as a whole. Hosea reminds us that they will be called to account:

> And they consider not in their heart that I remember all their wickedness: now their own doings have beset them about; they are before my face ... On the feast day the princes are sick with bottles of wine, and the king joins with scorners. (Hosea 7: 2, 5)

The nation has chosen corn and wine over the covenant and the consequence will be captivity (Hosea 7: 13–16).

Proverbs 31: 4 argues that those in political authority should not drink wine:

> It is not for kings to drink wine or for those who govern to crave strong drink.

This would affect their capacity to offer disinterested justice, leading to the oppression of the poor. Drink is viewed here in relation to the core purposes and principles of the king. The same passage goes on to suggest, ironically, that wine and strong drink can be given to the poor to help them forget. By implication, none of this is a substitute for justice.

Similar points are made in relation to church leaders, and avoiding drunkenness is one of the qualities expected of them:

> A bishop, therefore must be above reproach, husband of one wife, temperate, sober, courteous, hospitable, and a good teacher; he must not be given to drink or brawling, but be of a forbearing disposition, avoiding quarrels and not avaricious. (Timothy 3: 2–3)

In the Old Testament, drink was forbidden to priests on duty (Leviticus 19: 9), though they were given the best new wine from the first fruit offerings, to be consumed outside the temple. However, even ordinary worshippers had a leadership role, in that their behaviour can affect others. Hence, Paul argues that all Christians have a duty to think about their behaviour:

> It is right to abstain from eating meat or drinking wine or from anything else that causes a fellow Christian to stumble. (Romans 14: 20–1)

Paul also takes the Corinthians to task for getting drunk in the Eucharist (I Corinthians 11: 20–2).

Ascetic subgroups also include prohibitions of alcohol. The ascetic vow of the Nazirites, for instance, involved abstaining from wine, but also vinegar, grapes and raisins (Numbers 6: 3). However, at the completion of the vow, wine was included in the sacrificial offerings, and thus could be drunk, a practice adopted by John the Baptist. The ascetic practice of the Rechabites, a subgroup of the Kenites, who accompanied the Hebrews in the wilderness, was of a very different nature. They were not so much trying avoid the effects of alcohol, as to preserve their nomadic lifestyle (Jeremiah 35: 7).

There is a wider framework of shame within which drunkenness sits. In Genesis 9: 20–5, Noah plants the first vineyard and gets drunk on the first wine produced. As result, Noah suffers the shame of being seen naked in his tent by his son Ham. Ham suffers a curse for this, but the shame is clearly Noah's. Some argue that this is a parallel to the fall, with the nakedness of Adam and Eve revealed (Tomasino 1992). The association of shame and drunkenness was seen in prophetic metaphors, often commenting on the behaviour of the nation and its government. Hence, the judgement of God is to 'make Moab drunk' because the nation has defied the Lord:

> Let Moab overflow with his vomit,
> And become in turn a butt for derision. (Jeremiah 46: 26. See also Isaiah 19: 14)

In the story of David and Uriah the Hittite, drunkenness is seen as something that can lead to vulnerability, making easier for others to take advantage of one (2 Samuel 11: 13).

Cook (2006: 44) notes that there are several terms for drunkenness used in the New Testament, ranging from debauchery (*methe*), to drunkard (*methusos*), to be given to strong drink (*paroinos*), addicted to wine (*oino pollo prosecho*) to a slave to drink (*oino pollo doulo*). Hence, it is not simply addiction that is being targeted. The negative references to alcohol frequently refer to local problems of the Christian communities, and also to festivals held in honour of Dionysus. Hence, in I Peter 4: 3 there is a list of vices associated with drunkenness, including idolatry. In some cases, Paul seems to suggest that drunkenness leads to a number of vices, including debauchery, jealousy and strife (Romans 13: 13). He also relates drunkenness to intemperance (1 Corinthians 5: 11). Once more, accountability for actions in relation to alcohol is set in the context of the *eschaton*, the imminent return of Jesus:

Be on your guard, so that your hearts will not be weighed down with dissipation and drunkenness and the worries of life, and that day will come on you suddenly like a trap. (Luke 221: 340)

Let us behave decently, as in the daytime, not in orgies and drunkenness, not in sexual immorality and debauchery. (Romans 13: 13)

Paul further argues that not only will drunkenness lead to the person being caught unawares at the coming of the Messiah, it will also lead exclusion from the Kingdom:

Do you not know that the wicked will not inherit the kingdom of God? Do not be deceived, neither the greedy nor drunkards will inherit the kingdom of God. (I Corinthians 6; 9f.)

The acts of the sinful nature are obvious ... drunkenness, orgies and the like. I warn you, as I did before, that those who live like this will not inherit the kingdom of God. (Galatians 5: 19–21)

This could be seen in terms of God's immediate judgement or in terms of a form of self-exclusion, with drunkenness and associated vices making the person unaware of the presence of the Kingdom. Because of this, it becomes important not to associate with anyone who claims to be a Christian but who continues to abuse alcohol (I Corinthians 5: 11). Paul exhorts the Christian instead to be filled with the Holy Spirit, contrasting this experience sharply with drunkenness, as showing a domination of 'the flesh' (Ephesians 5: 18).

Alongside such negative views of drunkenness, there are several places where wine is used as a negative image. Drinking to the dregs a cup of strong wine and getting drunk are frequently presented as symbols of God's judgement and wrath (Psalms 60: 3; 75: 8; Isaiah 52: 17–23; Jeremiah 13: 12–14; Ezekiel 23: 28–33). Jesus uses the same image, applying it to the suffering of his sacrifice (Matthew 20: 22; Luke 22: 42) The winepress is also occasionally seen as an image of divine punishment, with the wine as the blood of the wicked trampled like grapes (Isaiah 63: 1–6). This was later used in the Battle Hymn of the Republic:

He is trampling out the vintage where the grapes of wrath are stored.

Later Christianity

In the early centuries of the Christian Church, there was little reference to wine. Intitially, it was confined to reflection on wine in the Eucharist, and how it was mixed with water to make the likeness of blood. Cook (2006: 109) argues that, up to the sixteenth century, the Church recognized drunkenness as a widespread sin, but saw no moral grounds for abstinence. Wine for medicinal purposes or for relaxation after work is acceptable for those who reasoned, and thus were not tempted by drunkenness. Clement, an early Church scholar, also encouraged the mixing of water with the wine to cut down on inebriation.

With Augustine and Aquinas, a focus on the psychology of drinking, and drunkenness as intemperance, emerges. Augustine was heavily influenced by Paul, seeing drunkenness as of the realm of the flesh, the fruit of living to please the self rather than God. It is impossible to become drunk with good intention (*Our Lord's Sermon on the Mount*, book 3, ch. 18, para. 59). Hence, getting drunk is blameworthy. Augustine thus can condemn Lot for getting drunk in Genesis 19: 30–5, because he accepted the alcoholic drink that his daughters kept making for him. However, Augustine distinguishes responsibility for being drunk from Lot's subsequent incest with his daughters. Being under the influence of drink he did not know what he was doing. Cook suggests that Augustine saw drunkenness as involving 'the inner struggle of a will divided against itself' (Cook 2006: 59). The idea of this inner struggle can inform the modern concepts of compulsion or craving. Deliverance from this intemperance requires the grace of God, and the determination of the drunkard.

Aquinas was influenced by Aristotle. He stresses the importance of reason and will, both of which enable the human being to develop agency and, thus, direct behaviour towards a good end. Human beings are created for the ultimate good (*rationi boni*) as their end. Drunkenness impairs man's capacity to reason and is therefore against this fundamental good. Aquinas argues that the sin of drunkenness is both drunkenness itself and that which leads to drunkenness. Intemperate drinking without knowing the strength of the alcohol involves a venial sin – a lesser sin that does not involve separation from God. Those who drink intemperately and do know the capacity of alcohol to intoxicate do so with intent. This is seen as a mortal sin involving complete separation from God, unless it is confessed and absolved. It is possible to be drunk without sin, and he cites Noah as blameless in this respect. Aquinas develops this further, arguing that if drunkenness was unintentional then the person is not deemed responsible for subsequent sins (*Summa Theologica*, part II, 2nd part, Q. 150.4, available online). If the drunkenness is intentional, then the person is deemed responsible for subsequent acts, though to a lesser degree. The point is that the first act of getting drunk involved an act of will, whilst the subsequent sin involved both diminished will and reason. Aquinas cites Augustine's use of the story of Lot in this.

Drinking wine, then, was in itself acceptable and 'lawful', provided that it was done with temperance. In this, Aquinas shared with Aristotle the view of the moral virtue as involving the mean between two extremes. Temperance in this case involves moderate consumption lying between abstinence and incontinence.

The journey into psychology is taken further by Luther who, like Paul, associates drunkenness with the realm of 'the flesh'. Luther sees little excuse for drunkenness or subsequent sins if it happens with intent. Luther's strong sense of orginal sin leads him to argue that drunkenness will always magnify and liberate the sinful tendencies that are kept in check when sober (*Table Talk*, Of Offences, para. 695). Hence, the person should be aware of the potential to unleash this sin if they become drunk. It is perhaps inevitable that the more negative view of human nature should lead some later Christian thinkers to stress the need to regulate behaviour and recommend abstention. They radically changed the more moderate view of temperance, identifying it with abstinence. However, these views have never been the mainstream Christian theology.

The nineteenth century saw the rise of the temperance movement and, with that, a redefinition of the term itself. As Cook (2006: 80) notes, part of the reason for this was a reinterpretation of temperance in terms of practical wisdom. This was seen as involving distinguishing the bad from the good. If alcohol was deemed to be bad, based on the view that it is an inherently addictive substance, then the right response was to abstain. Hence, the term 'temperance' became defined, in some circles, by what Aristotle took to be one of the two extremes either side of the mean: abstinence.

To sum up, the Judeo-Christian position remains largely positive. Alcohol is at the centre of community and ritual celebrations expressing something of the joy in creation and the covenant with God. Drunkenness is accepted as wrong, associated with a breakdown of moral meaning. Sometimes that breakdown is seen in terms of the collapse of the covenant with God, at other times the breakdown is seen in terms of its effect upon the nature of man – in particular, upon reason and the will. Amidst these broad views, there is a stress on the importance of individual responsibility, both in terms of imputability and accountability. The person has to take responsibility for not becoming drunk, to think through what he or she is doing and make a rational decision. Equally, the person is accountable to God, and takes the meaning of responsibility from the covenant. The spiral into drunkenness is when the person moves away from that community meaning into isolated practice focused on self-interest. By definition, then, personal responsibility is intimately connected to responsibility for and accountability to the community.

Once we turn to Islam, a more negative view of alcohol is found. Despite this, there is very similar view of responsibility.

Islam

It might be thought that the Islamic position on alcohol is straightforward. Islam prohibits alcohol, except in cases of necessity. This stress on abstinence would thus indicate that Islamic practice has little problem. However, there is great difference in terms of the legal control of alcohol in the Muslim world. At one extreme, in Saudi Arabia the law is Islamic, under a variant of Hanbali jurisprudence that forbids the consumption, production or sale of alcoholic beverage. Michalak and Trocki (2006, 534 ff.) report that, whilst this does not always apply to the consumption of alcohol in diplomatic missions, even some foreigners have been publicly whipped and deported for producing or selling alcohol. Alcohol is considered as equivalent to drugs, and so could theoretically lead to capital punishment.

At the other extreme, Turkey has a high Muslim population within a secular state. This allows commercial production and retail of wine and beer, with local spirits, including Turkish *raki*. On average, Turks consume a litre of alcohol a year (World Health Organization 2004), involving an increase in consumption of over 600 per cent between 1970 and 2003.

Given this wide range of responses to alcohol, it is difficult to ascertain whether there is a drink problem. In Saudi Arabia, for instance, the official figures show no alcohol consumption. The legal and moral context, of course, means that response to any research will tend to be negative. Respondents would hardly admit that they have broken a law. There is, however, a literature on alcoholism in Saudi Arabia that suggests that it is not uncommon (World Health Organization 2004). Much of the response to the alcoholism phenomenon sees it in moral rather than therapeutic terms, with the answer to be found in commitment to Allah. However, the World Health Organization estimated unrecorded drinking in Saudi Arabia as 0.6 litres per person per annum (Michalak and Trocki

2006: 536). More widely, there is evidence of major alcohol problems in several Muslim countries. The figures cannot be definitive. Hence, for instance, cases of cirrhosis of the liver are quite high in some Muslim countries, with over 35 per 100,000 in Egypt, though there might be other causes.

The general picture seems to stress two things. First, it is clear that behaviour and belief in the Muslim world varies according to local context and history. Second, it would appear that, in countries where there is a high pattern of abstinence, a high percentage of those who do drink become alcohol dependent. The World Health Organization (2004: 3) suggests, for instance, that 40 per cent of those who drink in Saudi Arabia are alcohol dependent.

It is ironic that Muslim chemists were responsible for developments in distillation, which they passed on to Europe through Spain. There has also been a strong if variable tradition of poetry that centres on alcohol, from Abu Nuwas (who glories in alcohol consumption) to Persian poets, exemplified by Omar Khyyam. Alcohol is even used in some Sufi poetry as a metaphor for the experience of ecstasy. However, the greater part of Islamic tradition is focused on abstention, a position that emerges from the *Qur'an* and the *Hadith*.

Alcohol, the Qur'an and Hadith

The negative view of alcohol emerged from a very positive view of health in Islam. There is a strong sense of the individual being responsible for his or her health, including the balance of physical and psychological health. Such health, in turn, contributes to the health of the Islamic community (*ummah*). In the light of that, alcohol, as does any other intoxicant, contributes to the breakdown of that health, the loss of sense and reason, social disharmony, neglect of prayer and, ultimately, to forgetfulness of and disobedience to Allah:

> O you who believe! Intoxicants and games of chance, sacrifices to [anything serving the function of] idols, and divination by arrows are a loathsome evil of Satan's doing: so turn wholly away from it that you may prosper. Satan only seeks to provoke enmity and hatred amongst you by means of intoxicants and games of chance, and to bar you from the remembrance of God and from the prayer. So, then, will you abstain? (*Qur'an* 5: 90–1)

In the early Islamic period, drinking was considered to be one of two offences against God, the other being illicit sex. Only the use of alcohol for medical, scientific, industrial and automotive purposes is allowed. This differs from the perspective of Aquinas, who as noted (p. 130) only sees drunkenness as a mortal sin if there is intent and an awareness of the effects of alcohol. This distinction might partly account for why two Abrahamic faiths differ so markedly in their response to alcohol.

There are five *ayahs* (sayings) that are against alcohol consumption through the *Qur'an*. The *Qur'an* is not in chronological order of revelation. Nonetheless, some Islamic scholars suggest that the five *ayahs* were part of an attempt by the Prophet to change gradually the pattern of alcohol consumption. The first reference places wine and gambling together (*Qur'an* 2: 219). It suggests that both involved great sin as well as profit for man, and that the sin is greater than the profit. The second (*Qur'an* 16: 67) acknowledges the wholesomeness of wine and food, but suggests that the wise will see the problem of intoxicants. The third more precisely begins to look at the consequences of intoxication, stressing that prayer should not be approached with a mind befogged (*Qur'an* 4: 43). The very term *khmer* (alcoholic beverage) has a broader meaning of 'to cause mental confusion' or 'disturb the mind'. Given that the Muslim practice is to pray five times a day, it is clear that the priority of keeping the mind clear for this was high. The final two *ayahs* see Muslims ordered to abstain from all drinking (5: 90–1). Muslims interpret these verses, in total, to forbid any intoxicating substance – whether it be wine, beer, or spirits. Over the years, the list of intoxicating substances has come to include modern street drugs.

Whilst the *Qur'an* is the word of God, the *Hadith* are the collected words of the Prophet. As with any Holy Scriptures, there are questions about the authenticity of these sayings. However, there are eight such sayings that refer to alcohol and are generally accepted as authentic. The first explicitly sees alcohol as *haram*, unlawful (*Hadith* 254). The second stresses the action of alcohol in befogging the mind (*Hadith* 255). This instructs followers to avoid any intoxicating substances, 'Of that which intoxicates in a large amount, a small amount is *haram*' (*Hadith* 256). For this reason, most observant Muslims avoid alcohol in any form, even small amounts that are sometimes used in cooking. *Hadith* 257 echoes this view. The next *Hadith* stresses the importance of not sitting at the same table where alcohol is consumed. The Muslim's accountability on the Day of Judgement causes him to take in account the possibility of being influenced by this or influencing others negatively. The remaining three sayings stress that the link to any aspect of alcohol consumption or sale is unacceptable and that it should not be used even as medicine. *Hadith* 260 states:

> Truly God has cursed alcohol and has cursed the one who produces it, the one for whom it is produced, the one who drinks it, the one who serves it, the one who carries it, the one for whom it is carried, the one who sells it, the one who earns from the sale of it, the one who buys it, the one for whom it is bought.

Such a judgement leaves little room for any aspect of the alcohol industry. Having said all that, it is clear that Islam is not a monolithic tradition, and that there are continued debates about the meaning and implications of any of the Scriptures. Islamic jurisprudence (*fiqh*) reflects these debates. There are differences between the major branches (the majority Sunni and Shia) and within them. Within Sunni Islam, there are four main schools of jurisprudence. At one extreme, the *Hanbali* School is very strict in its prohibition of all alcohol. At the other extreme, the *Hanafi* jurists have more limited definition of *khmer*. Hence, some allow spirits that did not exist at the time of the Prophet, and thus are not mentioned in the *Qur'an*. There are also examples in the *Qur'an* where there is a positive view of alcohol, often related to reward in heaven, including:

> As to the righteous, they shall drink a cup of wine mixed with camphor. (76: 5)

> They will be given to drink there a cup of wine mixed with ginger. (76: 17)

> Their thirst will be slaked with pure wine sealed. (83:25)

Scholars differ in their interpretation of these sentences. Some see the references as metaphorical or view the term pure as meaning non-alcoholic. It is important to note that there is no central body in Islam that can provide a final teaching on such issues. Hence, it is possible to get very different religious opinions from different Islam scholars.

The majority of Muslims do not drink alcohol. However, there are some who drink alcohol and still remain Muslims. The justifications for this behaviour vary. Michalak and Trocki (2006) note several attempts to interpret the *Qur'an* in a way that would allow this. The first argument suggests that alcohol is not forbidden as such but, rather *ijtinab*, not advised. The second points to the early *Qur'anic* injunctions that permit alcohol. The third argues that what is forbidden is drunkenness, not some drinking. Moreover, as noted above, *Hanafi* School interpretations of jurisprudence allow the use of spirits that did not exist at the time of the Prophet. This still leaves many questions about precise application of the *Qur'anic* verses, which for most people will be answered only by recourse to a *fatwa* (religious opinion) from a religious scholar.

To sum up, the Islamic position on alcohol is precautionary. It assumes that any alcohol has the potential for leading one astray and harming relationships with people and with God. Hence, Michalak and Trocki (2006: 523) stress the responsibility of the person to avoid alcohol and so avoid what it makes you capable of, quoting Aziz Omrane:

> Which is the worst deed: to kill a man, to rape a woman or to get drunk? Drunkenness is the worst, because the drunk will commit both rape and murder.

There has been no definitive explanation of why Islam should differ so markedly from the Judeo-Christian perspectives on alcohol. All have a strong theology of creation, community and final judgement. All include a plurality of views, and stress the need to reflect on particular practice. As noted, there are potential major differences in analysis. Some Muslim thinkers do not see the loss of will entailed in inebriation as a lessening of responsibility for any major sins committed whilst under the influence of alcohol. Such thinking might partly explain the view that drinking involves sin against God. Given that Aquinas and many Islamic scholars were influenced by Aristotle, it might be that Islam's view is simply a more heightened view of the need to retain reason. It could be argued that any loss of reasoning capacity robs one of capacity to respond to God in a free and open way. The practice of abstention might also reflect the identification of Islam, in some forms, with government, and therefore the need to regulate and control. Michalak and Trocki suggest that the development of the practice is probably a mixture of many things, such as the development of abstention from eating pork. Their argument is, in effect, that this is less a matter of theology and more one of practice that has developed over time as an expression of group identity.

Despite the fact that there are strong parallels in terms of any theology of responsibility, focusing on accountability and imputability. A good example in the Islamic world is found in the writings of the Turkish Ischolar Gülen. His view of responsibility is firmly set in accountability and, thus, in turn, is based in his creation theology. God created the world and appointed humanity to be the vicegerent (*Qu'ran* 2: 30). Humankind is, thus, responsible for the management of all that creation. The relationship with God the Creator also means that humanity is responsible on behalf of God. Humankind, in this sense, stands in for God, as deputy, but also stands before him. Hence, humanity is both responsible with God and responsible to God for the world in its fullness. This responsibility connects action to this world and the next. What we do now will have an effect on both realms and, thus, on our appreciation of both realms.

In order to fulfil this responsibility, God has made available all possible resources:

> If humanity is the vicegerent of God on Earth, the favourite of all His creation, the essence and substance of existence in its entirety and the brightest mirror of the Creator – and there is no doubt that this is so – then the Divine Being that has sent humanity to this realm will have given us the right, permission, and ability to discover the mysteries imbedded in the soul of the universe, to uncover the hidden power, might and potential, to use everything to its purpose, and to be the representatives of characteristics that belong to Him, such as knowledge, will and might. (Gülen 2004: 122)

Imputability in Gülen emerges from the framework of accountability. Personal autonomy and agency is a gift from God that enables the person to fulfil the role of steward. This agency gives the person freedom to transform society, so long as the source of that freedom and agency is acknowledged. God 'alone determines, apportions, creates, and spreads all out provisions before us' (Gülen 1999: 94). This, then, is a mediated agency, a limited form of subjectivity that is contingent on God's call. Imputability in all this is about rational reflection and freedom used to determine what is the best way of responding to that call. Hence, in this theology, alcohol could be seen as not simply negatively affecting prayer, but also disabling the response to God's call. At the heart of much of this is a great stress on action. Responsibility makes action critical. Gülen contrasts passive submission with active service. At the core of this is the concept of *hizmet*, a key principle about the ceaseless responsibility of putting values into practice. Any sense of free will, then, is very much in the context of the *hizmet*, focused on the example of the Prophet as a man of action. Again, alcohol could seriously affect the capacity to fulfil such action.

Bacchus

Throughout history, wine has been not simply seen as a positive aspect of a disciplined community but, rather, as something worthy of veneration. Greek civilization saw it as a critical part of its warrior culture, illustrated in the epic poems of the 'Illiad' and 'Odyssey'. Ceremonies and rituals included libations of wine. Drink even had the power to sanctify the words of warriors, enabling them to speak the truth. Hence, an oath sealed with wine had a stronger weight than a 'dry oath'. Not surprisingly, there was a God of wine, Bacchus. Bacchus was wild, and identified with liberation from communal constraint and the experience of ecstasy (Gatley 2008: 34). This experience enabled the person or group to transcend themselves, to feel truly that they were beyond their everyday experience.

Wine is thus seen as a gift from Bacchus, and the later Roman Dionysus, and a means of spiritual communion with him (Cook 2006: 37). Cook, however, suggests that the extreme view of these cults might be an overstatement. Dionysus was certainly a god of 'abundant life and liberation', but the ecstasy experience was not necessarily induced by alcohol. In any case, the excesses of the Dionysian cults were not accepted by the wider society, often being associated with anti-Roman activities.

The association of alcohol with ecstasy is something that writers on alcoholism have noted (Clinebell 1968: 14 ff.), with alcohol viewed as a substitute for the religious experience. However, in any of these cases the elevation of alcohol is not mainstream but, rather, associated with either eccentric behaviour or illness.

Conclusion

If we look to religions to clarify the nature of alcohol, or for guidance about the right behaviour, it is difficult to reach an easy conclusion. In one sense, they express the full range of ethical responses to alcohol and its consumption, from its importance to community and celebration to the need to regulate, and the need to remain free from the negative influence of alcohol. This diversity of views can be seen as positive. Fasching and Dechant (2001), for instance, argue that, at the core of healthy religion, is the constant wrestling between the call to obey the divine command and the nagging doubt about the claim of the moral particular, and the need to respond to that. This is summed up in the audacity of Job to question God, or Abraham to query the intention of God to destroy Sodom. It is also summed up in the internal dialogues and different practices in the Judeo-Christian cultures and the Islamic theology noted in this chapter.

Religion might provide us with the framework of the precautionary and of the celebratory. However, it also stresses the need to develop the virtues that enable the person to decide in relation to the particular problem at hand. It does not take away from the person the responsibility to decide how they will respond in relation to alcohol in a particular community context. Hence, for instance, good conservative Islamic friends of ours can happily choose to sit down with Christians in a pub and consume soft drinks, despite the *Hadith* that speaks against this. They have determined that they are not responsible for the behaviour of their friends and that the good of fellowship and dialogue is more important in that context than strict adherence to rules. They are also able to trust their friends not to abuse either the alcohol or their friendship.

The religions noted in this chapter all focus on the need to develop personal responsibility within a community framework, demanding the development of imputability and accountability, and freedom within community, and freedom to create beyond that community.

Finally, the voice of the different religions is important to include in the ongoing ethical debate, not least because the majority of the global population base their ethical identity in faith. As such, ethical debate and dialogue on alcohol needs to be sensitive not only to the plurality of religions, but also to how much of group identity is invested in this process. This takes ethical dialogue away from a simple rational reflection on the logic of any ethics, to a process that demands awareness of the cultural context of any ethical judgement and stresses the responsibility of the individual to set up a critical but non-threatening dialogue with that culture.

7
Addiction and Ethics

> God grant me the serenity to accept the things I cannot change; courage to change the things I can; and wisdom to know the difference.
>
> (Alcoholics Anonymous Prayer)

Thomas Reed (2006) suggests that the real focus of Robert Louis Stevenson's Jekyll and Hyde is alcoholism. The 'transforming draught' is alcohol. Alcoholism takes one beyond the simple idea of abusing alcohol into a relationship of psychological and physical dependency and, with that, a change in character. With that comes the sense of the person's will being overtaken by alcohol. Slowly but surely, the agency of the person is compromised. As the agency is compromised, so the negative effects of alcoholism begin to show.

At the heart of all this is the issue of responsibility. Alcoholism takes away any sense of responsibility and, thus, is seen as a form of illness. However, without a focus on the responsibility of the patient, it is hard to see how the condition can be effectively treated. Yet, is it possible to say that the person was not responsible in some way for the development of alcoholism? This is the moral tension that this chapter will begin to address.

Defining alcoholism

The US National Council on Alcoholism and Drug Dependence defined addiction to alcohol as 'a primary, chronic disease with genetic, psychosocial, and environmental factors influencing its development and manifestations. The disease is often progressive and fatal. It is characterized by continuous or periodic impaired control over drinking, preoccupation with the drug alcohol, use of alcohol despite adverse consequences, and distortions in thinking, most notably denial.'

The Council then unpacks the several layers of meaning. First, it reinforces the idea of alcoholism as a disease through the word 'primary'. This distinguishes the disease of alcoholism itself from any other pathology – psychological or physical – that might be involved in any particular case. Hence, alcoholism, as an addiction, is not seen as a symptom of any other disease, physical or psychological.

Second, disease is defined as 'an involuntary disability'. The term 'involuntary' sees the person involved as having no responsibility in the genesis of the condition. It happens to him or her. The term 'disability' stresses how persons who suffer differ from the norm, and are placed at a disadvantage. This is reinforced with the idea of impaired control, involving an 'inability to limit alcohol use' at any time or over a long period.

Third, the condition is progressive, in the sense that it leads to physical, emotional and relational changes over time. These might involve alcohol withdrawal syndromes, liver disease, gastritis, anaemia, neurological disorders, and psychological malfunctioning including impairments in cognition, changes in mood and behaviour. These lead to consequences in behaviour and practice in family relationships, including marital problems and child abuse, and breakdowns in workplace and educational relationships and performance, all of which can lead to legal, financial or spiritual problems. Untreated, it can lead to premature death through overdose; organic complications involving the brain, liver, heart and many other organs; and by homicide, motor vehicle crashes and other traumatic events.

Fourth, the term 'preoccupation' focuses on the obsessional nature of the condition, involving excessive focused attention on obtaining and consuming alcohol, leading to a diversion of energies away from important life concerns.

Finally, the definition focuses on denial as a key element in the 'disease' and a major block to recovery. This involves denial in the psychoanalytic sense of a defence mechanism that denies the significance of thoughts or practices, not least the extent of consumption. It also involves a broader range of strategies to hide the significance of behaviours.

The Council's approach focuses on the idea of alcoholism as an illness, an approach expanded by the International Classification of Diseases (ICD-10, World Health Organization 1992) and the Diagnostic and Statistical Manual (DSM-IV, American Psychiatric Association 1994)) which refer to it specifically as alcohol dependency syndrome. The DSM distinguishes alcohol abuse and alcohol dependence. Alcohol abuse is seen as a long-term pattern of 'maladaptive use of alcohol' leading to inability to fulfil long-term role expectations in work and home, and thus to frequent physical, interpersonal and legal problems. Alcohol dependence (first used as a term by Edwards and Gross, 1976) highlights a constellation of symptoms and indicators of maladaptive substance use. The key elements include:

Narrowing the drinking repertoire: The drinking patterns of most people vary over time and in context. With dependency, the pattern of drinking becomes invariable in type, quality and context.

Salience of drink seeking behaviour: Alcohol consumption becomes central to perceived well-being and functioning. Other activities from family to work receive less attention and suffer as a consequence. Large amounts of time are used in obtaining alcohol, finding the resources to obtain it, hiding alcohol and consumption, recovering from the effect of alcohol consumption.

Increased tolerance to alcohol: With increased consumption, the body develops tolerance of alcohol, such that tasks that would normally be impaired by high levels of drinking can be achieved. With the increase in tolerance, more alcohol has to be consumed to achieve the desired experience.

Repeated withdrawal symptoms: A period of abstinence will lead to so called 'withdrawal symptoms', probably the result of biochemical changes in the brain. These can include tremors, anxiety, nausea, and even experience of hallucinations.

Relief or avoidance of withdrawal symptoms by further drinking: Relief of withdrawal symptoms is found through further alcohol consumption. This is often summed up in the phrase 'the hair of the dog that bit you', the principle that like cures like (*similia similibus curantur*).

Subjective awareness of compulsion to drink: The alcoholic is aware of cravings that lead to impairment of control. There is agreement that this leads the alcoholic to consume more than was intended.

Reinstatement after abstinence: Generally, if there has been a period even of lengthy abstinence, it does not take long for the dependency to be re-established once drinking is renewed.

These developing symptoms reveal several things.

First, alcoholism is complex. The causes of addiction are complex and interactive, including:

Physiological and psychosocial factors: Atypical metabolic patterns have been established in some advanced cases of alcoholism, though it is still not clear if this predisposes the person to addiction or is caused by it.

Compulsive personalities or those who do not have effective ways of coping with stress can also be predisposed to addiction. There might also be other underlying mental health problems, such as depression.

Sociocultural factors: Alcohol abuse, reflected in high abuse and addiction figures, seems more prevalent in certain cultures, such as Ireland and France (Clinebell 1990). Some of this is seen in terms of peer and cultural pressure, not least the view that high alcohol consumption reinforces cultural identity. In this light, Clinebell suggests the possibility of spiritual dimensions, using the term 'spiritual' in its generic sense of habits, worldviews or relationships in which a person puts his or her faith. For some, the experience of alcohol is the equivalent of the religious experience. This involves using alcohol to 'feel good', to achieve a transcendence of the self. Alcohol can also be established as a foundation of faith. Alcohol consumption becomes the way of 'sorting out' problems, or trying to fulfil basic human needs, such as belonging or the need for security. In both cases, there is development of a false spirituality that denies responsibility for the self and others, and distorts reality, resulting in alienation from others. Behind both is a lack of purpose and spiritual meaning. Hence, Alcoholics Anonymous members speak of 'filling the empty bottle' – finding purpose and meaning that will replace the alcohol habit.

Second, a good deal of the definition is in terms of the consequences of the condition. It is precisely behaviour that significantly and adversely affects personal and professional life that provides the evidence of a problem.

Third, there is a moral context to all of the attempts at defining the term. In the case of the US National Council on Alcoholism and Drug Dependence, this involves a vigorous response to the stigma that is often associated with the condition. Stigma is, in effect, the result of a moralizing, judgemental or condemnatory approach that sees the sufferer as uniquely responsible for her condition. Charles Hewitt neatly summed up this attitude in 1943:

> Inebriety has been a simple moral problem for the layman for so long that the underlying problems are only now receiving attention from physicians. A Minneapolis newspaper recently printed a story about 'John Bones' who was sentenced to the workhouse for the 107th time. The tone of the article was one of whimsical despair at the unalterable depravity of 'Mr Bones' who has wilfully spent some 18 of the past 20 years as a guest of the city. (Quoted in Clinebell 1968: 27)

In fighting against this stigma, the Council focuses on terms such as 'involuntary disability', which clearly signals that the alcoholic is not morally responsible for the 'disease'. Hence, any definition of the term is morally neutral. It is a pathology experienced by the person and requires a therapeutic rather than a moral response. For many, this is part of objectifying the condition, making it easier to combat. In the DSM, there is equal concern to avoid stigmatization but an implicit acceptance of a moral framework in which the person is operating. Hence, it refers to obligations involved in different relationships and roles that the sufferer does not fulfil, the inability to learn effectively (hence the stress on maladaptive behaviour), and the negative consequences of behaviours, including harm to the self and others. At the very least, there are moral implications of the behaviour, and the moral world of the sufferer, and any underlying view of purpose or meaning is radically affected by his or her behaviour. Hence, the responsibility of the person has to be addressed as part of the treatment.

Such issues emerge in three major models of addiction, summed up by Cook (2006) as:

- *The moral model*: This suggests that addiction is developed because of the decision of the addict, that this is flawed because of the person's lack of moral virtues and, thus, that the person is culpable. This is often referred to as a 'judgemental approach'.
- *The disease model*: This sees addiction as a result of pathology. The person is not culpable for the development of the pathology, but has to be responsible for the behaviours that result from the disease. Developing such responsibility becomes a key part of the therapy.
- *The scientific model*: This is concerned with aetiology not culpability, focusing on neurological, psychological and physical causes.

As with most 'models', these are rather crude characterizations of what is involved. To begin with, the so-called 'disease model' has moral dimensions. The moral argument is that the person who suffers from the pathology is, in a sense, a victim and therefore should not be blamed. It also recognizes the importance of the patient developing responsibility as part of their therapy. Hence, it is not that useful to polarize these models.

Second, underlying the first two models is a moral tension that is there for all mental health therapy. Rogerian (or client-centred) therapists, amongst others, argue that therapy demands a non-judgemental response to the client (Robinson 2001). For Rogerians, this includes the view that the moral agenda should not even be raised. Therapy is not a space for transmitting values but, rather, for the client to discover his or her own values and build on them. Underlying this view of client-centred therapy is the belief that many mental health problems are caused by a sense of conditional worth; that is, that the person only feels a sense of worth if they fulfil certain conditions set by parents, peer groups and so on. The argument is that any reference to moral standards simply sets up further conditions for the person to have to work through, disabling any attempt to develop personal responsibility for values. Hence, the client has to be given space to experience and appreciate unconditional worth and build on that. This is a slightly more sophisticated version of the victim argument, in that the client was in a sense a victim, with the conditions of acceptance set by others, and therefore should not be deemed blameworthy.

Ranged against the attempts to exclude normative morality from therapy as a whole, there have been a number of arguments from Bellah *et al.* (1985), Billings (1992) and Reiff (1966). First, it is argued that the therapeutic approach is in danger of reducing the moral agenda to subjective preferences and moral relativity. Any moral position chosen by the patient is fine unless it harms another. For the alcoholic, this is difficult because there is a moral framework implicit in any treatment. This is focused on the harm that has been done, not simply to the person but also to the relationships in family and profession. It is those relationships that point to a moral substance that has to be more than personal preference.

Second, the therapeutic stance wants to avoid moral judgementalism but, in so doing, discourages moral judging. It is argued that, if clients are to locate their values they also have to be able to defend them clearly, and so provide reasons for making their own moral judgement. The strong version of this argument is that the best way to avoid judgementalism is to strengthen the capacity of the patient to make moral judgements for him- or herself.

Third, Reiff, Bellah *et al.* and Billings suggest that the lack of focus on moral issues in therapy will actually lead to a moral vacuum; one that will be filled by an emphasis, at best, on rights and, at worst, a general ethics of self-interest. Any action involves values and, if values are not tested and worked through, then self-interest will predominate.

All three arguments suggest that one of the key problems about the therapeutic model is that there is no basis for challenging the client. In terms of the alcoholic, it may be said that this is doubly disastrous. The alcoholic has developed a set of behaviours that are not worked out in a critical reflective way, and which are, by definition, centred on the self and not on any concern for others. If there is to be reinforcement of self-interest, and preference rather than critical reflection, then it is difficult to see how there can be change.

Fourth, it is argued that the therapeutic approach reinforces the identity of a victim. As such, this disempowers the person. Responsibility always lies elsewhere. Many of the writers go as far as to argue that the victim identity has become part of western culture (Martin 2006: 66).

Finally, the issue of guilt is faced head on (Billings 1992). Much of the therapeutic model around mental health suggests that raising issues of morality will cause guilt and shame to be accessed. By definition, it is argued, guilt and shame are negative, reinforcing a lack of self-worth. Against this, it is argued that it is possible to distinguish negative or even toxic guilt or shame based on a judgement on the person, from a sense of positive guilt, built on an awareness of responsibility for actions. Indeed, it is argued that such guilt or shame is necessary to motivate the client. Shame carries with it a stronger sense of guilt and the sense that the person can be seen by the rest of the world (Robinson 2001).

In fact, shame and guilt are both two-edged swords. Negative or toxic shame tends to be associated with shame about the person, focusing on the self that is not worthy. Shame, however, can be very healthy, enabling the person to reflect on what has been done and, because shame is connected to the awareness of others, it is tied to a healthy accountability. Either way, the therapist has to empower the client to critique the basis of toxic shame and to access healthy shame in such a way as to take responsibility.

The problem with many of the criticisms of the therapeutic model is that they tend to falsely stereotype the model itself. First, they fail to distinguish the idea of personal preference (Martin 2006: 64) from autonomous moral decision-making. The person centred therapy approach clearly stresses the autonomy of the client. The importance of not imposing a moral agenda on the client is seen in the light of enabling him or her to develop his or her own critical reflection. Second, the critics also fail to appreciate that the whole of the therapeutic relationship is set within the context of a moral framework; one that seeks to respect the autonomy of the client and provide a safe space for reflection, maintaining confidentiality, avoiding harm and so on. Robinson (2001) argues that the therapeutic contract itself provides a means to develop moral meaning and to enable the client to examine his or her moral meaning. Third, the idea that there is a victim culture encouraged by the therapeutic model has little actual evidence to substantiate it. Even in the

DSM approach, there is the caveat that one cannot use mental health pathologies to excuse people from responsibility (Martin 2006).

The criticisms of the therapeutic approach raise an important agenda, but it becomes apparent that any polarized view of alcoholism and its treatment is inadequate. Whilst dependency diminishes responsibility in the sense of agency, there is need to address the moral dimension of therapy in such a way that the moral autonomy of the patient is strengthened.

Clinebell (1968: 168) suggests that viewing alcoholism in terms of responsibility produces a more complex view of the moral options. Seen through the prism of pastoral theology, he offers seven different perspectives:

1 The alcoholic is responsible for all aspects of the condition.
2 Alcoholism cannot be seen as an illness that simply happens to the person.
3 Alcoholism begins with a failure of moral responsibility and then becomes an illness.
4 Alcoholism is primarily an illness.
5 Alcoholism leads to abuse and harmful consequences for which the person is responsible.
6 Alcoholism is an illness that involves a combination of moral responsibility and sickness.
7 Responsibility is shared. It is very much the alcoholic's responsibility for deciding to accept the value systems and identity of peer groups who abuse alcohol. However, such groups also share in responsibility for the development of alcoholism. Included in this responsibility are the government, the alcohol producers and retailers, and even the family. It might seem odd to say that the family of an alcoholic is partly responsible for the development of alcoholism. However, it is common that families are complicit in the denial of alcoholic behaviour, often seeking to protect the family member, or the reputation of the family as a whole.

This broad analysis is helpful as far as it goes. However, it raises as many questions about what is meant by responsibility. Hence, any view of alcoholism and responsibility has to provide such an analysis.

Responsibility

As noted in Chapter 4, there are several interconnected ways of viewing the responsibility concept suggested by Schweiker (1995), including:

- *Imputability*: Actions can be ascribed to a person. Hence, the person can seen have been responsible for those actions. This person is also responsible for making decisions that lead to action.
- *Accountability*: The person is responsible or answerable *to* someone.
- *Liability*: The person is responsible *for* something or someone.

To use the example of the medical profession, a doctor has responsibility for her actions as a professional. She is also responsible to a wide range of people, including any line manger or employing body, her professional body and her colleagues. She is also responsible for the health care of her patients, and possibly the broader community. We would add to this analysis a fourth mode that runs throughout, responsibility as social and shared. This is more than simply an additional reflection on collective responsibility, as distinct from individual responsibility. Rather, it a view that individual responsibility is also social, and requires an effective sharing of responsibility. This will have particular relevance to the issues in alcoholism.

Imputability

There are strong and weak views of imputability. The weak views (McKenny 2005: 242) simply refer to the causal connection between the person and any action. This shows that the person is technically responsible for the action – that the action can be attributed to the person. Such a view does not help in determining just how much the person is actually involved in the action and, therefore, fully responsible for the action. Stronger views suggest that responsibility involves a rational decision-making process that enables the person to own fully the action that arises from the decision. Taylor (1989) argues that this decision-making constitutes a strong valuation that connects action to deep decision-making, and is what constitutes the moral identity of the person. This stresses the unique response of the particular person.

In order to be fully responsible, the person would have to be aware of his social context, the significant relationships, and the mutual effect of those relationships. Other data would be necessary, such as awareness of the effects of alcohol on reasoned judgement. In turn, there would have to be the capacity for reflexivity and relating such reflection to practice. So, what is preventing this kind of reflective moral decision-making in the alcoholic? There are several possibilities. First, the person has simply not developed an effective method of moral decision-making.

The general liberal approach tends to look to the protection of the autonomy of the individual and, with that, to assume that the person has the means of making a moral decision. The work of Kohlberg (1984) and Fowler (1996) in charting spiritual and moral development suggests, however, that the capacity to make moral judgements is, in fact, tied to the development of maturity and, with that, to the development of moral virtues, such as courage, that enable such reflection and thought-out moral responses. Far from everyone having autonomy, in the sense of complete capacity for self-governance, individuals will be at different stages of developing autonomy.

Second, there is a tendency to actually avoid taking responsibility. This is exemplified in the tragedy of the *Herald of Free Enterprise* (Robinson 1992). The ferry was sunk because the bow doors were open as it left port. Several of the crew did see that the doors were open and did nothing about it for two reasons. The doors had often been open on sailing and therefore they did not have any sense of danger. They also assumed that the captain had all responsibility, and refused to take any responsibility themselves. The work of Milgram (2005) and Zimabardo (2007) reinforces this idea that a majority of people prefer to avoid responsibility. Milgram's experiments used participants who thought they were involved in an experiment about the relationship between pain and learning. Behind a screen was a subject (actually an actor) attached to 'electrodes' and the participant was in charge of administering shocks to the subject whenever he got the answers wrong. The participant was invited by a person in authority to increase the shocks on a regular basis. Over 60+ per cent took the shock to what was clearly marked as levels of high danger. Despite some initial questioning, they were content to deny their individual responsibility in the face of authority. Bauman (1989) develops this view and notes that the practice of the division of labour further reinforces such a dynamic. Once you decide not to accept responsibility, this affects how one perceives reality. The Milgram case suggests that the participant can see the effects that he is having on the person but simply does not ascribe any moral significance to them. That moral significance is something for the person in authority. In effect, this stronger view of responsibility is the recognition of moral significance and, thus, of one's obligation or duty in that situation.

Third, all views of data and the significance of that data, ultimately depend on the underlying values. Much of the ethical import of the parables in the New Testament Gospels is around this insight. The rich man of one parable (16: 20–27), for instance, does not see the poor man at his gate. This is not simply about a fear of taking responsibility, or of being accountable for that man but, rather, about a completely different set of values that dictate a concern for wealth and luxury, in the light of which a poor man, however close, is of no moral significance (Robinson 2007).

For the alcoholic, the primary value is often about self-esteem and social acceptance. Behind that is often conditional value, such as the need to drink to be accepted by a group or to cope with a situation. There may be other bases to worth, such as the male myth that one should be a hard drinker and so on. In each case, the dominant value, based in self-esteem, provides the social and psychological environment within which the person operates, and issues about consequences, immediate or long-term are secondary. Similarly, perception of data will be influenced by the underlying value; hence, for instance, the minimization of alcohol consumption reported by the alcoholic. The person simply cannot see truth of the situation. In particular, this will make the person unaware of the consequences of actions, possible and actual, and of their moral significance. This is why the idea of reality testing becomes a key part in any therapy. By enabling the person to focus on reality, this provides the basis for the alcoholic to take responsibility for his or her data and, at the simplest level, to provide a way into perceiving at least the weakest sense of imputability. In taking responsibility for the actions, this inevitably invites the person to assess the moral significance of those actions and to make sense of any incongruities.

Cook (2006) suggests that the idea of the divided self, originally set out by Augustine and developed by Frankfurt, might explain the problem of responsibility and the alcoholic. In Frankfurt's terms, this suggests that there are first- and second-order desires and volitions (Cook 2006: 156). First-order desires are simple desires to do one thing or another. Second-order desires are about a more reflective choice that supports the first-order desire. It is possible, then, to speak of an 'unwilling addict', who has a second-order desire to stop the behaviour but cannot prevent the first-order desire being carried out. However, it is not clear how coherent or useful this distinction is. First, it could be argued that first-order desires or volitions, such as those of the addict, are based on second-order volitions, but that these second-order volitions are actually not worked out in a reflective or critical way. For instance, the second-order volition might have a strong sense of ethical value, but one that is based in affective need, such as the desire to gain approval through drinking. This carries with it a whole set of moral assumptions about conditional worth, and often also about the need to demonstrate independence and to avoid any dependence. It is precisely the latter that often makes the alcoholic – indeed, many other mentally ill patients – feel ashamed to seek help.

Hence, the root of the problem is not about a conflict between first and second order but, rather, about a lack of responsibility for second-order thinking. It is precisely this that stops the patient from genuinely engaging first-order volitions, and thus truly engaging the will.

Second, the first- and second-order model is essentially individual-ist. However, the behaviour of the addict takes place in the context of relationships. These set up a framework of accountability and, beyond that, of liability. Any attempt to challenge the alcoholic's behaviour is not just about the division between first- and second-order desires or volitions. It is also about how the person characterizes and responds to those relationships, and how he or she perceives their worth, and his or her worth in relation to them. This leads us to the two other modes of responsibility: accountability and liability.

Accountability

Accountability is most often based in formal or informal contract rela-tionships. The contract sets up a series of mutual expectations. These expectations, as the DSM implied, set up different moral frameworks and broad and specific duties or obligations. At one level, these are about discernible targets. Hence, there will be key work targets that form the basis of any job, and without which the competence of the person might be questioned. One target might itself ensure continuous staff develop-ment of competence. The family might set up a number of targets – not least amongst them, care and provision of finance. Second, there will be broader moral expectations of how one should behave in any con-tract. This would include the importance of openness, transparency in relationships, and other such behaviours that provide the basis for trust.

The underlying problem for the alcoholic with such accountability is that, once more, he or she might not be fully committed to such relation-ships; that is, might have entered them without fully working through the implications of the contract. Once more, then, the broader sense of value tied to alcohol consumption causes the person simply not to see the significance of their behaviour and, therefore, not to accept account-ability. They might claim to do so from some unrealistic and ill-thought through view of the relationships but, in fact, do not do so. As noted, it is precisely at this point that the family often draws lines around the alco-holic. For many reasons, the family may collude in attempting to 'hide' the reality of the situation. Once more, this is often based in condi-tional worth. Hence, some spouses feel ashamed that this has happened because they feel that it is a failure on their part, or because they feel that others will see them responsible for a failed marriage. Hence, the very basis for accountability can become blurred. The signals that this sends to the alcoholic are that there is no real accountability in the relationship. Whatever he or she does will be sorted out by somebody else.

Liability

Liability goes beyond accountability into the idea of caring for others, a sense of wider liability for certain projects. The alcoholic is responsible for the well-being of his or her family and him- or herself and, beyond that, has broader civic and environmental responsibilities. There are major questions about where one draws the line, and how one might reasonably fulfil such responsibility. It is not surprising, then, that the some philosophers suggest that one has to begin with the view of responsibility for everything. Bauman (1993) and Levinas (1998) argue this is based around view of shared responsibility for common humanity. The workability of such a view of responsibility is quite another thing. At one level, this is really about being aware of others. At another level, it is the ground for effectively negotiating responsibility. This means that no one can be responsible for everything, but that such responsibility can be shared and that the proper way forward is to negotiate it. The alcoholic precisely finds that difficult because he or she thinks that they do not need to share responsibility. They feel the need to be responsible for their own behaviour and ashamed to be dependent on someone else, and thus discount what they actually do and its effect on others. Sharing responsibility is seen as failure.

Given this threefold view of responsibility, in what sense might the alcoholic not be responsible? In the weak sense of imputability, he or she clearly is responsible. They have decided to form a relationship with alcohol and this has led to a variety of negative consequences that are attributable to the alcoholic. In the stronger sense of imputability, they are not fully responsible, in the sense that their value base has led them not to be aware of their surrounding context or the moral significance of what they have done. More importantly, one might want to say that the alcoholic has actually also denied any sense of responsibility, for the self or for others. In that frame of mind, the alcoholic will often blame others. There is no sense of the awareness of the hold that alcohol has on him or her. Once the dependence is established, then the core dynamic of denial is further reinforced. It is not clear that the dependence itself actually causes that dynamic.

In this light, it is difficult to see the alcoholic as simply a victim; that is, as someone who has no responsibility for his or her situation.

The simplistic view of the victim who cannot and should not be blamed therefore has to be revised. Martin (2006) suggests four different kinds of blame:

- *Judgement blame*: This notes that people are culpable for actions that are attributed to them.
- *Attitude blame*: This focuses on the person and on expressing the feelings about the person who is responsible.
- *Censure blame*: This involves public reprimand or condemnation.
- *Liability blame*: This involves assigning liabilities, in the sense of costs, penalties or punishments.

In the light of the reflection on responsibility, it is reasonable to apportion the first level of blame to the alcoholic. At one level, this is uncontested. This person was responsible for these consequences. At another level, one might suggest a form of blame at the deeper level of not working through the implications of behaviour, and lacking critical reflection. Attitude blame is precisely the one that is problematic. Focused as it is on expressing feelings to the patient, it is precisely harmful to any therapy.

Censure blame, if focused in the therapy, becomes simply another form for judgementalism. However, such blame is inevitable in the context of accountability in relationships. The person cannot be shielded from this and has to deal with it if he or she is to recover. Indeed, it could be said that a critical part of recovery is learning how to deal with implied or explicit censure.

The final blame is tied closely to the development of a response to accountability relationships. It might involve legal reparation, if actions have broken the law, or might look to ways of making amends in relationships that have been adversely affected. Hence, again, this has to be worked through by the alcoholic.

In all this, the moral dimension of alcoholism involves far more than simply accepting moral responsibility for the consequences of any action. To accept that fully means the patient taking the personal responsibility for such actions. If, for instance, the alcoholic drives a car whilst drunk, leading to a major road accident that causes the death of another, this would mean accepting moral liability. Doubtless, the person would agree that driving in this way could lead such a consequence. The point is that the person in question has not made the link between the act and consequences as something that applies to them, something involving personal responsibility. This would require both a sense of shared liability and a sense of identification. It would also require some sense of accountability to those of his or her core groups who might be affected by any such act and consequence. This is not unique to the alcoholic. Hence, in any treatment the agency of the patient has to be focused on and enabled, along with the connected sense of accountability and liability. This applies over past, present and future.

For therapy, this means that several things have to be addressed (Robinson 2001):

- *The truth of the situation*: Given the propensity for denial, this means a strong emphasis in therapy on reality testing – never simply accepting the testimony of the patient, and always checking out the truth and implications of the patient's perceptions. At the heart of this is the unconditional support of the therapist that enables the patient to articulate and reflect on a narrative that might be painful and morally problematic.
- *The ethical meaning*: What are the values of the patient and how do they relate to the actions? This avoids moral censure and works from the assumption that the patient has his or her own value base. More positively, reflection on value and action focuses on imputability and, thus, aims to empower the patient in developing personal responsibility. Key to this is allowing the patient to articulate incongruities between value and practice, and to deal with those him- or herself. Hence, the therapeutic process avoids judgementalism and strengthens the patient's own ethical capacities. It is important in this to recognize that the patient already has a strong ethical base. As noted, for many alcoholics this involves a belief in freedom and self-reliance, allied to the belief that dependence on others is a personal failure. Awareness of the possible moral censure often leads to attempts to morally justify, play down or deny patterns of behaviour. Hence, it is important to enable the patient to articulate these values alongside the broader story, so that contradictions can emerge and the patient take responsibility for dealing with them.
- *The question of accountability*: This is raised through reflection on the patient's relationships. This focuses, potentially, on several role related areas of responsibility. The family is perhaps the most obvious starting point, involving an exploration of the patient's view of his or her role and the actual relationship, and the patient's effect on the relationship. This demands a careful move away from toxic shame, involving a reinforcing of shame about failure attached to a role that

might simply worsen the patient's sense of shame (Robinson 2001). It does not preclude the patient accepting guilt and beginning to handle that guilt. The same process might be there in other areas of responsibility, including professional, corporate and civic responsibility. Each of these has underlying values that the person might well identify with closely. An engineer, for instance, might have a strong sense of concern for society and safety in construction. The reflection on responsibility will enable that person to reflect on value and action, and so begin to see how alcohol consumption has affected professional competence and, thus, professional identity. The key point is that the patient cannot begin to accept responsibility for past or future actions until he or she has begun to look at identity, value and practice. The incongruity between these and how that affects what might be a prized professional identity provides the dissonance that enables the person to learn. Similar issues would be there for business persons and so on.

- *Therapy*: This, then, has to deal with how identity is reshaped or restored. At the heart of this is the focus on accountability and how the patient can begin to mend relationships. The relationship might not be capable of being rebuilt, but even this does not preclude working at reconciliation. This might involve a clearer understanding and negotiation of responsibilities, leading to growth and change in the patient and others. In the family, for instance, it could lead to the negotiation of a new family contract that spells out the needs of all parties and how they can be fulfilled together. This will require change and commitment from the alcoholic and challenge the family to move beyond simply protecting the alcoholic.

There are, of course, many different approaches to the treatment of alcoholism. However, the general point is that working through moral meaning, with responsibility at its heart, is central to successful recovery.

Much of this dynamic is also found in the experience of Alcoholics Anonymous (AA).

Alcoholics Anonymous

We have suggested that the development of ethical thinking is central to successful therapy. Nowhere is this more apparent than in AA's Twelve Step programmes (see Box 7.1). Some estimate as many as 3.5 million people attend such programmes in America alone. The Twelve Step approach offers a clear ethical perspective on both the nature of the problem and the way to recovery. Research demonstrates that these programmes lead to improved psychological functioning and to a genuine commitment to change, and that they work well in coordination with other forms of therapy and counselling (Tonigan *et al.* 2003).

Box 7.1   The original twelve steps, as published by Alcoholics Anonymous

We admitted we were powerless over alcohol – that our lives had become unmanageable.

Came to believe that a Power greater than ourselves could restore us to sanity.

Made a decision to turn our will and our lives over to the care of God *as we understood Him.*

Made a searching and fearless moral inventory of ourselves.

Admitted to God, to ourselves, and to another human being the exact nature of our wrongs.

Were entirely ready to have God remove all these defects of character.

Humbly asked Him to remove our shortcomings.

Made a list of all persons we had harmed, and became willing to make amends to them all.

Made direct amends to such people wherever possible, except when to do so would injure them or others.

Continued to take personal inventory and when we were wrong promptly admitted it.

Sought through prayer and meditation to improve our conscious contact with God *as we understood Him*, praying only for knowledge of His Will for us and the power to carry that out.

Having had a spiritual awakening as the result of these steps, we tried to carry this message to alcoholics, and to practice these principles in all our affairs.

Spirituality

Spirituality is often seen as an exclusively religious phenomenon and there is no doubt that the original AA document saw religion and ethics as closely tied together. However, this has been increasingly modified in recent Twelve Step approaches to provide a more generic spirituality, focusing on the faith system that underlies any ethics.

The first spiritual belief expressed in the Twelve Step programme is belief in a higher power. This is a very broad view of a transcendent reality, designed to be inclusive. This is a generic spirituality involving an awareness of the Other and of one own limitations in relation to the Other. The *Big Book of AA* sees a generic God concept as being there in every person, accessed through reflection (Alcoholics Anonymous 1976: 55).

A second 'spiritual axiom' is the need to form a relationship with the higher power. At one level, this is about the development of a mechanism against relapse, with meditation and prayer as a means of maintaining awareness of the Other. Perhaps more importantly, it sets out awareness of the limitations of the self and the need to rely on another. Hence, there is a stress on the person him- or herself as powerless over alcohol (Alcoholics Anonymous 1976: 25).

A third axiom is the need for constant renewal. This accepts that there is no cure and that, therefore, the person must at all times be aware of his or her needs and of the dangers of resting on laurels (Alcoholics Anonymous 1976: 85).

A final axiom is the need to examine the self and to take seriously any sense of discord in the self. This focuses centrally on the integrity of the person and the need to remain constant to the purpose that they have chosen for their life.

The moral dynamics

The spiritual axioms are reflected in the practice of the Twelve Step programme and the moral development that has, at its heart, the development of responsibility. This includes:

- *A fearless and searching moral inventory*: This is directly about facing up to the actions and to the person's responsibility for them.
- *The articulation of the person's narrative, in the context of the AA meeting*: The stress on the working with the AA community sets up a network of relationships to which the person is accountable. Initially, accountability is learned in practice through this relationship to the group and involves public articulation of the person's narrative.
- *The embodiment of repentance, through seeking forgiveness and to make amends*: More widely, there has been the development of forgiveness therapy (Sanderson and Linehan 2003). For some religious patients, the practice of confession can be used for enabling forgiveness. However, for those with a high level of toxic shame this is often not effective.

- *Criticism*: One of the criticisms of AA is that whilst this helps to develop the person's identity, the identity tends to be negatively focused in the alcoholism. In one sense, this is true. Focus for the rest of the alcoholic's life is on nature of the condition as not curable. However, at the heart of the Twelve Step approach is the development of mutuality in therapy with the person who has been helped becoming an active part of the healing community. In other words, the responsibility is practised, enabling the development of a new identity. The identity itself remains positive, based in the service given to others and the development of a more balanced, accepting and critical approach to life. At the heart of such practice is acknowledgement that there is no point at which the person has overcome the problem of addiction and that he or she therefore has to commit him- or herself to disciplines that will keep him or her morally focused.

Virtues

The subjective experience of the treatment process in addiction self-help groups focuses on the development of several key virtues (Tonigan *et al.* 1999: 122). Virtues are the elements of the morally mature character. Miller (2003) argues that the development of the virtues is central the successful recovery in a range of conditions, including alcoholism. The immediately obvious virtues are those referred to in the so-called 'serenity prayer', set out at the head of this chapter.

Serenity

This virtue lies at the base of the AA prayer – requesting the 'serenity to accept the things I cannot change'. Calmness, tranquillity, composure, repose, calmness, equanimity, steadiness of mind under stress, and *ataraxia* (or 'peace of mind') characterize this virtue. The process enables the patient to accept the reality of his or her self and his or her situation. It also gives a sense of release at not having to face a purpose based upon conditional acceptance.

Humility

The capacity to accept things that cannot be changed is, at least in part, about the virtue of humility. Humility is often seen as false modesty. However, it is a virtue involving realistic awareness of both strengths and limitations (Robinson 2007). As Aristotle notes of the virtues, they can only be learned through practice. Hence, the AA programme places it at the centre of their community of practice, from the initial acceptance of limitations to the continual renewal of the self through making amends to others. Much of the problems about alcoholism have been precisely about the absence of this virtue. As the dependence on alcohol is developed, the person tends to believe that he or she can overcome problems or is in control of the alcohol consumption.

Courage

Aristotle suggests that virtues involve the mean between extremes. Hence, courage is found between cowardice and foolhardiness. The AA prayer begins with this, precisely because of the importance of courage in facing up to the reality of what the person has done. The denial noted in the definitions seeks to avoid that. This is the courage to take responsibility. The subjective experience of courage will vary. Those who have developed and continue to practise the virtue of courage might not feel very courageous, partly because it has become second nature to them. Those facing major problems and new challenges will certainly feel anxiety that comes with exercising such courage. Such anxiety might almost be compared to the aching muscles in physical training. The example of AA forcefully gets this across. Not only is courage required to admit this to oneself, there is the added courage required to state this in public. Even this has two levels. The simple act of public speaking might, for many people, be very difficult. Hence, there is almost a ritualised approach about the sharing of the person's story, empowering the person to work through the initial formula of 'I am ... and I am an alcoholic.' This sets up a community base that empowers the person to take that courage. In doing that on a regular basis, the person then begins to practice that courage. But the practice of courage continues to develop in the way in which the person is encouraged to work through the different relationships. It is one thing to admit to the self or even a group of strangers; it is another to admit to the person whom you have injured and to begin to work through the issues.

Gratitude

This develops both with the awareness of the concern and help of others, and also with the release from debt and wrongdoing. Importantly, this ties to the acceptance of the need of others. The concept of acceptance of gift is at the heart of this idea, distinguishing it from a view of a right to recovery.

Wisdom

Views about the provenance of the AA prayer differ, from Augustine or Aquinas to Reinhold Niebuhr. Quite what was meant by the term 'wisdom' is not clear. However, Aristotle and Aquinas provide an important meaning. Aristotle saw wisdom as essentially practical (*phronesis*). This is the capacity to reflect on the values and purpose of any action and relate it to practice. On the face, it this seems to be a simple and obvious intellectual activity. However, as the brief reflection on therapy shows, it is a virtue that is very difficult to develop, not least because it can very quickly question how we view value and practice and, thus, question our identity.

Temperance

As noted in Chapter 6, this does not involve abstinence – from drink or anything else – but, rather, moderation, balance and self-control. This is important for effective judgement, self-reliance and the acceptance of responsibility. Plato's *sophrosunê* ('temperance' or 'self-control'), Reid (2006) suggests, corresponds to discipline. Discipline, in the sense of keeping to training or eating regimes, is, however, only part of this virtue. It also includes a sense of balance, of not moving to extremes, and is therefore critical to the exercise of judgement.

Hope

The virtue of hope is given little space in ethical reflection. However, it is a key virtue in the empowerment for change and, thus, repays a more detailed analysis. For many people, the idea of hope is about the giving of hope to someone and about the ground of that hope. This is often seen as a theological virtue, with the ground of hope being some divine activity or promise, such as salvation. Hope, however, is more complex than a passive acceptance of the work of the Other, involving existential as well as doctrinal dimensions. Hope is about the capacity to envision and take responsibility for a significant and meaningful future. As such, it is a genuine virtue, and is distinct from a generalized attitude of optimism. The experience of hope develops in and through the counselling or broader caring relationship, and the language of hope emerges from the practice of dialogue and reflection on that experience. The primal ground of hope is not in the future but in the present and, above all, in another. Many people have a sense of being 'hope-less'. They feel this largely because they have internalized the explicit or implicit judgement of significant others. The ascription 'hopeless' actually means that they have no value and, therefore, by definition have no future: indeed, for many the future simply involves the repetition of patterns of behaviour that always fail to achieve the goal of acceptance (Robinson 1998). The need here, then, is for the person to feel a significant sense of hope in the self, something that can only be supplied by the unconditional acceptance of another. However, hope, as Lester (1995) notes, cannot thrive on deceit or untruth. It has to be realistic, with a sense of how the vision of the future might be achieved. Snyder (2000) suggests that the development of this virtue depends on three factors: goals, pathways and agency.

Goals: The capacity to hope is generated through a sense of morally significant purpose. Such good hope provides meaning that affirms the worth of the person. Hence, hope in those who are dying can be embodied in concern for right relationships with significant others. In the light of such purposes, realistic goals need to be set out. Hopefulness develops goals that can be achieved.

Pathways: Hopeful thinking looks to find ways to the goals. This involves a development of the creative imagination to be able to see what ways forward there are. This is enabled through the development of method and through practice, not least the widening of possibilities through negotiation of responsibilities. The use of imagination enables the person to project future narratives and work through the different possibilities. Snyder (2000) notes that hope is associated with the development of multiple pathways. Such pathways increase through collaborative work with others, which is enabled as resolution and shared responsibility is achieved.

Agency: Hope centres in the experience of the person as subject, capable of determining and achieving the goals he or she looks to. This is achieved, to begin with, through the development of the narrative and its related skills. In particular, hope is generated when the person finds he or she is able to own and take responsibility for the feelings of shame and fear that have dominated his or her life. Hope is also achieved by the owning of values, the development of one's own method and by the practice that demonstrates capacity in the relationship.

Hope, then, has several elements. It is not a discrete virtue but one that is gradually developed along with others. It depends upon several factors including reflectivity, process and dialogue. At its base, hope depends on the discovery of faith in another and the development of responsibility.

Work with alcohol addiction has moral awareness and development at its centre, focusing on the person taking responsibility for him- or herself and, through his or her awareness of the condition he or she is suffering from, responsibility for others. With that comes a critical change in spiritual and moral awareness, with the person learning concern for the self. Indeed, concern for the self is a key starting point for the programme, with a concern to change not for the sake of someone else but for the self. This leads to a renewal of identity and purpose, and development of a new lifestyle that includes service to others as a key purpose. In and through the practice of the articulation, critical reflection on value and practice, the development of responsibility and response to the different groups and persons involved in the patient's life, the virtues are practiced and developed.

In all of this, the person begins to develop integrative thinking, with the final virtue of integrity at its core.

Integrity

Solomon (1982) argues that integrity is a collection of virtues, rather than a single virtue. Brown (2005), as noted in Chapter 4, outlines a view of integrity at a corporate and personal level that includes consistency, relational awareness, inclusiveness and purpose. Robinson *et al.* (2003) argue for integrity as involving integration, consistency, transparency, responsibility and the capacity to critique the self. All see integrity as central to the identity of the self or group.

Taking these ideas together suggests the following description of integrity:

- *Integrative thinking*: This involves integration of the different parts of the person: emotional, psychological and intellectual. This leads to holistic thinking, and an awareness of the self alongside awareness and appreciation of external data.
- *Consistency*: This entails consistency of character and operation between: value and practice; past, present and future; and in different situations and contexts. The behaviours will not necessarily be the same in each situation, but will be consistent with the ethical identity of the person. Closely related to consistency is the idea of *transparency*. This involves ensuring that values and practice are open to scrutiny and reflection, something that the alcoholic avoids.
- *Relational awareness*: Identity is not individualistic but is based upon a plurality of relationships. These include cultural, interpersonal, organizational, social, and natural (Brown 2005, Robinson *et al.* 2003). Hence, consistency and integration are played out in this plurality.
- *Responsibility*: All of the elements above demand the development of responsibility in its three modes. First, responsibility for articulating and developing thinking about values, purpose and practice. Second, there is responsibility as accountability. This looks to those relationships that have some contractual basis, from the work contract to

the professional or the family contract. Finally, there is responsibility as liability. Such responsibility is for people and projects in the past, present and future.

• *Learning and self-criticism*: Absolute integrity is impossible to attain. Hence, an important virtue is humility, the acceptance of limitations, of weakness as well as strengths. Equally important, therefore, is the capacity to reflect; to evaluate, practice and be self-critical; to be able to cope with criticism; and to alter practice appropriately. This capacity to learn means that integrity should not be seen as simply maintaining values and ethical practice come what may but, rather, as involving a core process of learning. This relates closely to practical wisdom.

In this light, integrity can be seen as a complex, lively and robust idea rather than something precious that has to be handled with kid gloves. On the contrary, integrity thrives off and is developed by critical reflection and conversation. In effect, it is developed through the immediacy, reflexivity and mutuality of the therapeutic experience. Precisely because such integrity involves continual learning and no simplistic path to development, there is always need for the community that enables the reflection and response.

Conclusion

We began this chapter by looking at the balance between non-judgemental therapy and responsibility in alcoholism. Is the alcoholic to blame or is he or she suffering from a medical condition, a dependency? This chapter concludes that it is not a matter of either/or engaging morality or being value neutral. No therapy can be value neutral, having at its heart the concern for health as well as autonomy. At the simple level of imputability, the alcoholic is responsible for his or her actions, and could be said to be blameworthy. At a deeper level of imputability, the alcoholic can be said to have the capacity for making rational decisions affected by the condition of dependence. However, there is little doubt that alcohol dependence cannot be addressed and worked through without addressing the moral identity of the patient and enabling him or her to fully take responsibility for values, identity and practice. This demands the development of the deeper level of imputability. It also demands that the patient develop a sense of accountability and, thus, respond to the needs of key relationships. Moral meaning is therefore at the centre of the recovery of the alcoholic, and such moral meaning is most effectively addressed through enabling the development of critical reflection on values and practice. This suggests that the development of a sense of guilt, and even shame, is a healthy part of therapy. This should not be guilt imposed by the therapist but, rather, owned by the patient as he or she reflects on value and practice. If therapy is to be successful, it does require the development of virtues and this, in turn, requires clear purpose and discipline. AA provides a good example of how this can be achieved but other therapies address this.

All of this squarely places the alcoholic as being involved in the ethical debate and as being part of the web of responsibility. It also reinforces the central issue of personal responsibility in the wider debate about alcohol. However, it also, as with the religious reflections, places personal responsibility in a community context.

8
Ethics and Alcohol in the Twenty-first Century

This book has begun to develop a view of the ethics of alcohol that focuses on responsibility and the importance of developing responsibility in all who are involved in the production, sale, consumption and regulation of alcohol, and who deal with the social effects of alcohol consumption. In this final chapter, we will review the arguments, focusing on the need to develop partnerships of responsibility. We will note some good examples of this working together, and conclude that perhaps the most important element in the whole debate is establishing an environment that enables the individual to reflect on their personal responsibility. In all of this, we suggest that the example of the alcohol industry takes the wider ethical debate about the nature of corporate responsibility well beyond the parameters of the past thirty years. Hence, we shall begin this final chapter by setting out the thinking in that wider debate – a debate that applies to any industry.

Corporate responsibility

Corporate responsibility (CR) is, in one sense, no new phenomenon. Without explicit CR policy, it has been practised by business for centuries (Robinson 2008). In the final quarter of the twentieth century, the term 'corporate social responsibility' (CSR) began to be used explicitly, focusing largely on how the company contributed towards the local, and possibly wider, community. The twenty-first century has seen CR expanding to take in an awareness of, and responsiveness to, all aspects of business life in the social and physical environment, and in the company itself – a view that stresses interconnection and interdependence. Hence, the International Business Leaders Forum (IBLF) define CR as:

> open and transparent business practices that are based on ethical values and respect for employees, communities and the environment. It is designed to deliver sustainable value to society at large, as well as to shareholders. (http://www.iblf.org/csr/csrwebassist.nsf/content/a1.html)

The liberal view of CR, however, would question this.

The liberal view of CR

Milton Friedman (1983) argued that the role of business is the creation of wealth and, thus, the prime responsibility of business is to make a profit. The exclusive duty of the company is to its owners, usually the shareholders. In this, the executive acts as 'an agent serving the interests of his principal' (Friedman 1983: 240). The interest of the principal is profit maximization, and involvement in any activities in the community outside this sphere would be a violation of trust and, thus, morally wrong. Ultimately, any money used by a company executive for social concerns is the shareholders' and, therefore, cannot be used other than for making profits for them. Friedman does not argue against the social involvement of the company as such, rather, simply, that the company – and the owners, especially – can decide to do what they think is fit. There can be no moral or legal constraint on the company to be more socially aware, and no question of the rights of the community or groups within the community taking precedence over the company, so long as it is pursuing legal ends.

If the company executive does decide to become involved in a community project, Friedman argues that this is not the payment of an obligation but, rather, a means of achieving the company aims. Thus, giving donations to a local medical project, for instance, is not fulfilling obligations but, instead, improving the image and reputation of the company and, thus, contributing to improving profits.

Friedman notes the negative consequences of pursing social responsibility. It would involve costs that would have to be passed on to the customer, possibly to the shareholder in reduced dividends, and to the employee in reduced wages. Not only is this unfair, it also constitutes a form of taxation without representation and is, therefore, undemocratic. Moreover, it is both unwise (because it invests too much power in the executive) and futile (because it is likely that the costs imposed by this approach will lead to a reduction in economic efficiency).

Finally, Friedman argues that the executive is not the best person to be involved in making decisions about social involvement. He or she is neither qualified, nor mandated to pursue social goals. Without the skills and experience of social administrators, it is difficult to see how the executive could understand the needs of the local community or begin to determine local priorities. Such a task is better suited to local government and social concern groups, whose roles and accountability is directly related to these tasks. For business to enter this field, then, would lead to a confusion of roles and the raising of false expectations.

Friedman's argument focuses on the primacy of the goals of profit-making (written into the contracts of the executive), the obligations of the executive within such a contract, the freedom of the executive to pursue company goals, and the local government as the proper focus for social activity. This approach is a good example of contract ethics, in that responsibility is determined by the freely entered contract.

Elaine Sternberg (2000) takes Friedman's argument further. Sternberg argues from a strong theoretical ethics basis: that of the *telos*. Aristotle argues that the idea of the good arises from reflection on the *telos*, the underlying purpose or end. Applied to business, Sternberg suggests that the *telos* of business is to make profit and to stay within the law. Hence, any attempt to go beyond that basic *telos* would be teleopathic – involving pursuit of a wrong purpose.

Albert Carr (1968) provides an even narrower and more severe view of CR. He argues that the ethics of everyday encounter have no part to play in business. Carr sees the so-called 'ethics of business' as analogous to poker, a game where participants can reasonably aim to deceive other players. All the participants know the rules of the game and accept that they apply only in that situation. On this basis, business people can acceptably deceive those in the business world, including the customer, with respect to advertising. All expect to be deceived and operate accordingly. So, social responsibility takes second place to the game, and the purpose and rules of the game.

All three arguments are based on what Berlin (1967) calls a negative view of freedom; that is, freedom from oppression or interference. Hence, they seek to protect the agent and the shareholder from attempts to determine what they should do. They also rest on the purpose of business, and a narrow view of that purpose is defended. Finally, they rest on the freedom to operate in the marketplace, which, for some, is seen as the place where individual effort and effective distribution of wealth come together.

Michael Novak develops this in a different way. He suggests that the freedom to do one's duty is central to the argument, not merely negative freedom, and that the duty of the business person is of a high moral nature. The very activity of enterprise is a moral good. Novak (1990: 12) argues, first, that every human being has the right to personal economic activity. Indeed, the capacity for enterprise is a fundamental virtue that Novak infers is basic to human development and fulfilment.

Second, in this context the business person is serving society and wealth creation in a socially responsible activity, both in the practice of his or her skill and in the distribution of wealth.

Third, underlying this, Novak links the moral perspective of the marketplace. The market actually enables not only the distribution of wealth, but also the development of community. 'Markets' argues Novak, 'draw people out of isolation into reasoned, civil voluntary interchange with their fellows' (1990: 10). Markets, in other words, enable community. It is possible to argue from that, that contracts enable empowerment and freedom. Individuals enter the contract freely and operating in the market empowers them. Novak, then, sees the marketplace as, in itself, ethical and responsible; a basis for the development of autonomy, distribution of wealth and building community. In such a context, there is little need for a policy on CR, because the business person is directly enabling society as a whole to grow, financially and as a community.

The argument set out by these writers is not simply based in self-interest, but has a variety of philosophical underpinnings involving underlying values, views of society and different ideas about purpose. Several arguments can be made against them. First, with respect to the view of society, Novak and Friedman have an idealized view of the market. In Novak's case, this assumes an underlying equality, ignoring the power imbalances within the market that militate against simplistic community building, especially seen at a global level. All ignore the complexity of the relationship between the marketplace and society, and the subsequent responsibilities that emerge. Hence, whilst the market is an important mechanism, more and more commentators prefer to look to ways in which the market can work with society (Buchholz and Rosenthal 2002).

Second, two key underlying values are 'freedom' and 'creativity'. Freedom is important but, as R. H. Tawney (1930) notes, it requires the balance of other values. The freedom of any person affects the freedom of another. The negative view of freedom tends to assume an individualistic view of the person. Against this is a view of humanity as interdependent. This suggests neither a collectivist view of society nor an individualistic one. Creativity, in that view, is very much about partnership and working together with the community.

Third, Sternberg's view of the purpose of business is simplistic. It assumes a single purpose in relation to the immediate task of the business person. However, there is no reason why the business person cannot have several different purposes, each of equal importance; care for shareholders, clients, the physical environment and so on. Perhaps the biggest problem with the arguments from different purposes is the assumption that shareholders have a single purpose. It is certainly true that one aim of shareholders is to make a profit. However, it is not clear that shareholders do not have an equal concern for the environment or for the community in which they live. This can only be tested in dialogue with each group of shareholders, and in the light of the nature of the business and its effects on society.

Fourth, behind much of this is another assumption: that the different ethical worlds of social concern and business are discrete, quite separate. In fact, the different value worlds are many and varied, and are connected. It is not possible simply to say that there is a clearly defined wall between them. The shareholder, for example, is also a member of the community, with concerns for that. Equally, as a business works in other countries, it encounters a great many other cultural and religious values that affect different stakeholders and which, in turn, will affect how the company does business in that context. In this sense, the company has to be aware of the plurality of roles and values, and be prepared to negotiate and work with them.

Fifth, in this light it becomes difficult to predetermine what the responsibility of the business person or the business should be – no less difficult than it is possible to be precise about the responsibility of, for instance, local or national government. In practice, there are broad responsibilities but these are continuously being debated and negotiated. An example of this, in government terms, is the issue of respect. The responsibility for identifying and developing respect has traditionally been seen to be that of the school or the family. At the beginning of 2005, the UK government also began to argue that it had an important part to play in encouraging the definition and practice of respect (http://www.labour.org.uk/respect). The issue of respect is one for which all groups in society have a concern, including business.

Stakeholder theory, ethics and social responsibility

Traditionally, so-called 'stakeholder theory' has been used as the basis for arguing against the liberal view of CR. A stakeholder was initially defined in terms of those groups that were critical to the survival of the business, including employees, customers, lenders and suppliers (Sternberg 2000: 49). This concept has been further widened to include 'any individual or group who can affect or is affected by the actions, decisions, policies, practices or goals of the organization' (Carroll and Bucholtz 2000: 315). This results in a much more complex situation, encompassing the government, community and beyond.

Heath and Norman (2004) suggest there are in fact several different stakeholder theories (SHTs) within this, including:

- strategic SHT, a theory that attention to the needs of stakeholders, will lead to better outcomes for the business.
- SHT of governance is a theory of how shareholder groups should be involved in oversight of management; for example, placing shareholders on the board. This is built around positive ethical views of democracy and leadership (Noam Cook 2005).
- deontic SHT, a theory that analyzes the legitimate rights and needs of the different stakeholders, and uses this data to develop company policies. This is often expressed as demanding a response from the company to fulfil such needs.

The debate continues as to whether there really are many different theories, or whether they are parts of one major view of how business relates to society. Sternberg (2000: 49ff.) argues against the forms of theory that assert the rights of the stakeholder on several grounds:

- The argument that stakeholders should have equal representation on the board mistakenly confuses business with government.
- SHT rests on a confusion about accountability. Whilst business should take many groups into account, it is not accountable to them. Sternberg's argument rests on the meaning of 'being called to account'. If it is used for all stakeholders, then the meaning of it becomes unclear.
- Faced by the many competing interests of the stakeholders, there are no criteria offered by the theory for deciding how to handle conflicting interests.

These arguments do not recognize the many different perspectives of stakeholder theory. Perhaps, more importantly, they arbitrarily confine the definition of responsibility to accountability.

Carroll and Bucholtz (2000) suggests a way of looking at CR that holds together the different elements of responsibility, suggesting that it involves four areas: economic, ethical, legal and philanthropic. Carroll argues that these different responsibilities are set in layers within a company, with CR involving and addressing all four layers consecutively.

Corporations have an economic responsibility towards their shareholders to be profitable, and provide reasonable returns on shareholders' investments. Economic and financial gain is the primary objective of a corporation in a business sense, and is the foundation upon which all the other responsibilities rest. This is required by society.

At the same time, businesses are expected to comply with the laws and regulations as the ground rules and legal framework under which they must operate. A company's legal responsibilities are seen as coexisting with economic responsibilities as fundamental precepts of the free enterprise system. This also required by society.

Ethical responsibilities within a corporation ensure that the organization performs in a manner consistent with expectations of ethics in society. It is important to recognize and respect new or evolving ethical trends adopted by society, and that good corporate citizenship can be defined as doing what is expected morally and ethically. It must be noted, however, that the corporate integrity and ethical behaviour of a company go beyond mere compliance with laws and regulations, and is the obligation to do what is right and fair, and to avoid harm. This is expected by society.

Philanthropic responsibilities include corporate actions that are in response to society's expectation that businesses be good corporate citizens and activities or programs to promote human welfare or goodwill. Philanthropy, 'love of fellow humans', is highly desired by society, argues Carroll; however, it is not ultimately necessary. This desired by society.

Carroll's view is comprehensive, and usefully brings together different views of CR. However, the distinction between desirability and necessity in the fourth area is not clear. It simply assumes that business is not primarily concerned with the promotion of human welfare. However, human welfare might at any point be a critical issue in the life of a business. If a subsidiary is directly abusing the human rights of its workers, for instance, then human welfare is not only desirable, but also a moral demand. How one answers that moral demand will depend on the situation. Carroll's contention that CR will operate in a manner consistent with the ethics of the wider society is also questionable. Does this mean that businesses should accept, without question, the ethical framework of a fascist society? A less extreme example might be a society that is undergoing transition, and with no fixed ethical expectation. There are increasing examples of business contributing towards the ethics of wider society rather than following it, including involvement in peace build-ing (see Robinson 2008). Hence, CR might involve engaging with issues of justice. The point is that any business will have to make a decision about this in context.

As Buchholz and Rosenthal (2002: 316) note, feminist ethics, in par-ticular, argue for a web of stakeholder relations that stress connectivity, interdependence, power sharing, collective action and conflict reso-lution. In this view, business is a part of society and its identity is established through how it relates to society, not least in its conduct with those who are affected by it, and who affect them. Hence, the iden-tity of the company is continually developing, and has to be worked on. This is further stressed by Heath and Norman (2004). They note how the view of shareholders' interests as opposing stakeholders' is false. Learning lessons from disasters such as the Enron case, the real problems emerged from problematic managers who kept their actions secret from the share-holders. Hence, the shareholders were not able to be part of an adult conversation about values, purposes and the practice of the business. The message is this: when business, or any corporation, is not transpar-ent, or is also fragmented, then the sense of responsibility of members, or the corporation as a whole, is easily lost.

All corporate activities and decisions have social impacts associated with them. These impacts can have positive and negative implications associated with them, and normally surface when providing products, services, employment and other corporate activities or business transac-tions (Crane and Matten 2004). It is precisely here that reflections on the alcohol industry come into play.

The alcohol industry

As noted, alcohol is no ordinary commodity. The alcohol industry pro-duces a product that has a massive negative effect on the health and well-being of individuals and organizations, and is a significant drain on the health, social care and legal resources of society. The effect of the product has to be taken into consideration. In this sense, the com-pany has, at the least, to be aware of the potential negative effects of its product. In particular, it has to be aware of the effect that the marketing of its product has on behaviour of the customer. This accepts a weak view of imputability: that the company is responsible for its products. Such a view, however, simply makes the connection between the business and the product and its use. The stronger view of imputability would take the company to be responsible for knowingly encouraging excessive drinking, thus making it blameworthy in relation to the effects of alcohol consumption on society. This distinction suggests that the alcohol company is responsible for producing a product that has potential negative effects on health and well-being, and that it has a responsibility for either minimizing those effects or, more positively, for encouraging a responsible and life enhancing use of alcohol. In the light of all this, two points emerge. First, the company cannot argue that responsibility can only be seen in terms of accountability to the shareholders. The nature of the product sets out a moral liability for how the product is presented and how the company relates to potential customers and the wider society. Friedman wants to characterize such moral liability as not being a genuine responsibility, in the sense of not demanding any moral response for the business. The business can be involved with this, but it is instrumental; that is, it is a means by which to achieve the core end of the business: to make a profit. Second, however, regardless of how one defines the purpose of business, the moral liability that surrounds the product of alcohol requires a response from the company; it is not *necessarily* connected to the making of profit. Moreover, this liability cannot be characterized, as Sternberg would suggest, simply in terms of adhering to the law. There are clearly legal frameworks to which companies have to adhere. In addition, there are self-regulatory codes. Even such voluntary codes, however, do not demand simply a minimal response from the company. As Brown-Forman showed, in the case of product placement, the company has to interpret such codes and, in doing so, might well go beyond simply fulfilling minimum standards. The criterion for response is not about profit but, rather, the moral liability. Such liability provides the moral context within which the company works and makes its profit. Moreover, it is precisely such moral liability that lies beneath codes such as the BCAP. Such a code provides a framework for judging the way in which, in this case, the advertisement might affect not only the customer, but also wider social groupings and cultural perceptions.

All of this places the alcohol company in an interesting position. On the one hand, it cannot be characterized as responsible for all the ills of alcohol abuse in terms of strong imputability. At the same time, however, it cannot restrict itself to responsibility as accountability to the shareholders. It remains morally liable for how it markets the product. Interpreting what this means in practice therefore requires relating to several different stakeholders. It would be a mistake at this point to assume that this approach rests on a simple application of stakeholder theory. As noted, there are several different stakeholder theories. However, moral liability goes beyond those. Moral liability operates in several ways with stakeholders.

First, it does not simply seek to fulfil the needs or rights of the stakeholder. The practice of the company should clearly not contravene the rights of any stakeholder. However, at the same time, moral liability addresses the responsibility of the stakeholder. Hence, the alcohol company seeks not simply satisfy the customers' need for alcohol; it also seeks to ensure responsible use of the product, focusing on the moral responsibility of the customer. As noted, this demands careful attention to marketing, but might also involve more broadly educational work. Regulatory codes from such as the BACP take the company beyond fulfilling responsibility simply by warning about the effect of irresponsible drinking, thus focusing on informed choice. The way in which a product is advertised can actively influence the choice of values involved in making a choice, especially in relation to the more vulnerable members of society. Hence, moral liability demands that the company be constantly aware of how it influences or empowers stakeholders.

Second, moral liability in this area is, by definition, shared. The government shares part of this moral liability through social policy concerns and the need to respond to the negative effects of alcohol consumption – as do alcohol retailers, public houses and wider members of the alcohol industry. As we have observed, there are many other groups who share this moral liability, from the media to educational institutions, to local authorities and so on. The key question, then, is how all these work together to respond.

One way of trying to capture this idea around CR has been to view the corporation as a citizen (Zadek 2001). This neatly locates the business in a wider network of citizenry, all of whom share responsibility in their role as citizens. However, this does not really clarify the plurality of responsibilities that are there within society. The responsibility of the professional is not *qua* citizen, but of the professional who, by dint of his or her role, is responsible to the client, his or her own profession and professional body, and to wider society. In the case of law, for example, this wider responsibility is to uphold justice, a value that transcends any particular interest. In the case of corporate responsibility, the nature of the business tends to define the area of responsibility. It will always involve responsibility to workers in the business, and might involve responsibility to the wider industry and, even again, for areas of wider society. Hence, for instance, an alcohol company might have responsibility to the wider industry in the sense of ensuring good practice across the industry that would affect how people view the industry in general.

Civic responsibility is responsibility *qua* citizen and the contract between the citizen and civil society. The corporation might act as citizen at points, supporting democracy or community events. In everyday operation, it also supports the civic or familial responsibility of workers; for example, in providing space to fulfil parenting roles (Brown 2005). Given, then, that responsibility is related to role and purpose, it is difficult to sum up the business responsibility purely in terms of citizenship. Given also that it is difficult simply to restrict responsibility to accountability, the corporation has to work out its responsibility in context and in relation to the other agencies in that situation. We have argued that this demands that the alcohol company has to work together with the other stakeholders to respond to the problem raised by patterns of drinking, and that involves ensuring that all groups involved focus on and develop their responsibility in relation to the situation.

Responsibilities

All this means that the company, along with the other agencies, has to take seriously all areas of responsibility, and each of the modes of responsibility.

Personal responsibility

We have argued that personal responsibility remains critical in the discussion about alcohol. There has to be proper consideration given for those who are vulnerable – those who, because of age and condition, can be deemed to be more vulnerable to group pressures to abuse drink. Chapter 5 was a reminder that the young are not simply vulnerable, but, potentially, are at volatile stage of development. In that respect, they actually need to have the different narratives about values and alcohol, so that they can begin to develop critical thinking and, thus, take responsibility for their own thoughts and values. A key narrative in this is provided by the legal framework, which provides limits to acceptable behaviour. At the same time, this framework requires interpretation and a creative community response, if responsibility is to be encouraged. That framework reinforces the need to develop personal responsibility, and this is reinforced by public information campaigns to discourage drink-driving and the abuse of alcohol. The key point about such campaigns is that they focus on imputability, accountability and liability, looking both at the consequences of misuse on innocent victims, as well as effects on the person's relationships and roles (HM Government 2007). There is a parallel dynamic with the question of binge or extreme drinking where the different responsibilities of the person, as a citizen, a family member and so on can be stressed. Some research into drug taking in sport suggests that an effective way of changing behaviour is to focus on the identity of the person in relation to other groups or communities (Backhouse *et al.* 2007). A company, for instance, could support this strongly by stressing to its employees that public drunkenness can affect the reputation of the firm, reinforcing the person's responsibility to the firm. There has been much discussion about the naming and shaming of such behaviour. The dynamic of shame is most effective in relation to a group where one is known.

We have also argued that the stress on personal responsibility is further reinforced with the argument that its development is at the heart of addiction therapy. Again, this demands taking responsibility for reflection such that the patient begins to acknowledge both the reality of his or her behaviour, the underlying values and the nature of his or her identity. It is important to remember that raising the moral agenda for the alcoholic does not involve asserting something new. On the contrary, the alcoholic's response to any challenges about his or her behaviour is already value-laden. Typical liberal moral arguments are that his or her behaviour is not affecting anyone else and therefore is not wrong – 'I can do what I like with my body'. Underlying such arguments is often a strong sense that, if there is a problem, then he or she is quite able to deal with it, expressing a fear of depending on others and an assertion of personal responsibility and the importance of individual freedom. Therapy, from Twelve Step programmes to cognitive-behaviourist (Robinson 2001), looks to test perceptions of reality and enable reflection on values and practice. As such, it does not condemn but, rather, enables the patient to give an account of his or her situation and, through that, to examine accountability. Part of that involves developing the capacity to critique the person's values and practice. The therapeutic process takes time and, inevitably, involves attempts by the patient to deny responsibility or to place responsibility onto others. This is precisely why the commitment of the therapist or therapeutic community is necessary (Robinson 2001).

Just as the ordinary drinker is encouraged to look at the multiple responsibilities of the person – from citizen to professional, reinforcing the public, accountable identity – also, in therapy, the development of responsibility involves locating and responding to such responsibilities.

Hence, in one case, for example, 'B' began to focus on taking responsibility through reflecting on how alcohol had adversely affected her work as a schoolteacher. Her work with children was a critical part of her identity, and her addiction had caused her to deny any problems at work. Only once she had faced that reality – and, with that, the great challenge to her core values – did she begin to take personal responsibility for dealing with the condition. This suggests that the issue is less about a divided self (Cook 2006) and more about dealing with the plural responsibilities of the self and the relation of value to practice.

There has been an ongoing debate amongst philosophers (Widerker and McKenna 2003) around whether moral responsibility is compatible with any form of determinism. In particular, the principle of alternate possibilities argues that a person can only be held to be morally responsible if he or she could have done otherwise. If there were no alternatives open to him or her, then he or she could not have been morally responsible for his or her action. Focusing on the logic of this argument, Frankfurt (2003) argues against it on the basis that a person can be intuitively responsible for his or her behaviour even if he or she could not have done otherwise. Responsibility can only be denied if the person is completely coerced. In relation to alcohol dependence, it is clear that dependence, whilst impairing the will and determining the decision of the addict, cannot be counted as coercion. In any case, it can be argued that there is always one key choice, no matter what the range of options available to the person; that is, to respond or not to respond to the issue or challenge at hand. This remains true of the ordinary drinker who, even after several drinks, is sufficiently rational to decide not to drive.

Government responsibility

We have argued that it is reasonable for government to go beyond the liberal model of public policy to a stewardship model. It is reasonable to provide coercive frameworks to ensure that the vulnerable do not develop abusive patterns of behaviour. However, we have also argued that the stewardship model should focus more on community, and the support of personal and professional responsibility.

Corporate responsibility

We have argued that the alcohol company is not responsible for all the ills of alcohol; neither can it restrict its responsibility to its immediate contract with shareholders. The examples we have given of corporate responsibility focus on marketing that does not simply look to contain the problems associated with alcohol abuse but, rather, seeks to develop the responsibility of the consumer.

Civic responsibility – civil society

We have noted the importance of working with civil society. This includes more effective work with NGOs.

The responsibility of the industry

We have argued that it is important to develop the responsibility of the alcohol industry as such. At one level, this is difficult. It would be reassuring to see the industry as something of a professional body. However, the context is not about a shared profession so much as a free market. As such, it is hard to develop either a sense of shared professional identity or any effective 'self-regulation'. New companies are not bound by professional registration. This therefore demands further development of regulation that seeks to reinforce responsibility across the industry, such as that recommended by Baggott (2006). The focus in the Queen's Speech, setting out UK legislation for 2009 (3 December 2008) is on the retail part of the industry. Hence, at the point of writing, the UK government aims to institute a mandatory code to target irresponsible practices, such as promotions for cheap drinks in clubs and pubs, and cheap deals in supermarkets. There is no doubt that promotions, such as 'Drink all you can for £10', work against the broader concern to develop responsible drinking. In developing such additional regulation, it remains important that the focus should remain on empowering the responsibility of all persons involved. A good example of this is the idea of having the Know Your Limit logo at the point of sale. All this asks important questions about the responsibility of the supermarkets. Some continue to offer very cheap alcohol. Their justification seems to be around basic liberal arguments about freedom to make a profit and respect for competition laws. As we have argued, neither of these are adequate ethical arguments, largely because they refuse to explore their moral liability.

Ethics and responsibility

In ethical terms, ethics and responsibility moves away from the debate about ethical concepts, such as freedom versus the best interest of the consumer or business, to a debate that focuses more on a community of practice that seeks to enable responsibility at all the levels. As such, the ethical framework of the debate has moved away from either a deontological approach, stressing the core principles at issue, or a utilitarian approach, stressing the need to maximize the good for the greatest number. Elements of both of these are important in understanding moral value and developing policy. However, the stress on the responsibility of all involved takes us, rather, to a form of virtue ethics in which the capacity of the person or organization to respond to the social and physical environment becomes central. As we have argued, such development is central to successful therapy. In therapy, it demands the development of community within which responsibility and the related virtues can be practised. It is equally important to develop a framework for the practice of virtues across all the different areas of responsibility and, at its centre, would be the development of integrity, both personal and corporate. For the young person facing the pressure to drink excessively, this would also include focusing on virtues such as courage (to stand against prevailing views) and practical wisdom (*phronesis*) the capacity to reflect critically on the purpose of the action before one.

One illustration of how aspects of this can be achieved is found in the report of a Health Forum Key Note Seminar that took place on 21 October 2008 (see Box 8.1).

Box 8.1   'Alcohol and Responsibility' – Westminster Health Forum Key Note Seminar

On 21 October 2008, guests ranging from Crispin Acton (Programme Manager, Alcohol Policy Team, Department of Health), Kate Blakely (Head of Social Responsibility, Diageo GB) and Don Shenker (Chief Executive, Alcohol Concern) came together to discuss the positive social and health benefits that alcohol has in our society. The negative consequences of violence, long-term ill health, and the drain on hospitals and enforcement agency resources were also presented. The purpose of the forum was to gain a collective understanding of the consequences of excessive and harmful drinking, and share the many initiatives that should pave the way for a less hazardous, more enjoyable night-time economy.

One of the speakers was Chief Inspector Shaun de Souza Brady, Chief Inspector, Your Team, Safer Neighbourhoods Unit, Metropolitan Police Service. As his title implies, he was concerned with keeping his local neighbourhoods safe and secure. He acknowledged that he had limited staffing resources during the evenings and early mornings – a time when demand for those resources is at its highest. But he needed to ensure that he used the resources in his borough effectively to reduce crime, disorder, violence and thefts, in line with the Violent Crime Reduction Act. Chief Inspector de Souza Brady presented to the forum an account of how he gained community spirit amongst residents, licensees of the local pubs, taxi drivers, and the Safer Neighbourhood Team in Haringey.

Haringey, de Souza Brady explained, is a borough that had an east–west divide; the less affluent people lived on the east side and the more affluent lived on the west side. The night-time economy consisted of only five pubs and a small retail parade. However, five late-night pubs in close proximity brought a series of incidents that went 'out of control'. Virtually every night, Haringey turned into a danger zone. Revellers were fighting each other in the excessively long queues for taxis; no buses ran late at night or early in the morning. It was noisy, people were being robbed, and gangs began to move into the area where the pubs were in order to join in the melee.

Chief Inspector de Souza Brady relied on the intelligence he was receiving from the Safer Neighbourhood Team and decided he wanted to add to this intelligence through a public meeting. Past experience of public meetings had always been disappointing; hence, the police force expected few residents to join the meeting. De Souza Brady was surprised when 150 residents arrived to air their grievances. The residents added to the intelligence by stating that fights were happening, not only outside the pubs, but also in their flowerbeds and driveways; drunken people were being sick, urinating or just collapsing into their gardens or by their front doors. Littering and damage to the cars of residents were also nightly occurrences. Those revellers who had brought cars to the pub often parked them in the residential areas and brought their party atmosphere back into their cars by playing music at a deafeningly loud level, singing, shouting, revving engines, flashing lights and sounding their car horns. And, more importantly, the residents stated they never went out of their own homes after 8pm, as it was not safe to do so.

Clearly, something had to be done, and de Souza Brady and his team began to realize that some of his limited resources were being deployed in the wrong areas. Therefore, police began to move in and around the residential neighbourhoods as well as by the pubs and taxi ranks. The police force also enlisted the help of the five licensees, who have a radio link to each other so that any trouble or violent behaviour can be alerted to each pub and the police quickly. A dress code was also introduced at the licensed premises, together with a policy of admitting only those over-21 years of age. Local taxi companies were also contacted and enlisted. The taxi companies now have contracts with the five pub licensees, and they make themselves available to take revellers away from the premises quickly, thus cutting down long taxi queues. At the same time, a night warden with a Blackberry phone pre-books taxis for people so that they can also get home quickly and safely.

This joint forum of police, licensees, the general public and taxi firms enables all to discuss their point of view and work together to bring a safer night-time economy. The success of the community forum has enabled de Souza Brady to reduce the number of officers in the Haringey area, and it has significantly reduced anti-social behaviour and violent crime in that borough. The local press in Haringey has praised this initiative, expressing thanks for making the area safe.

Following Chief Inspector de Souza Brady's address, questions were taken from the floor. Norman Lamb MP asked the Chief Inspector if the five licensed public house managers were as happy as the residents in the actions being taken. The reply was that licensees were initially concerned that their takings might fall due to the original news that there would be extra policing in the area. However, media coverage reassured people that Haringey would benefit through cooperation rather than through enforcement. Dr Alexandra Kenyon from Leeds Metropolitan University asked if he would prefer such partnerships to continue, or would he prefer further legislative powers. The Inspector replied that local authorities and police services are now, for the first time, being held accountable for the way in which they deal with local crime and disorder. Therefore, he felt that working together, embedding communication and dialogue throughout the community, and working with other voluntary services brings strong partnerships that are effective. De Souza Brady felt this model was preferable to additional legislation at this moment.

Source: Information taken from the transcripts to the Westminster Health Forum Keynote Seminar 'Alcohol & Responsibility'.

This case provides something of a framework for the practice of responsibility that can be set out in terms of the core modes of responsibility. First, a strong sense of imputability involves the development of agency, and this demands an awareness and appreciation of one's social and physical environment, and the issues related to that. This is more than simple data collection. It involves an awareness of the context within which any relevant data is collected. The Haringey case (Box 8.1) illustrates the importance of bringing together all involved to describe the situation. In this case, it meant that the overall picture was clear and that a more effective response could be plotted.

More broadly, this recognizes that the social environment affects any perception of data; that social environment involves different agencies, including civil society and the government. Hence, there is a need to work closely with these different agencies. Even understandings of responsibility amongst different agencies can affect perceptions of data. NGOs, for example, often perceive themselves as responsible for defending wider civil society, especially the most vulnerable members. Such a view of responsibility easily leads to an assumption that other agencies are not fulfilling their responsibility, and to a skewed view of the data (Entine 2002). More complex situations can demand an awareness of how the company relates not only to the immediate situation, but also to broader aspects, such as the supply chain and how subsidiaries do business.

Alongside awareness of the situation, strong imputability involves an understanding of the values and beliefs that underlie any decision made by the company. This demands that the company or community articulates its values. In one sense, this is about giving an account of the story of the firm and, with that, an understanding of its value and what it values. It is also about giving an account – in effect, justifying those values. This becomes central to the development of the ethical identity of a company or community. Once again, this underlines that, whilst codes are important, CR cannot be summed up in codes – involving, as it does, continued interaction with the different agencies in any situation. Managing values, however, involves more than stating the core values of the company, and enabling others to share and embody them. The business environment includes many different values and raises questions about how they are handled. Any business might have a number of conflicting values that have to be held together, or face a situation where a choice has to be made between values. The response of the Haringey licensees is a good example of this. Initially, they feared that this kind of community involvement would affect their profits – raising a conflict of values. However, they stood out for a community response. In effect, the acceptance of shared responsibility led to the addressing of shared interests. This required purposeful reflection in practice.

We have noted that part of giving account in the alcohol industry has to involve an awareness of the moral ambiguity of the product. We also noted how this ambiguity was reflected in religious perspectives that held alcohol at the centre of community celebration and historical identity, but also saw it as an evil that required abstention throughout the community. Part of the nature of communities, as McIntyre (1981) notes, is that they give account of their meaning and practice through stories. McIntyre argues that this enables virtues to be identified and practised. Hence, part of the responsibility of the alcohol industry is to respond to the negative effects of alcohol, and also to show examples of how alcohol can be used well in the community and, indeed, embody something of that community itself. In the Haringey case, the representatives of the alcohol industry included themselves in the wider community narrative. Accounting for values and practice is most often focused in annual CR reports, often independently assessed. These relate stories that can engage the imagination, and can also usefully focus on targets, all of which enables the company to learn and develop any CR policy. However, the Haringey case suggests that accountability is mutual, and that a key means of accounting has to be relational, focused, in that case, in the regular community forums. The effect of shared practice reflection in that context was also to develop trust between the different agencies, and this began to establish a disciplined framework of direct accountability. This, in turn, takes the company or industrial perspective beyond accountability to immediate agents, and into a sense of shared responsibility for the situation, thus connecting accountability to the third mode of responsibility: moral liability.

The Haringey case illustrates the way in which the process moved from shared responsibility for dialogue about the situation and the identification of the key issues to a shared responsibility for the broader community, and, from that, to a negotiation of responsibilities and a creative response. Responsibility negotiation is a key element in deciding what a particular CR response might include. First, this involves identifying the stakeholders in any situation. Second, there is an analysis of the stakeholders in terms of power and responsibility. This enables a full appreciation of constraints and resources in the situation. This leads to an awareness of creative possibilities. Third, responsibilities are negotiated. This does not simply look to the development of goods for all stakeholders but, rather, looks to enabling all to identify their particular responsibility in practice, enabling a maximization of resources for social responsibility through collaboration.

In this process, several things can be achieved:

- the further development of ethical identity of the company or community
- the development of trust and of a sense of shared values with the stakeholders
- reflection on appropriate levels of responsibility, and areas where responsibilities and roles overlap. In areas such as human rights, for instance, this is clearly the responsibility of elected governments. However, firms might be faced with abuses in their supply chains that demand response. Without a response, the abuses are, in effect, being condoned. The firm then has to work out what its responsibility might be – to withdraw, to confront the agencies involved, and so on
- reflection on how the power of the company can respond to the effects that they have on the physical and social environment, and how it might enable other stakeholders who have little power to fulfil their responsibility.

The Haringey case neatly shows how the negotiation of shared responsibilities can mutually reinforce the response of all the agents, enabling each to take responsibility and contribute to the most creative overall response. It might be argued that this approach does little to develop the personal responsibility of the drinkers themselves. However, it does provide a framework of practice that enables an effective response to the critical problem. It also establishes a shared moral framework in which the major players model responsible actions, and which sets out expectations for civic behaviour. Furthermore, it retains the legal framework, and targets the law enforcement response that will continue to demand personal and civil responsibility. All this can be reinforced by practice that challenges and encourages the development of reflective personal responsibility in marketing and at points-of-sale.

Conclusion

The approach to corporate and industry responsibility argued for in this book is focused in the particular context of the alcohol industry recognizing the particular nature of alcohol. As such, it can be seen to be of relevance to all companies who deal in areas where there is ambivalence about a product. However, the argument that CR should include all agents in any situation in the creative development of responsibility applies more broadly to CR in all firms and industries. It links personal responsibility to corporate and community responsibility, arguing that these reinforce each other. It focuses on virtue and, in particular, integrity, and how this is practised corporately and in the community. As such, it positively links freedom, autonomy and community. Finally, it looks to the development of shared moral leadership and, in this case, the alcohol industry's part in that. In becoming involved in this, the alcohol industry can share a moral leadership that extends beyond the issue of alcohol to society itself.

References

A.D.W. (1919) 'The Control of the Drink Trade in Britain. A Contribution to National Efficiency During the Great War, 1915–18', *Journal of the Royal Statistical Society*, 82, 4, July: 590–1, from writings by Henry Carter, Lord D'Abernon.

'Adolescent Alcohol Use', Australian Institute of Family Studies Research Report 10, November.

Ahlström, S.K. and Österberg, E.L. (2004/05) 'International Perspectives on Adolescent and Young Adult Drinking', *Alcohol Research & Health*, 28 (4): 258–68.

AHRSE (2004) 'Alcohol Harm Reduction Strategy for England', available at http://www.cabinetoffice.gov.uk/media/cabinetoffice/strategy/assets/caboffce%20alcoholhar.pdf (accessed 13 May 2006).

Alcohol Concern (2005) *Health Select Committee on the Public Health White Paper: A Response from Alcohol Concern* (London: Alcohol Concern).

Alcohol Concern (2007) 'Mortality and Alcohol', Factsheet, 9 August.

Alcoholics Anonymous (1976) *Alcoholics Anonymous*, 3rd edn (New York: Alcoholics Anonymous World Services).

Alexander, D. (2001) '"Beer Brewing Paralleled the Rise of Civilization", in conversation with Kurt Stoppkotte', *National Geographic News*, 24 April, available at http://news.nationalgeographic.com/news/2001/04/0424_kurtbeer.html

American Psychiatric Association (1994) *Diagnostic and Statistical Manual* (Washington, DC: American Psychiatric Association).

Anderson, P. and Baumberg, B. (2006) *Alcohol in Europe A Public Health Perspective* (London: IAS).

Andersson, B., Hibell, B., Beck, F., Choquet, M., Kokkevi, A., Fotiou, A., Molinaro, S., Nociar, A., Sieroslawski, J. and Trapencieris, M. (2007) 'Alcohol and Drug Use Among European 17–18 Year Old Students. Data from the ESPAD Project' http://www.espad.org/documents/Espad/ESPAD_reports/17_18_Year_Old_Students_Full_Report.pdf, available at (accessed 1 December 2008).

Andrews, J., Tildesley, E., Hops, H. and Li, F. (2002) 'The Influence of Peers on Young Adult Substance Use Health Psychology', *American Psychological Association*, 21 (4): 349–57.

Ariza-Cardenal, C. and Nebot-Adell, M. (2000) 'Factors Associated with Problematic Alcohol Consumption in Schoolchildren', *Journal of Adolescent Health*, 27(6), 425–33.

ASA (2003) 'The British Code of Advertising, Sales Promotions and Direct Marketing', available at: www.asa.org/NR/rdonlyres/A44808F1-1573-482A-AOE5-D8045943DA57/0/The_CAP_cODE_Ed11_20060901.pdf

ASA (2008) Adjudications, available at http://www.asa.org.uk/asa/adjudications/public/ (accessed 18 November 2008).

Asthana, A. (2005) '"One Bar, Three Hours – I was sold enough drink to kill me: Even before 24-hour drinking arrives", Anushka Asthana finds that bar staff will happily let customers buy one round. And another. And another', 23 October, *The Observer*: 8.

Babor, T., Caetano R., Casswell, S., Edwards, G., Giesbrecht, P., Graham, K., Grube, J., Gruenewald, P., Hill, L., Holder, G., Homel, R., Österberg, E., Rehm, J., Room, R. and Rossow, I. (2003) *Alcohol: No Ordinary Commodity. Research and Public Policy* (Oxford: Oxford University Press).

Backhouse, S., McKenna, J., Robinson, S. and Atkin, A. (2007) *Attitudes, Behaviours, Knowledge and Education – Drugs in Sport: Past, Present and Future*, Prepared for World-Anti-Doping Agency, Canada.

Baggott, R. (2006) *Alcohol Strategy and the Drinks Industry: A Partnership for Prevention?* (York: Joseph Rowntree Foundation).

Barrett, C. (1978) *The Gospel According to St John*, 2nd edn (London: SPCK).

Bauman, Z. (1989) *Modernity and the Holocaust* (London: Polity).

Bauman, Z. (1993) *Postmodern Ethics* (Oxford: Oxford University Press).

BBC (2004) Available at http://news.bbc.co.uk/1/hi/health/4133099.stm

BBC News (2005) 'Smooth Start to 24-hour Drinking Saturday', 26 November, GMT.12.40 http://news.bbc.co.uk/2/low/uk_news/4472432.stm (accessed 15 October 2008).

BBC Research, available at news.bbc.co.uk/1/hi/health/7598288.stm

Bede (1990 [731]) *Ecclesiastical History of the English People*, trans. L. Sherley-Price (London. Penguin Classics).

Bellah, R., Madsen, R., Sullivan, W., Swidler, A. and Tipton, S. (1985) *Habits of the Heart* (Berkeley: University of California Press).

Benhabib, S. (1992) *Situating the Self.* London: Polity Press.

Berlin, I. (1967) *Four Essays on Liberty* (Oxford: Oxford University Press).

Berlin, I. (1969) 'Two Concepts of Liberty', in A. Quinton (ed.), *Political Philosophy* (London: Penguin): 141–53.

Berridge, V. (2005) *Temperance: Its History and Impact on Current and Future Alcohol Policy*, JRF Drug and Alcohol Research Programme, Joseph Rowntree Foundation.

Billings, A. (1992) 'Pastors or Counsellors?', *Contact*, 108 (2): 3–9.

Bloomfield, K., Ahlström, S., Allamani, A., Choquet, M., Cipriani, F., Gmel, G., Jacquat, B.J., Knibbe, R., Kubicka, L., Lecomte, T., Miller, P., Moira Plant, M. and Spak, F. (1999) *Alcohol Consumption and Alcohol Problems among Women in European Countries*, Institute for Medical Informatics, Biostatistics and Epidemiology (Berlin: Free University of Berlin).

BMA Report (2008) *Tackling Alcohol Misuse*, available at http://www.bma.org.uk/ap.nsf/Content/HubAlcohol

Braidwood, R.J., Sauer, D., Helbeck, H., Mangelsdrof, P.C., Culter, H.C., Coon, C.S., Linton, R., Steward, J. and Leo, A. (1953) Symposium: Did Man Once Live by Beer Alone? Oppenheim Source: *American Anthropologist*, New Series, Vol. 55 No. 4 (October, 1953), pp. 515–26. Published by Blackwell Publishing on behalf of the American Anthopological Association.

British Beer & Pub Association (2006) *EU Beer Duty Rates as at 11.10.2006.* http://www.beerandpub.com/statistics_eubeerdutyrates.aspx (assessed 23 December 2003).

British Code of Advertising Practice (2005) Available at http://www.asa.org.uk/NR/rdonlyres/A44808F1-1573-482A-A0E5-D8045943DA57/0/The_CAP_Code_Ed11_20060227.pdf (accessed 17 November 2008).

Brown, A. (2007) 'Advertising, Ethics and the Environment: A Personal View, Market Review', *Journal of the Marketing Society*, 36, Spring: 1.

Brown, A.G. (2002) 'Learning from the Past: Palaeohydrology and Palaeoecology', *Freshwater Biology*, 47: 817–29.

Brown, M. (2005) *Corporate Integrity* (Cambridge: Cambridge University Press).

Brown-Forman (2008) *Our Long-Term Perspective: Brown-Forman Corporate Social Responsibility* (Louisville: Brown-Forman).

Browning, D. (2006) *Christian Ethics and Moral Psychologies* (Grand Rapids: Eerdmans).

Buchholz, R. and Rosenthal, S. (2002) 'Social Responsibility and Business Ethics', in R. Frederick (ed.), *A Companion to Business Ethics*: 303–22 (Oxford: Blackwell).

Butcher, A.D. (1989) *Ale and Beer: A Curious History* (Toronto: McClelland & Stewart).

Cabinet Office (2004) *Reduction Strategy for England. Prime Minister's Strategy Unit* March (London: HMSO): 14.

CAMRA (2003) 'Licensing – a Brief History' and 'Opening Hours in Other European Countries), *Ale*, Spring, 309, available at http://www.cambridge-camra.org.uk/ale/309/licensing-history.html

Carr, A. (1968) 'Is Business Bluffing Ethical?', *Harvard Business Review*, 46 (1), January/February, 143–53.

Carroll, A.B. and Buchholtz, A.K. (2000) *Business and Society: Ethics and Stakeholder Management* (London: Thompson).

Chapman, J. (2005) 'Lunacy of 24-Hour Drinking', *Daily Mail*, 10 August: 1, 10.

Clinebell, H. (1968) *Understanding and Counseling the Alcoholic* (Nashville: Abingdon).

Clinebell, H. (1990) 'Alcohol Abuse, Addiction and Therapy', in R. Hunter (ed.), *Dictionary of Pastoral Care and Counseling* (Nashville: Abingdon Press).

Commission of the European Communities (2006) 'Communication From The Commission to The Council, The European Parliament, The European Economic and Social Committee and The Committee of the Regions', available at http://ec.europa.eu/health/ph_determinants/life_style/alcohol/documents/alcohol_com_625_en.pdf (accessed 24 October 2008).

Connor, S. (1989) *The Post Modern Culture* (Oxford: Blackwell).

Cook, C. (2006) *Alcohol, Addiction and Christian Ethics* (Cambridge: Cambridge University Press).

Cooper, C. (2008) 'Alcohol, Young People and Family Breakdowns', e-mail with A.J. Kenyon.

Cornellisen, F. and Cronje, T. (2006) 'Young People and Alcohol in South Africa', Third International Conference on Alcohol and Harm Reduction Conference Report Cape Town, South Africa, 22–25 October.

Crane, A. and Matten, D. (2004) *Business Ethics – A European Perspective – Managing Corporate Citizenship and Sustainability in the Age of Globalisation* (Oxford: Oxford University Press).

Cuthbertson, L. (2008) 'RCP: Direct Link found between Alcohol Sponsorship and Hazardous Drinking among Sportspeople', Press release Tuesday, 18 November, 12:00, available at http://www.politics.co.uk/opinion-formers/press-releases/opinion-former-index/culture-media-and-sport/rcp-direct-link-found-between-alcohol-sponsorship-and-hazardous-drinking-among-sportspeople-$1249853$365674.htm (accessed 27 November 2008).

Deacon, A. (2002) *Perspectives on Welfare* (Buckingham: Open University Press).

Department for Children, Schools and Families (2008) 'Use of Alcohol among Children and Young People', Final Report, Define Research & Insight, Published by the Department for Children, Schools and Families, available at www.dcsf.gov.uk/research (accessed 23 November 2008).

Department of Culture, Media and Sport (2002) 'Tessa Jowell Praises Pub Industry And Promises Reform', Archive April 2002, available at http://www.culture.gov.uk/reference_library/media_releases/2903.aspx (accessed 13 May 2008).

Department of Health (2005) *National Liver Transplant Standards*, available at www.dh.gov.uk/assetRoot/04/11/78/55/04117855.pdf DHSS (1980) *Inequalities in Health* (London: DHSS).

Diageo CSR Policy, available at http://www.diageo.com/en-row/Corporate Citizenship/

Dineley, M. and Dineley, G. (2000) 'Neolithic Ale: Barley as a Source of Sugars for Fermentation', in A. Fairbairn, (ed.), *Plants in the Neolithic and Beyond* (Oxford: Oxbow Books): 137–54.

Dornbusch, H.D. (2006) *History, Brewing Techniques, Recipes (Classic Beer Style)* (US: Brewers Publications).

Drink Pocket Book, The (2006) World Advertising Research Council and AC Neilson Oxon: WARC.

Drummond, D.C. (2004) 'An Alcohol Strategy for England: The Good, the Bad and the Ugly', *Alcohol & Alcoholism*, 39: 377–9.

Edwards, G. and Gross, M. (1976) 'Alcohol Dependence: Provisional Description of a Clinical Syndrome', *British Medical Journal*, 1 (1): 1058–61.

EGTA (2008) 'Strategies to Reduce the Harmful Use of Alcohol', Document A61/13, available at http://www.egta.com/documents/egta%20comments%20WHO%20Strategy%20to%20reduce%20the%20harmful%20use%20of%20alcohol%20FINAL.pdf (accessed 23 October 2008).

English Football Association Respect Campaign, available at http://www.thefa.com/TheFA/Respect/

Entine, J. (2002) 'Shell, Greenpeace and Brent Spar: The Politics of Dialogue', in C. Megone and S. Robinson (eds), *Case Histories in Business Ethics* (London: Routledge).

ESPAD Report (2004) 'Alcohol and Other Drug Use Among Students in 35 European Countries', ESPAD Report (2003) (Stockholm: Swedish Council for Information on Alcohol and Other Drugs).

Eurobarometer (2007) 'Attitudes towards Alcohol European Commission', available at http://ec.europa.eu/health/ph_determinants/life_style/alcohol/documents/ebs272_en.pdf

Eurocare (2007) EUROCARE press release on the EU Alcohol Strategy http://www.epha.org/IMG/pdf/EUROCARE_press_release_after_adoption_EU_Alcohol_Strategy.pdf (accessed 24 October 2008).

Fairbairn, A.S. (2000) 'On the Spread of Crops across Neolithic Britain, with Special Reference to Southern England', in A.S. Fairbairn (ed.), *Plants in Neolithic Britain and Beyond* (Oxford: Oxbow Books).

Fasching, D. and Dechant, D. (eds) (2001) *Comparative Religious Ethics* (Oxford: Blackwell).

Forrester, D. and Skene, D. (1988) *Just Sharing* (London: Epworth).

Fosters *Community Responsible Marketing* 2005 www.fosters.com

Fowler, J. (1996) *Faithful Change* (Nashville: Abingdon).

Foxcroft, D.R., Lister-Sharp, D. and Lowe, G. (1997) 'Alcohol Misuse Prevention for Young People: A Systematic Review Reveals Methodological Concerns and Lack of Reliable Evidence of Effectiveness', *Addiction*, 92: 531–8.

Frankfurt, H. (2003) 'Alternative Possibilities and Moral Responsibility', in D. Widerker and M. McKenna (ed), Moral Responsibility and alternative Possibilities (Aldershot: Ashgate). Friedman, M. (1983), 'The Social Responsibility of Business is to Increase Its Profits', in T. Donaldson and P. Werhane (eds), *Ethical Issues in Business* (New York: Prentice-Hall): 239–43.

Friedman, M. (1983) 'The Social Responsibility of Business is to Increase its Profits', in T. Donaldson. and P. Weherne (eds), *Ethical Issues in Business* (New York: Prentice Hall): 239–43.

Gateley, I. (2008) *A Cultural History of Acohol* (London: Gotham Books).

Gilligan, C. (1982) *In a Different Voice* (Cambridge, MA: Harvard University Press).

Gourvish T.R. (1997) 'The Business of Alcohol in the US and the UK: UK Regulation and Drinking Habits, 1914–39', *Business and Economic History*, 26 (2), Winter: 609–16.

Gourvish, T.R. and Wilson, R. (1994) *The British Brewing Industry 1830–1980* (Cambridge: Cambridge University Press).

Greenaway, J. (2003) *Drink and British Politics since 1830: A Study in Policy Making* (Basingstoke: Palgrave Macmillan).

Greenfield, T.K. and Rogers, J.D. (1999) 'Who Drinks Most of the Alcohol in the U.S.? The Policy Implications', *Journal of Studies on Alcohol*, 60: 78–89.

Grindal, R. (1979) 'Measure for Measure', *British Journal on Alcohol and Alcoholism*, 14 (3): 128–31.

Gülen, F. (1999) *Key Concepts in the Practice of Sufism, Vol. 1* (Fairfax: The Fountain).

Gülen, F. (2004) *Towards a Global Civilization of Love and Tolerance* (New Jersey: The Light).

Habermas, J. (1992) *Moral Consciousness and Communicative Action* (London: Polity).

Hawkins, J.D., Graham, J.W., Maguin, E., Abbott, R., Hill, K.G., and Catalano, R.F. (1997) 'Exploring the Effects of Age of Alcohol Use Initiation and Psychosocial Risk Factors on Subsequent Alcohol Misuse', *Journal of Studies on Alcohol*, 58 (3): 280–90.

Hayes, L., Smart, D., Toumbourou, J.W. and Sanson, A. (2004) 'Parenting Influences on Adolescent Alcohol Use', Australian Institute of Family Studies Research Report, 10, November.

Heath, J. and Norman, W. (2004) 'Stakeholder Theory, Corporate Governance and Public Management: What can the History of State-Run Enterprises Teach us in the Post-Enron era?', *Journal of Business Ethics* 53 (3): 247–65.

Hibell, B., Andersson, B., Bjarnason, T., Ahlström, S., Balakireva, O., Kokkevi, A. and Morgan, M. (2003) 'Alcohol and Other Drug Use among Students in 35 European Countries', ESPAD Report (2003) (Stockholm: Swedish Council for Information on Alcohol and Other Drugs (CAN)).

Highet, G. (2005) 'Alcohol and Cannabis: Young People Talking about how Parents Respond to their Use of these Two Drugs', *Drugs, Education, Prevention and Policy*, 12 (2), April: 113–24.

HM Government (2007) *Safe. Sensible. Social. The Next Steps in the National Alcohol Strategy – A Summary*, August, available at http://drugs.homeoffice.gov.uk/publication-search/drug-strategy/alcoholsummary2?view=Binary

HM Revenue & Customs (HMRC) (2008) *Alcohol Factsheet*, July (London: HMRC).

Holden, A. (1736) *The Trial of the Spirits* (London: T. Cooper).

Home Office (2007) 'Underage Alcohol Sales Down', Press release, 12 October, available at http://press.homeoffice.gov.uk/press-releases/underage-sales-down (accessed 13 May 2008).

Hopkins, P. (2008) Whitwell Local History Group, available at http://www.wlhg.co.uk, updated 25.08.2008 (accessed 5 October 2008).

Hornsey, I.S. (2003) *A History of Beer and Brewing* (Cambridge: RSC Paperbacks).

Hough, M., Hunter, G., Jacobson, J. and Cossalter, S. (2008) *The Impact of the Licensing Act 2003 on Levels of Crime and Disorder: An Evaluation*, March, available at http://www.homeoffice.gov.uk/rds/pdfs08/horr04b.pdf (accessed 13 May 2008).

House of Commons Home Affairs Committee (2008) 'Policing in the 21st Century', Seventh Report of Session 2007–08, Volume I, Report, together with formal minutes Ordered by The House of Commons, 30 October.

IAS (2003) 'Alcohol and Advertising Factsheet', March, available at http://www.ias.org.uk/

IAS (2005) 'Alcohol and Advertising Factsheet': 1–17 available at http://www.ias.org.uk/

IAS (2008) 'Alcohol And Health Factsheet': 1–16, available at http://www.ias.org.uk/

ICAP (2002) *Industry Views on Beverage alcohol Advertising and Marketing, with Special Reference to Young People*, Prepared for the WHO: 8, 23–30.

ICAP (2007) Blood Alcohol Concentration Limits Worldwide, available at http://www.icap.org/PolicyIssues/DrinkingandDriving/BACTable/tabid/199/Default.aspx (accessed 5 December 2008).

Ikonomidis, S. and Singer, P. (1999) 'Autonomy, Liberalism and Advance Care Planning', *Journal of Medical Ethics*, 25, 522–7.

Interface Inc., available at http://www.interfaceinc.com/goals/sustainability_overview.html

International Center for Alcohol Policies (2007) Blood Alcohol Concentration Limits Worldwide http://www.icap.org/PolicyIssues/DrinkingGuidelines/GuidelinesTable/tabid/204/Default.aspx (accessed 5 December 2008).

International Chamber of Commerce (2006) 'International Code of Advertising', available at http://www.iccwbo.org/uploadedFiles/ICC/policy/marketing/pages/330_Consolidated_Code.pdf (accessed 21 September 2008).

International Harm Reduction Association (2006) 'Conference Report', Third International Conference on Alcohol and Harm Reduction Cape Town, South Africa October 22–25.

James, L. (2008) 'An Analysis of UK Alcohol Advertising Expenditure and Consumption', WARC online Exclusive, February: 1.

Järvinen, M. and Room, R. (2007) 'Youth Drinking Cultures', in M. Järvinen (ed.), *Youth Drinking Cultures: European Experiences* (Aldershot: Ashgate).

Joffe, A.H. (1998) *Current Anthropology*, 39 (3): 297.

Jonas, H. (1984) *The Imperative of Responsibility* (Chicago: Chicago University Press).

Journal of Studies on Alcohol and Drugs (2008) 'Guidance for Authors on the Policy of the *Journal of Studies on Alcohol and Drugs* regarding the Appropriate Use of the Term "Binge"', available at http://www.jsad.com/jsad/static/binge.html.%5D

Katz, S.H. and Voigt, M.M. (1986) 'Bread and Beer', *Expedition*, 28 (2): 23–34.

Kenyon, A.J. (2008) 'When Should Parents Let Their Child Have A Drink', from *Looking at West Yorkshire Life the Liver Way*, Graham Liver, BBC Radio Leeds available at http://www.bbc.co.uk/iplayer/episode/p001qv8q/Graham_Liver_11_12_2008/

Kenyon, A.J. (2009a) 'Benefit Segmentation in UK Pubs and Bars', Masters Dissertation (Unpublished).

Kenyon, A.J. (2009b) 'Exploring Alcohol Strategies and Binge Drinking: Cases from UK and Poland', Sixth International Conference for Consumer Behaviour and Retailing Research, Centre for International Research in Consumers Location and their Environments (CIRCLE) (Austria: Vorarlberg University of Applied Sciences).

Kevany, S. (2008) 'French Group Demands Sarkozy Action on Anti-alcohol Lobby', *Decanter.com*, 5 March, available at http://www.decanter.com/news/196079.html (accessed 10 March 2008).

Key Note (2006) 'Drinks Market', February, available at www.keynote.co.uk

Key Note (2007) 'Sports Sponsorship Competitors Analysis', November, available at www.keynote.co.uk

Key Note (2008) 'Drinks Market', available at www.keynote.co.uk

Koehn, D. (1998) *Rethinking Feminist Ethics* (London: Routledge).

Kohlberg, L. (1984) *Essays on Moral Development, Vol. 2: The Psychology of Development* (San Francisco: Harper & Row).

Kreis, S. (2004) 'The History Guide Declaration of the Rights of Man and the Citizen', (August 1789), Last revised 13 May 2004, available at http://www.historyguide.org/intellect/declaration.html (accessed 21 December 2008).

Kung, H. (1991) *Global Responsibility* (London: SCM).

Leading National Advisors Index; Bureau of the Census cited in ICAP (2002) *Industry Views on Beverage alcohol Advertising and Marketing, with Special Reference to Young People*, Prepared for the WHO: 7.

Lester, A. (1995) *Hope in Pastoral Care and Counseling* (Louisville, KY: Westminster John Knox Press).

Levinas, E. (1998) *Entre Nous: On Thinking-of-the-Other* (New York: Columbia University Press).

Lintonen, T., Ahlström, S. and Metso, L. (2004) 'The Reliability of Self-Reported Drinking in Adolescence', *Alcohol & Alcoholism*, 39 (4): 362–8.

Lintonen, T., Rimpelä, M., Vikat, A. and Rimpelä, A. (2000) 'The Effect of Societal Changes on Drunkenness Trends in Early Adolescence', *Health Education Research*, June, 15 (3): 261–9.

Luty, J. (2005) 'UK Alcohol Policy-pure Genius', (editorial), *Psychiatric Bulletin*, 29: 410–12.

Malcolmson, R.W. (1981) *Life and Labour in England* (New York: St Martin's Press).

Martin, M. (2006) *From Morality to Mental Health* (Oxford: Oxford University Press).

Martinic, M. and Measham, F. (2008) *Swimming with Crocodiles: The Culture of Extreme Drinking* (London: Routledge).

Mason, N. (2001). "'The Sovereign People Are In A Beastly State": The Beer Act of 1830 and Victorian Discourse on Working-Class Drunkenness', *Victorian Literature and Culture*, 29: 109–27.

Masterman, G. (2007) *Sponsorship For a Return on Investment* (London: Butterworth-Heinemann).

McCrae, N. (2004) 'The Beer Ration in Victorian Asylums', *History of Psychiatry*, 15 (2): 155–75.

McGue, M., Iacono, W.G., Legrand, L.N., Malone, S. and Elkins, I. (2001) 'Origins and Consequences of Age at First Drink. I. Associations with Substance-use Disorders, Disinhibitory Behavior and Psychopathology, and P3 amplitude', *Alcoholism: Clinical and Experimental Research*, 25 (8): 1156–65.

McIntyre, A. (1981) *After Virtue* (London: Duckworth).

McKenney, G. (2005) 'Responsibility', in G. Meilaender and W. Werpehowski, *Theological Ethics* (Oxford: Oxford University Press): 237–53.

Measham, F. (2002) '"Doing gender" – "Doing drugs": Conceptualising the Gendering of Frugs Cultures', *Contemporary Drug Problems*, 29: 335–73.

Michalak, L. and Trocki, K. (2006) 'Alcohol and Islam: An Overview', *Contemporary Drug Problems*, 33 (4): 523–62.

Michel, R.H., McGovern, P.E. and Badler, V.R. (1992) 'Chemical Evidence for Ancient Beer', *Nature*, 5 November, 360: 24.

Milgram, S. (2005) *Obedience to Authority* (New York: Pinter & Martin).

Mill, J. (1989) *On Liberty and Other Essays* (Cambridge: Cambridge University Press).

Mill, J.S. (1943 [1859]) *On Liberty*, R.B. McCallum (ed.) (Oxford: Blackwell).

Miller, W. (ed.) (2003) *Integrating Spirituality into Treatment* (Washington, DC: American Psychological Association).

Minihan, M.A. (1967) *Dostoevsky: His Life and His Work*, trans. Konstantin Mochulsky (Princeton: Princeton University Press).

Mintel (2006) 'Brand Communication and Promotion in Cider', available at www.mintel.com

Mintel (2007) 'Brand Communication and Promotion in Flavoured Alcoholic Drinks', available at www.mintel.com

Mirror, The (2004) 'The Yob Squads', 8 July: 4.

Mirror, The (2008) 'Manchester United Xmas Party', available at http://www.mirror.co.uk/sport/pictures/2008/12/15/manchester-united-xmas-party-115875-20972768/ (accessed 17 December 2008).

Mitchell, B.R. and Deane, P. (1962) *Abstract of British Historical Statistics* (Cambridge: Cambridge University Press): 371, 357–8.

Moeller, K. and Erdal, T. (2003) *Corporate Responsibility Towards Society: A Local Perspective* (Brussels: European Foundation for the Improvement of Living and Working Conditions).

Moskowitz, H. and Fiorentino, D.A. (2000) *Review of the Literature on the Effects of Low Doses of Alcohol on Driving Related Skills*, Pub. No. DOT HS–809–028 (Springfield, VA: US Department of Transportation, National Highway Traffic Safety Administration.

Mustakova-Possardt, E. (2004) 'Education for Critical Moral Consciousness', *Journal of Moral Education*, 33, September: 245–70.

National Health Service (2008) 'The Health Dangers of Drinking Too Much', available at http://www.units.nhs.uk/healthHarms.html#didYouKnow (accessed 13 May 2008).

Nelson, J.P. (2001) 'Alcohol Advertising And Advertising Bans: A Survey Of Research Methods, Results, And Policy Implications', in M.R. Baye and J.P. Nelson (eds), *Advances in Applied Microeconomics, Volume 10: Advertising and Differentiated Products* (Amsterdam: JAI Press & Elsevier Science): 239–95.

New York Times (1887) 'The Last of the Ale Tasters', 17 July.

New York Times (1915) 'America Unready says Lloyd George', 1 March http://query.nytimes.com/mem/archive-free/pdf?_r=1&res= 9D02EFDF1E3FE633A25752C0A9659C946496D6CF&oref=slogin (accessed 23 July 2008).

Nicholls, J.C. (2003) 'Gin Lane Revisited: Intoxication and Society in the Gin Epidemic', *Journal for Cultural Research*, 7 (2): 125–46, 129.

Nicholls, J.Q. (2006) 'Liberties and Licences Alcohol in Liberal Thought', *International Journal of Cultural Studies*, 9 (2): 131–51.

Nicholson, S. (2005) 'Change in Drinks Laws Will Lead to an Alcoholic 'Free-for-all', *Daily* Mail, 11 August: 6.

Nielsen Media Research GmbH, 'European Association of Television and Radio Sales Houses Response to the Public Consultation Strategies To Reduce The Harmful Use Of Alcohol', Document A61/13: 8, cited in EGTA (2008).

Noam Cook, S. (2005) 'That Which Governs Best: Leadership Ethics and Human Systems', in J.B. Ciulla, T.L. Price and S.E. Murphy, *The Quest for Moral Leaders* (Cheltenham: Edward Elgar).

Novak, M. (1990) *Morality, Capitalism and Democracy* (London: IEA Health and Welfare Unit).

Nozick, R. (1968) *Anarchy State and Utopia* (Oxford: Blackwell).

Nuffield Centre for Bioethics (2007) *Public Health: Ethical Issues* (London: Nuffield Centre for Bioethics).

O'Daniel, W. (1859) 'Victorian London – Entertainment and Recreation – Drinking – Temperance Movement – "No-one Drinks Water", Ins and Outs of London', compiled by L. Jackson, *The Victorian Dictionary*, available at http://www .victorianlondon.org/

Office of National Statistics (2006) 'Smoking and Drinking among Adults', General Household Survey (2005), available at http://www.ons.gov.uk/search/ index.html?newquery=smoking+and+drinking+among+adults (accessed 26 May 2007).

Olsen, G. W. (1994) 'Physician Heal Thyself: Drink, Temperance and the Medical Question in the Victorian and Edwardian Church of England 1830–1914', *Addiction*, 89: 1167–76.

Our Lord's Sermon on the Mount (1949) (New Jersey: Paulist Press).

Palazzo, G. and Richter, U. (2005) 'CSR Business as Usual? The Case of the Tobacco Industry', *Journal of Business Ethics*, 61 (4), 387–401.

Piacentini, M.G. and Banister, E.N. (2006) 'Getting Hammered? Students coping with Alcohol, *Journal of Consumer Behaviour*, 5: 145–56.

Pitt, M. (2005) 'Pots and Pits: Drinking and Deposition in Late Iron-Age South-East Britain', *Oxford Journal of Archaeology*, 24 (2): 143–61.

Plant, M. and Plant, M. (2006) *Binge Britain Alcohol and the National Response* (Oxford: Oxford University Press).

Polish Investment and Foreign Investment Agency (2006) 'Advertising', available at http://www.paiz.gov.pl/index (accessed 13 December 2007).

PriceWaterhouseCoopers (2007) *From Sao Paulo to Shanghai New Consumer Dynamic the Impact on Modern Retailing 2006/07*, 5th edn.

Queen's Speech (2008) Setting out UK legislation for 2009, 3 December, available at http://news.bbc.co.uk/1/hi/uk_politics/7762594.stm

Rabikowska, M. (2008) 'Commercial Consumer TV Advertising in Poland', University of Glasgow, available at http://www.arts.gla.ac.uk/Slavonic/Epicentre/Marta%20art.htm (accessed 11 May 2008).

Raistrick, D., Hodgsen, R. and Ritson, B. (1999) *Tackling Alcohol Together: The Evidence Base for a UK Alcohol Policy* (London: Free Association Books).

Reed, T. (2006) *The Transforming Draught* (Jefferson, NC: McFarland).

Reid, H. (2006) 'Olympic Sport and its Lessons for Peace', *Journal of the Philosophy of Sport*, 33: 205–14.

Reiff, P. (1966) *The Triumph of the Therapeutic* (Chicago: Chicago University Press).

Riley, H.T. (1861) quoting from *Liber Albus* (The White Book of the City of London): 1419.

Ringhold, D.J. (2008) 'Responsibility and Brand Advertising in the Alcoholic Beverage Market: The Modelling of Normative Drinking Behaviour', *Journal of Advertising*, 37 (1), Spring: 127–41.

Robinson, S. (1992) *Serving Society: The Responsibility of Business* (Nottingham: Grove).

Robinson, S. (1998) 'Helping the Hopeless', *Contact*, 127: 3–11.

Robinson, S. (2001) *Agape, Moral Meaning and Pastoral Counselling* (Cardiff: Aureus).

Robinson, S. (2002) 'Nestlé Baby Milk Substitute and International Marketing', in C. Megone and S. Robinson (eds), *Case Histories in Business Ethics* (London: Routledge).

Robinson, S. (2007) *Spirituality, Ethics and Care* (London: Jessica Kingsley).

Robinson, S. (2008) 'Can the Marketplace be Ethical?', in P. Wetherly and D. Otter (eds), *The Business Environment* (Oxford: Oxford University Press).

Robinson, S. and Dixon, R. (1997) 'The Professional Engineer, Virtues and Learning', *Science and Engineering Ethics*, 3, (3), 339–48.

Robinson, S., Dixon, R., Moodley, K. and Preece, C. (2007) *Engineering, Business and Professional Ethics* (London: Butterworth-Heinemann).

Robinson, S., Kendrick, K. and Brown, A. (2003) *Spirituality and the Practice of Healthcare* (Basingstoke: Palgrave).

Room, R., Jernigan, D., Carlini-Marlatt, B., Gureje, O., Mäkelä, K., Marshall, M., Medina-Mora, M.E., Monteiro, M., Parry, C., Partanen, J., Riley, L., and Saxena, S. (2002) *Alcohol in Developing Societies: A Public Health Approach* (Helsinki: Finnish Foundation for Alcohol Studics).

Rowan, S. (2007) 'More Young People Hooked on Alcohol and Gambling', in *Alcoholics Anonymous Review*, available at http://www.aa-uk.org.uk/alcoholics-anonymous-reviews/2007/08/more-young-people-hooked-on-alcohol-and.htm (accessed 14 December 2008).

Rowley, J. and Williams, C. (2008) 'The Impact of Brand Sponsorship of Music Festivals', *Marketing Intelligence & Planning*, 26 (7): 781–92.

Samuel, D. and Nesbitt, M. (1996) 'From Staple Crop to Extinction? The Archaeology and History of the Hulled Wheat', in S. Padulosi, K. Hammer and J. Heeler (eds), *Hulled Wheats* (Rome: International Plant Genetic Resources Institute).

Sanderson, C. and Linehan, M. (2003) 'Acceptance and Forgiveness', in W. Miller (ed.), *Integrating Spirituality into Treatment* (Washington, DC: American Psychological Association): 199–217.

Saul, A. and Colom, J. (2001) 'From Paris to Stockholm: Where does the European Alcohol Action Plan Lead To?', *Addiction*, 96: 1093–6.

Schweiker, W. (1995) *Responsibility and Christian Ethics* (Cambridge: Cambridge University Press).

Sherratt, A.G. (1987) 'Cups that Cheered', in W. Waldren and R.C. Kennard (eds), B.A.R., Oxford, *Bell Beakers of the Western Mediterranean*, cited in I.S. Hornsey (2003), *A History of Beer and Brewing* (Cambridge: RSC Paperbacks).

Sims, R.R. and Brinkmann, J. (2003) 'Enron Ethics (Or Culture Matters More than Codes)', *Journal of Business Ethics*, 45 (3): 243–56.

Snyder, C. (2000) 'The Past and Possible Futures of Hope', *Journal of Social and Clinical Psychology*, 19 (1): 11–28.

Solomon, R. (1982) *Ethics and Excellence* (Oxford: Oxford University Press).

Spear, L.P. (2002) 'Alcohol's Effects on Adolescents', *Alcohol Health and Research World*, 26 (4), 287–91.

Sternberg, E. (2000) *Just Business* (Oxford: Oxford University Press).

Styles, O. (2007) 'Sarkozy: I Will Relax Wine Advertising Regulations', *Decanter.com*, 27 February, available at http://www.decanter.com/news/111170.html (accessed 10 May 2008).

Table Talk (2005) (Philadelphia: Lutheran Publication Society).

Tawney, R.H. (1930) *Equality* (London: Allen & Unwin).

Taylor, C. (1989) *Sources of the Self* (Cambridge: Cambridge University Press).

Titmuss, R. (1973) *The Gift Relationship* (London: Penguin).

Tomasino, A. (1992) 'History Repeats Itself: The "Fall" and Noah's Drunkenness', *Vesus Testamentum*, 42: 1288–130.

Tonigan, J., Toscova, R. and Connors, G. (2003) 'Spirituality and the Twelve Step Programs: A Guide for Clinicians', in W. Miller (ed.), *Integrating Spirituality into Treatment* (Washington, DC: American Psychological Association): 111–33.

Toynbee, P. (2005) 'Comment and Analysis: Only Raising Prices will End our Love Affair with Booze: arguing over opening hours won't remove the fetishism from drink', *The Guardian*, 24 August: 20.

Turner, J. (1980) 'State Purchase of the Liquor Trade in the First World War', *Historical Journal*, 23 (3), September: 589–615.

UK Government (2005) Available at http://www.direct.gov.uk/en/Government citizensandrights/Yourrightsandresponsibilities/DG_4002951

UK Ofcom Code, available at http://www.ofcom.org.uk/tv/ifi/codes/bcode/

Unger, R.W. (2004) *Beer in the Middle Ages and the Renaissance* (Philadelphia: Philadelphia University Press).

US National Council on Alcoholism and Drug Dependence, available at http://www.ncadd-detroit.org/whatsaddictions.htm

Valverde, M. (1998) *Diseases of the Will: Alcohol ad the Dilemmas of Freedom* (Cambridge: Cambridge University Press).

van Hoof, J., van Noordenburg, M. and de Jong, M. (2008) 'Happy Hours and other Alcohol Discounts in Cafés: Prevalence and Effects on Underage Adolescents', *Public Health Policy*, September, 29 (3): 340–52.

Webb, S. and Webb, B.P. (1903) *The History of Liquor Licensing in England Principally from 1700 to 1830* (London: Longmans, Green & Co).

Westminster Health Forum Keynote Seminar (2008) 'Alcohol & Responsibility', 21 October.

Widerker, D. and McKenna, M. (2003) *Moral Responsibility and Alternative Possibilities* (Aldershot: Ashgate).

Williams, F. (2004) *Rethinking Families* (London: Calouste Gulbenkian Foundation).

Winters, K.C. (2008) 'Adolescent Brain Development and Drug Abuse Research indicates that Brain Development is Still in Progress during Adolescence; Immature Brain Regions may place Teenagers at Elevated Risk to effects of Drugs', TRI Science Addiction, available at http://www.tresearch.org/headlines/2008Jan_TeenBrain.pdf (accessed 16 December 2008).

Wired for Health (2008) 'National Healthy Schools Status', available at http://www.wiredforhealth.gov.uk

Wood, M.D., Read, J.P., Mitchell, R.E. and Brand, N.H. (2004) 'Do Parents Still Matter? Parent and Peer Influences on Alcohol Involvement Among Recent High School Graduates', *Psychology of Addictive Behaviors*, 18 (1): 19–30.

World Health Organization (1992) *The ICD-10 Classification of Mental and Behavioural: Clinical Descriptions and Diagnostic Guidelines* (Geneva: World Health Organization).

World Health Organization (2006) 'WHO Expert Committee on Problems Related to Alcohol Consumption', WHO Technical Report Series, no. 944, Geneva, 10–13 October.

World Health Organization (1998) 'Report of the 48th Session Regional office for Europe Copenhagen Regional Committee for Europe', 14–18 September 1998, available at http://www.euro.who.int/document/rc48/ereport.pdf (accessed 21 December 2008).

World Health Organization (2002a) http://www.who.int/hpr/NPH/docs/whr_2002_risk_factors.pdf (accessed 12 December 2008).

World Health Organization (2002b) *World Health Report 2002: Reducing Risks, Promoting Healthy Life*, ch. 6: 65.

World Health Organization (2002c) World Health Report http://www.who.int/dietphysicalactivity/publications/facts/en/gsfs_ppt_rf.pdf (accessed 12 December 2008)

World Health Organization (2004) 'Global Status Report on Alcohol', http://www.who.int/substance_abuse/publications/global_status_report_2004_overview.pdf (accessed 12 December 2008) table 3: 11 and 12.

World Health Organization (2007) *Drinking and Driving* – An International Good Practice Manual, available at http://www.who.int/roadsafety/projects/manuals/alcohol/en/index.html

World Health Organization (2008) 'Strategies to Reduce the Harmful Use of Alcohol', Sixty-first World Health Assembly, available at http://www.who.int/gb/ebwha/pdf_files/A61/A61_13-en.pdf (accessed 15 December 2008).

World Health Organization (2008a) 'Alcohol', available at http://www.who.int/topics/alcohol_drinking/en/ (accessed 9 May 2008).

World Health Organization (2008b) 'Strategies to Reduce the Harmful Use of Alcohol', Report by the Secretariat, Sixty-first World Health Assembly, A61/13 Provisional agenda item 11.10 20, March 2008, available at http://www.who.int/gb/ebwha/pdf_files/A61/A61_13-en.pdf

YFJ (2002) 'Development of the Youth Sector in the European CIS Countries', Position Paper adopted by the Bureau of the European Youth Forum, Warsaw, Poland, 22 June.

Zadek, S. (2001) *The Civil Corporation: The New Economy of Corporate Citizenship* (London: Earthscan).

Zimbardo, P. (2007) *The Lucifer Effect* (London: Rider).

Index